I DARE SAY

I DARE SAY

A Gerald Horne Reader

Edited by Tionne Alliyah Parris

O/R

OR Books
New York · London

Published by OR Books, New York and London

Visit our website: www.orbooks.com

First printing 2024

Library of Congress Cataloging-in-Publication Data: A catalog record for this book is available from the Library of Congress.

British Library Cataloging-in-Publication Data: A catalog record for this book is available from the British Library.

Typeset by Lapiz Digital.

paperback ISBN 978-1-68219-363-1 • ebook ISBN 978-1-68219-422-5

CONTENTS

A Note from the Editor   vii

Introduction   1

PART I: RACISM   9

Hell in the City of Angels: 1965 and 1992   11

Race Backwards: Genes, Violence, Race,
    and Genocide   25

"Myth" and the Making of "Malcolm X"   45

Who Lost the Cold War? Africans and African
    Americans   65

The Dawning of the Apocalypse: The Roots of Slavery,
    White Supremacy, Settler Colonialism, and
    Capitalism in the Long Sixteenth Century   89

PART II: INTERNATIONALISM   135

Rethinking the Lumpen: Gangsters and the
    Political Economy of Capitalism   137

Hands Across the Water: Afro-American Lawyers
    and the Decolonization of Southern Africa 161

Things Fall Apart: China and the Decline of US
    Imperialism   191

From Crisis to Catastrophe? What is to be Done in
    Eastern Europe   205

PART III: RESISTANCE   **211**

TOKYO BOUND: African Americans and Japan
    Confront White Supremacy   213

Shirley Graham Du Bois: Portrait of the
    Black Woman Artist as a Revolutionary   237

"The White Republic": Response by Gerald Horne   267

Permissions   275

A NOTE FROM THE EDITOR

Tionne Alliyah Parris

I was born in Scotland in 1996 and lived there until 2019 before moving down to England. I was always encouraged to know and appreciate both sides of my heritage—Scottish and African American. Growing up of Mixed/Black heritage in Scotland was not easy, and so I often identified with African American icons to bolster my sense of self. My earliest studies were always geared toward Black history. When I turned thirteen my mother bought me a copy of *The Autobiography of Malcolm X* by Alex Haley. From then on, I ventured eagerly down the rabbit hole of histories of the Black radical tradition in the United States. Malcolm X and the Black Panther Party were both enticing figures for me as a teenager. Their stories of rebellion and resistance to the status quo have long inspired many. I still remember reading about the Black Panther Party's Rainbow Coalition spearheaded by Fred Hampton, and about Malcolm X's Organisation of Afro-American Unity's petition to the United Nations. It was through these histories that I began to understand how international outreach was central to fights against entrenched imperialism, colonialism and systems of white supremacy.

When I began my first history degree at the University of Dundee in 2015, I resolved to study as much of U.S. Black history as possible. As a result, both my Undergraduate and Masters studies included an exploration of the Black Panther Party versus the Federal Bureau of Investigation, and later the rise of the prison abolitionist movement of the 1970s. Angela Davis, the most well-known Black Communist woman in the world, naturally featured in my writings. In her autobiography, Davis wrote about her incarceration in the New York Women's House of Detention, when she was loaned a book that may have been in the hands of Claudia Jones, a prominent Communist political activist, around two decades prior. I was fascinated by this detail. From then on, I became interested in the generation of Black radical women that had preceded Davis—those whose stories had been side-lined in the grander narratives of twentieth century history. My PhD study looks at the members of this network of Black radical women, their impact, and investigates how early strategies of U.S. Black Communists were passed (knowingly or unknowingly) to a new generation of activists. My work emphasises the often-obscured connections between generations of the 1930s and 1970s and will, I hope, contribute to our understanding of tactics that can be used for future liberatory agitation.

I first encountered Gerald Horne's work through his biography of Benjamin J. Davis—*Black Liberation/Red Scare: Ben Davis and the Communist Party*—in the early months of my PhD. I wanted to ground myself in the environment that had been the catalyst in the rise of Claudia Jones, and many other women in my work, that brought them to the forefront of radical activism. *Black Liberation/Red Scare* provided this. Horne's book showed that the life of Ben Davis was frequently interspersed with the presence of women like Eslanda Robeson, Audley Moore and, of course, Jones. It also highlighted his interactions with Paul

Robeson, William Patterson and later, Martin Luther King, Jr. Most importantly, it underscored the rampant repression Davis and those in his network faced as a consequence of their radicalism. From that point Horne's scholarship became central to my understanding of twentieth century Black radical history, and the complexity Civil Rights struggles more broadly. His biographies of W. E. B. and Shirley Graham Du Bois, William Patterson, Paul Robeson, and Ben Davis illuminated an extensive network of Black radicals who were active in both domestic and international struggles. These books led me to the vast contributions Horne has made to the wider histories of U.S. internationalism, and movements often led by marginalized activists seeking allies for their causes from abroad.

This reader is, therefore, made up of short pieces which we believe encapsulate the pinnacle of Horne's writings, and many remain—even decades after their release—foundational pieces for historians, young and old, who seek to grasp the nuance of African American and African diasporic histories. As an entry point to this genre, we have included in part 1 many pieces that journey through Horne's study of the Cold War, and the Red Scare which preceded it. The article *Who Lost the Cold War? Africans and African Americans*, for example, is a valuable synthesis of Horne's major contributions to historiography of Black Communists in the United States. The theme of internationalism ripples throughout the selection of writings in this book, and in the process of collating these pieces I saw how Horne's craft has developed over the years. For example, part 2 shows the origin of Horne's early activism by including speeches which were given during his time working with the National Conference of Black Lawyers (NCBL), and in *Hands Across the Water: Afro-American Lawyers and the Decolonization of Southern Africa*, we see how Horne's transnational interests persisted beyond his university days. The scope of Horne's work is always, quite rightly, one which chronicles the national and international ramifications of racism and resistance—whether considering their effects on the early settlement of colonies in America, or indeed on the outbreak of the war in Ukraine in early 2022. To combat racism, international collaboration is key. However, articles included in the final section of the book— like *Tokyo Bound: African Americans and Japan Confront White Supremacy*—serve as cautionary stories highlighting the consequences of misalliances. In the closing *Against Left Wing White Nationalism: Gerald Horne's Response to 'The White Republic' and the Struggle for Racial Justice*, Horne ties together many of his current concerns, including the recent white supremacist fervor spreading throughout the United States and Europe— and of course—how to resist it. Also included is an excerpt from Horne's 2020 book *The Dawning of the Apocalypse: The Roots of Slavery, White Supremacy, Settler Colonialism, and Capitalism in the Long Sixteenth Century*. Although many earlier pieces in the *Reader* span twentieth century history, Horne's later career turned towards examining the foundations of white supremacy in America's settler colonies. As Angela Davis once stated, "radical simply means grasping things at the root"—and Horne's recent studies of sixteenth and seventeenth century American history grapples with these unfortunate roots. His scholarship remains a timely reminder of the work that must be done to combat reactionary fables about the United States, and beyond.

I Dare Say displays the breadth of Horne's work, and highlights how collaborative, transnational resistance is a necessary strategy to defeat the harms of white supremacy in the United States, and the impact of its many tendrils across the globe. Horne's work brings to the fore the tangled history of U.S. capitalism with analysis that should encourage readers to consider why the events covered are still very much relevant today. In contrast to the strictly 'empirical' or 'objective' approach which is often drilled into students of history, Horne shows that one can in fact pick a side. In the case of Horne's scholarship, this is what is so appealing to so many. To borrow from the saying often attributed to Malcolm X: Gerald Horne 'makes it plain.' Reflecting on my own work as a young woman of Black/mixed heritage who has always been in predominantly white institutions and environments, Horne's scholarship has inspired me not to fear stating a bias—especially when writing about histories of injustice, of repression, and of violence against people of Africa and the African diaspora.

Finally, this leads me to the personal lasting impact of this project. The intergenerational exchanges of activism which I probe in my own work have, fortuitously, leaped off the page and become central to my own development as a historian. For the last two years, I have been a coordinator at the Young Historians Project—an organization led by volunteers who are creating resources about the history of Black people in Britain. Additionally, the organisation addresses the woeful lack of Black British historians by training and developing the skills of young people of African and Caribbean heritage. We hope that some will go on to study history as a result, but simply learning about our place in Britain is a grounding and enriching exercise in itself. Through this, and through the range of scholars I have been introduced to since starting my PhD, I have gained a greater understanding of the mentorship and support that is required for Black youths to thrive, both in Britain and globally. The collaboration with Professor Gerald Horne in these pages has been the zenith of my experience so far. It is the perfect example of different generations aligning under one banner to expand knowledge and platform justice. Although we are separated by experiences and geography, Professor Horne extended the opportunity to collaborate on this project as a method of passing along knowledge, and of sharing space with a young scholar. For that alone, I will always be grateful.

INTRODUCTION

Professor Gerald Horne is, as the late Professor Manning Marable stated, "one of the most gifted and insightful historians on racial matters of his generation."[1] With a career spanning four decades, Horne has created his own distinguished approach to both national and international histories and situated his works within the canons of history. His work interrogates mainstream narratives, and astutely shows how these narratives have led to our current crises with regards to the sustained resurfacing of white supremacist protests, and the everlasting struggle the global majority are waging against it.

The depth of research exemplified across the selection of pieces in *The Gerald Horne Reader* highlights Horne's attention not only to establishing new narratives of African American and African diasporic histories, but also to reorienting mainstream narratives of European histories to unravel the layers of white supremacy woven throughout centuries of modern societal development. The collection is an instructive snapshot of Horne's multifaceted approach to writing history—showcasing a range of topics as Horne seamlessly reaches into the past and looks forward to the future throughout his contributions.

* * *

1   Manning Marable in NYU Press review of *Race War! White Supremacy and the Japanese Attack on the British Empire*, NYU Press.Org, 2005.

Gerald Horne was born on January 3, 1949, in St. Louis, Missouri. Horne's parents Flora and Jerry Horne, he recollects, "were of hearty Mississippi peasant stock, and their parents, who were of hearty Mississippi slave stock, are worthy representatives of a community that allowed a worker like myself to grow, flourish, and produce."[2] As a child, his mother encouraged Gerald's older sisters to excel academically and, witnessing their success, he followed suit. Horne recalled the influence his sisters had on his development: "I read what they read. I learned the songs they did—I still know a lot of Johnny Mathis's songs and lyrics."[3] Growing up in racially segregated Mill Creek Valley, Missouri, Horne was an avid reader and regular visitor at his local library. Historian Ula Taylor writes: "In many ways Horne's library card was a passport. Books gave him access to the world beyond his racially segregated environment."[4] He was an ardent sports fan and supported the St. Louis Cardinals, much to the chagrin of his Mississippi-born parents who instead cheered for the Brooklyn Dodgers and their star player Jackie Robinson.

Fueled by an early interest in sports and inspired in particular by Bill Bradley—a young basketball player for the Princeton Tigers—Horne seized the opportunity to enter further study and applied to Princeton. In 1966 he began undergraduate studies in law with the backdrop of nationwide desegregation,

2   Gerald Horne, *Black and Red: W. E. B. Du Bois and the Afro-American Response to the Cold War, 1944–1963,* (New York: State University of New York Press, 1985), p.xii.

3   Ula Taylor, "Introduction: The Shaping of An Activist and Scholar," Gerald Horne Symposium: Contributions to African American and African Diaspora Studies, *The Journal of African American History* Vol. 96, no.2, (Spring 2011), p.207.

4   Ibid., p.204.

and international decolonization, spurring him on. Although the student population was majority Euro-American, Horne says that he never felt the pressures of being in the minority and found many external influences to buttress his interests. There, at Princeton, Horne was faced with the "memory and majesty of Paul Robeson." Once, in W. E. B. Du Bois's estimation—"the best known American on Earth"—there is no doubt that the young Gerald Horne was influenced by the omnipresence of Robeson on campus, despite the fact Robeson was not admitted to Princeton and instead went to Rutgers.[5] Decades later Horne would pen a range of biographies which set the record straight on the rampant repression of Robeson and his network of comrades throughout the 1950s.[6] Similarly, another interest was sparked by Horne's time at University, where he'd spend his spare time frequenting jazz clubs in Manhattan "...with my late black classmate and fellow Missourian (Kansas City in his case) Darryl Johnson, checking out Ornette Coleman, Archie Shepp, and Albert Ayler and developing a lifelong interest in their jazz music."[7] Again, one can observe how Horne's

---

5   W.E.B. Du Bois, in Gerald Horne, *Paul Robeson: The Artist as Revolutionary* (London: Pluto Press, 2016), p.13.

6   For more, see Gerald Horne's numerous works - *Race Woman: The Lives of Shirley Graham Du Bois* (New York: New York University Press, 2000), *Paul Robeson: The Artist as Revolutionary* (London: Pluto Press, 2016), *Black Revolutionary: William Patterson and the Globalization of the African American Freedom Struggle* (Urbana, Chicago and Springfield: University of Illinois Press, 2013), *Black Liberation/Red Scare: Ben Davis and the Communist Party* (New York: International Publishers, 2020), *Communist Front? The Civil Rights Congress, 1946–1956* (New York: International Publishers, 2021).

7   Gerald Horne, in foreword to Stephen Bradley's *Upending the Ivory Tower: Civil Rights, Black Power, and the Ivy League* (New York: New York University Press, 2018), p.x.

ever-growing catalogue of works developed as a reflection of his various passions—specifically in his 2019 book *Jazz and Justice: Racism and the Political Economy of the Music.*

As a talented student, and emerging lawyer, Horne interned during his studies at Capitol Hill under Congressman Bill Clay. However, in the summer of 1968, as the internship came to an end—he found himself "quasi-homeless" and relied on friends to spare a couch for the night on many occasions. Traversing from Philadelphia, to Atlantic City, to Columbia, and back in this period shaped Horne's wandering spirit—a trait which came in handy in the decades following whilst he traveled the globe in search of archival materials. Horne was also shaped, in his undergraduate years, by the shift in the Civil Rights Movement, which by 1968 was overshadowed by the explosion of the Black Power Movement across the nation. Horne was involved in a range of student protests, concerning both national and international issues. He noted that during this time: "I attended the massive rally in New Haven on behalf of Black Panthers then on trial, which then led me as a law student at Berkeley to do legal work for the BPP and teach classes at Vacaville State Prison."[8] Crucially, although perhaps unbeknownst to himself at the time, Horne was following in the footsteps of the extraordinary lawyer and radical Black activist William Patterson, who would later become the subject of his 2013 biography *Black Revolutionary: William Patterson and the Globalization of the African American Freedom Struggle.* Additionally, during his studies, Horne became a founding member of Princeton's Association of Black Collegians, and supported challenges against Princeton University's institutional complicity in South

8   *Ibid.*, p.xi.

African Apartheid by taking part in building takeovers on campus. These challenges were formative for Horne, and he wrote that they crystallized within him ". . . an abiding interest in global trends, particularly in Africa, which led me to eventually reside in Zimbabwe."[9]

Once Horne achieved a J.D. in Law from Berkeley, he went on to pursue graduate studies in history at Columbia, where more activism ensued. There he led the National Conference of Black Lawyers and continued his protest against South African apartheid in the 1980s, alongside fellow students. While heavily involved in a range of extracurricular activities, Horne completed his Ph.D. dissertation in 1982. This would later become his first book *Black and Red: W. E. B. Du Bois and the Afro-American Response to the Cold War, 1944–1963* (1986). Reflecting on his undergraduate and graduate studies, Horne wrote:

"I think some of the most valuable lessons I learned at Princeton and Columbia were outside the classroom, such as how to navigate seemingly awkward situations (being quasi-homeless), how to raise funds for causes (Orangeburg, Namibia), how to use personal experience to enhance understanding of book topics (African liberation, Hong Kong, the South Seas, labor history, etc.), and most of all, how to survive in a society where white supremacy remains more than a cipher."[10]

In the years following his freshly awarded doctorate, Horne worked in a wide range of capacities. He taught at Sarah Lawrence College in Bronxville, New York, whilst consulting

9   *Ibid.*, p.xi.
10 *Ibid.*, p.xii.

for the hospital workers' union in New York City, and juggling legal cases. Additionally, in this decade Horne continued to broaden the scope of his concerns beyond the national, seizing more opportunities to be a part of global campaigns. He free-lanced as a journalist, interviewing Yasser Arafat in his bunker in Beirut in the early 1980s and covering the unwinding of apartheid rule in Namibia in 1989. He also worked as a legal observer at the criminal trial of Walter Rodney in Guyana and worked with the Union of Arab Jurists in the mid-1980s to mediate the Sudanese Civil War. While continuously developing as a historian, lawyer and activist, Horne traveled extensively—going wherever there were happenings in that tumultuous decade—traversing the Philippines, Cyprus, Lisbon, Luanda, Puerto Rico, Moscow, Havana, Libya, Dar es Salaam, Tanzania, and Chile. Horne wrote: "I even found time to moonlight as a blues singer in Baku, Azerbaijan, and in the city then known as Leningrad."[11] Horne also entered the 1992 race for U.S. Senate against Dianne Feinstein in California and garnered 305,000 votes for the Peace & Freedom Party in the Golden State. He lost the race; but winning it would have been a diversion to what was clearly his true calling.

During the early 1990s, when Nelson Mandela was finally emancipated, and with the European landscape shifting rapidly following the fall of the Berlin Wall and the signing of the Maastricht Treaty ushering in the European Union, he made a definitive effort to dedicate his talents to full time historical study:

---

11 Gerald Horne, *One Historian's Journey*, The Journal of African American History, Vol. 96, No. 2, (Spring 2011), p.249.

"It was clear to me then that the old order had evaporated, a new world was emerging and that my time might be better spent analyzing, on a full-time basis, domestic—and particularly global—trends."[12]

This expansive range of experiences, and volunteering his multidisciplinary talents, undeniably sculpted Gerald Horne into the scholar he is today. His travels informed his transnational outlook, his legal work no doubt influenced his analysis of the myriad of lawyers and organizations he would later explore in his works, and his activism gave him valuable insight into the machinery of grassroots organizing. In the decades that followed, Horne wrote both richly detailed and impressively researched historiographical books, as well as journal articles and journalism for myriad outlets.

* * *

In recent decades, Horne has consolidated his position as perhaps the most generative historian of our time. Having written more than forty books in the last three decades, he has made an indelible contribution to the topics of race, internationalism and resistance in historiographies of the last four centuries.

Divided into three parts, *The Gerald Horne Reader's* contents summarize key themes that are often present throughout all of Horne's works: racism, internationalism, and resistance. The citations accompanying the pieces here often lead to Horne's book-length contributions to historiography. Readers should consider each piece an invitation to explore Horne's larger works.

12   Gerald Horne, in foreword to Stephen Bradley's *Upending the Ivory Tower: Civil Rights, Black Power, and the Ivy League* (New York: New York University Press, 2018), p.xi.

Ultimately, the hope is that *The Gerald Horne Reader* will inform, influence, and inspire its audience to follow in the footsteps of Horne—which at this current juncture in the twenty-first century seems imperative. Horne himself exemplifies the spirit we should carry with us in saying: "I am confidently optimistic about the future—notably about the terminal crisis of white supremacy, a multi-headed hydra which has created so much misery for so many."[13] By instructing us all on how white supremacy has functioned historically, and how it has been overcome in the past through transnational organizing, we can continue to follow these historic examples, and build upon Horne's scholarship to continue our resistance.

---

13   Gerald Horne, "One Historian's Journey," *The Journal of African American History*, Vol. 96, no. 2, (Spring 2011), p.253.

PART I: RACISM

HELL IN THE CITY OF ANGELS: 1965 AND 1992

The Guild Practitioner Volume 49, No. 3, Summer 1992

"The more things change, the more they remain the same" is a frequent aphorism. In a pithy fashion, it reflects the trajectory of history which involves both continuity and change. The "civil unrest" that gripped Los Angeles in 1965 and 1992 reflects this tendency. For although there has been some positive, evolution for national minorities and the working class generally in Southern California, it would be a mistake to emphasize this trend to the exclusion of others.

Gangs and Arms

It is striking that in 1992 an immediate cause for concern by the press has been the alleged increase of weapons in the hands of street organizations, often referred to as gangs. Apparently, a number of gun shops were burglarized in the Pico-Union and South-Central areas of Los Angeles. Moreover, a number of suburbanites engaged in panic purchases of firearms, fearing that the "darker hordes" would invade their idyll. A similar development took place in 1965. While the fires were still raging, the Los Angeles Times on 17 August 1965 reported on the front page that pistol sales that past weekend had jumped 250%. Somehow the paper was able to obtain the statistic that of the 2038 sales, only 68 of the buyers were African American.

Even prior to that, there seemed to be a proliferation of weapons. On 15 August 1965, the Times reported that "hundreds of white citizens were arming themselves. Gun shops and sporting goods stores . . . exhausted their supply not only of guns but also of ammunition. . . . At the Brass Rail Gun Shop, 711 N. La Brea Avenue, an armed clerk—in the manner of the Old West—searched customers entering the shop to forestall a possible holdup." Said one gun shop owner, "'They don't even know which shoulder to put a gun to, but they want a gun to protect themselves.'" A week after the height of those days of tumult, then Attorney General Thomas C. Lynch reported that gun sales had jumped "500%;" again, it was noted that ". . . . less than 2% of the purchasers were Negroes . . ."[1]

Though this "domestic arms race" characterized both 1965 and 1992, it is striking that interpretations of this phenomenon varied at crucial points. In 1965, Southern California had already established a reputation as headquarters of the ultra-right, a reputation it still maintains.

Yet, as the political spectrum in this country has moved steadily to the right, what was at one time perceived as the ultra-right, has now migrated to the border of the mainstream. Nevertheless, in 1965—as in 1992—the question of arms proliferation was discussed in terms of the alleged threat from predominantly African American gangs, an emphasis misplaced during both periods.

1   *Los Angeles Times*, 25 August 1965.

In 1965, John Rousselot, then national public relations director of the John Birch Society—and later a Congressman—claimed 2000 officers of the L.A. Police Department were distributing Bircher propaganda from patrol cars. Meanwhile, throughout the 1960's and into the 1970's, L.A. led the nation in bombings with ultra-rightists heavily involved. August 1965 was the pretext for the formation of SWAT teams within the LAPD and the accelerated militarizing of the police function—a tendency only beginning to ebb with the ascendance of Willie Williams as the city's first African American police chief. [2]

History seems to be repeating itself. The headlines from 1965—"Negro hoodlums and juvenile gangs may be storing them underground for use in future times of violence"—could have been lifted from today's headlines.[3] Meanwhile, the press has taken an indifferent attitude to the recent revelation by Judge Terry Hatter that the L.A. Sheriff's Department contained a white supremacist gang. This is even more unfortunate in light of the fact that today's ultra-rightists continue to pay maximum attention to the turmoil of Los Angeles. A few years ago, it was revealed that Robert Matthews, a leading ultra-right racist leader, wanted to blow up power lines and telephone lines in L.A. and "drop a tub of cyanide into the aqueduct. Matthews was impressed. He'd dreamed of a repeat of the urban riots of the 1960's and wanted to capitalize on the strife to recruit frightened whites."[4] The continual focus on gangs and arms and

2   *Village Voice*, 16 April 1991.
3   *Los Angeles Times*, 18 August 1965.
4   Kevin Flynn and Gary Erhardt, *The Silent Brotherhood: Inside America's Racist Underground*, (New York: Free Press, 1989), p. 359.

the relative ignoring of the ultraright and weapons is one of the more unfortunate aspects of the events of 1965 that has been grafted on to 1992. It also reflects how the shifting of the political spectrum to the right in this country has led to a relative indifference to the question of arms in the hands of the ultra-right.

Xenophobic Nationalism and Population Increase

By 1965, the Red Scare had been in place for some time and despite the progressive winds brought about by the nascent civil rights movement, it had become difficult to blame the uprising in Los Angeles on "Communists" and other "outside agitators." However, as in Eastern Europe, the decline of left influence set the stage for the rise of right-wing influence among whites and xenophobic nationalism among minorities. Something of a "Black Scare" developed as ruling elites sought to blame the Nation of Islam—and not police brutality, unemployment, racism, etc.—for the uprising. Ironically, this enhanced the influence of this sect, which has lost some influence since February 1965 after being implicated in the assassination of Malcom X who had earlier defected from their ranks. Marquette Frye, whose arrest on 11 August 1965 had led directly to the conflagration, eventually joined the NOI.[5]

Yet, the rise of xenophobic nationalism had significance beyond the augmentation of the ranks of the NOI. In 1948, Los Angeles was the home of a thriving multi-ethnic, multiracial chapter of the Civil Rights Congress—a left-led formation

5   *Muhammad Speaks*, 27 August 1965.

that specialized in fighting racist and political repression. By 1956, it had been harassed into extinction as a result of the Red Scare.[6] By 1965, Congressman Gus Hawkins, a founder of the Congressional Black Caucus who represented South Central L.A. in Washington, D.C., was afraid to enter his district for fear that his light skin would lead someone to mistake him for "white" and thereby attack him: "'I recall once in Will Rogers Park, I was walking from the clubhouse out of my automobile and some fellow ran down to attack me on the basis of "here's whitey in our neighborhood"' . . . Hawkins said friends who knew he is Black rescued him. He did not report the incident, he said, but it taught him a lesson."[7]

In 1992, as noted, the ultra-right—William Dannemeyer, Ronald Reagan, William F. Buckley, Jr., William Rehnquist, et al.—has become part of the mainstream. Meanwhile, xenophobic nationalism continues to flourish as reflected in some of the popular tunes of rappers like Sister Souljah and L.A.'s own Ice Cube. In particular, the ideological tendency has been a complicating factor in establishing a civil discourse between Korean Americans and African Americans.

The increase in the Korean American population has been one of the more notable differences between 1965 and 1992. Likewise, a salient distinction between 1965 and 1992 has been the increase in the Latino—particularly Central American—population. Just as 1965 was preceded by an enormous growth in the African American population after World

6   Gerald Horne, *Communist Front? The Civil Rights Congress*, (London: Associated University Presses, 1988).

7   *Los Angeles Times*, 28 September 1989.

War II, 1992 was preceded by a similar staggering increase in the Latino population.

The Rand Study

Nevertheless, there has been a regrettable tendency to view the events of 1992 in the familiar Black-white tones of 1965. Yet, a study conducted recently by the Rand Corporation found that of the 5,633 adults arrested during the 1992 unrest, 18–24-year-old Latinos predominated. In all fairness, it should be noted that the Rand study did not include arrestees processed through the courts in Downey, Culver City, Inglewood, and Compton, which presumably would have included a higher proportion of the African Americans. Still, the Rand Study is indicative of a new demography that cannot be ignored; 30% of California's population is Latino and this may grow to 50% within twenty years. This is a reality and a challenge not presented so dramatically in 1965.[8]

Yet, this is not to deny that such a challenge was absent, even before 1965. It should never be forgotten that although African Americans participated in the founding of Los Angeles in 1781, the 1880 census revealed that only 100 Blacks were in L.A. County. The origins of a mass African American community in this area actually begins with World War II, when the need for Black labor in the defense plants of Southern California sparked a mass migration from Louisiana, Texas and Oklahoma. A useful metaphor encapsulating this process is the fact that an early Black community in L.A. had its origins with the internment of Japanese Americans as "Little Tokyo" became "Bronzeville."

8   *Los Angeles Sentinel*, 25 June–1 July 1992.

Historical Ignorance

At the same time, the unrest of 1965 and 1992 was preceded by the so-called "Zoot Suit riots" of 1943, which involved racist attacks on Mexican Americans in L.A. An understanding of California and its history must encompass an understanding of the displacement of the indigenous population and the conquest of this region from Mexico. Testifying before the commission headed by former CIA Director John McCone that investigated the 1965 uprising, Chicano analyst Ralph Guzman recalled, "as late as 1898 California had a higher incidence of unsolved homicides than all the states in the Union put together and the Los Angeles area had a higher incidence than the rest of the state. In most instances the people were being killed by lynch mobs." And the majority of those so treated were either indigenous, Mexican or both.[9]

Sadly, this history is little known. Such ignorance has contributed to ethnic tensions in L.A., a phenomenon noted by the well-known Chicano scholar Rodolfo Acuna: "A byproduct of the Watts riots was a further shift in control of poverty funds to Blacks . . . In turn, many Blacks felt that the poverty programs generally resulted from their civil rights movement . . . White politicians encouraged tensions between the two groups by playing them against each other."[10] Chicano politicos testifying before the McCone Commission were concerned that the only way for their community to be noticed and receive justice was

9   *Governor's Commission on the LA Riots*, Volume 7, 27 October 1965. Testimony of Ralph Guzman.

10   Rodolfo Acuna, *A Community Under Siege: A Chronicle of Chicanos East of the Los Angeles River, Los Angeles*, UCLA-Chicano Research Center Publications, 1984, p. 132.

"to riot in order to become recognized by the appropriate officials so that the poverty problems they have could be resolved." This forecast of what happened in 1992 was underscored by the fact "that there is a greater number of Mexican-Americans living in a state of poverty in Los Angeles County than there are Negroes."[11]

A Question of Class

The attempt to elide the Latino Question is part and parcel of an overall tendency by U.S. ruling elites to ignore the question of class and take advantage of centuries of ingrained Afro-phobia by portraying all manner of societal ills as "Black Issues." Sweeping Latino Questions under the rug facilitates this nefarious process. Also facilitating this trend has been the process—exacerbated by the Red Scare—of destabilizing class-based organizations, especially trade unions. Naturally, this tendency is reflected most starkly in U.S. foreign policy, particularly the effort to destabilize regimes that stressed the question of class conflict and sought to base themselves on the working class.

Justice or Hysteria

Yet, it remains true that the 1965 uprising was overwhelmingly an African American phenomenon. The typical juvenile arrested in 1965 was a 17-year-old Black native Californian male, coming from a family with an income of $300 per month. Those detained included 41 boys and girls under the age of 13.

---

11   *Governor's Commission on the LA Riots*, volume 16, 27 October 1965, Report of Interview with Eduardo Quevedo, Manuel Ruiz and Frank Paz.

All told, there were over 4000 arrests of juveniles and adults, with over 80% felony counts and more than 90% were African American.[12] Stanley Malone, president of the predominantly Black Langston Law Club complained at at the time about how judges had "hysterically punished and prejudged" the defendants due to "'racial overtones'" and an "'overall hysteria.'" Though bail for misdemeanors was typically set at $1000, this time it was raised 100% to to $2000.[13]

There were over 450 boys and 72 girls arrested during this period. The Times concluded, "Never in the history of the county's juvenile court system have so many youngsters been arrested in so short a period."[14] National Lawyers Guild stalwart Ben Margolis recalled later, "There was a near hysteria in the courts at that time. People were being arrested at the drop of a hat. There was almost something like a kind of civil war going on."[15] Even Evelle Younger, who subsequently served as the State Attorney General concluded in his inimitable fashion that judges raised bail "so high that probably the only ones that made bail were the Muslims and professional hoods."[16]

---

12   "Watts Riot Arrest: Los Angeles; August 1965. A Statistical Accounting as of 30 June 1966 of Procedures . . . " Prepared in Bureau of Criminal Statistics-Department of Justice, State of California. (Urban Policy Research Institute, 3301 C St. Sacramento, California 95807).

13   *Los Angeles Times*, 19 August 1965.

14   *Los Angeles Times*, 26 August 1965.

15   Ben Margolis, 17 May 1985, UCLA Oral History.

16   *Governor's Commission on the LA Riots*, volume 14, 28 October 1965, Testimony of Evelle J. Younger.

Just as the authorities were little concerned about weapons in the hands of ultra-rightists and hysterical about the prospect of gangs obtaining them, those participating in racist riots received a veritable slap on the wrist for their behavior. Edwin O. Guthman, special assistant to the U.S. Attorney General during the time of the violent protests against integrating the University of Mississippi in the early 1960's, recalled that "after the riot at Oxford we did not condemn all southern whites. In fact, under Mississippi justice, not one rioter was convicted of anything—not even disturbing the peace."[17]

Apparently, few lessons were learned from the gutting of civil liberties in 1965. This was the sad conclusion reached by NLG leader Cathy Dreyfuss after an exhaustive investigation of the aftermath of the events of 1992: "Faced with thousands of defendants, many of whom were guilty of nothing more than being Black or brown and in the wrong place at the wrong time, the justice system has responded by suspending due process and convicting them as a class. . . . The people arrested in the days after the verdict have been denied their rights at every step of the process—from unconstitutional delays in arraignment, denial of a speedy trial, excessive charging and bail policies, prosecutions without sufficient evidence, and extreme sentences. This 'Judicial emergency' shows us just how quickly many of our constitutional protections are dispensed with when the authorities believe they are under attack."[18]

---

17   *Los Angeles Times*, 22 August 1965.

18   Cathy Dreyfuss, "What the Crackdown has done to Defendants' Rights," NLG LA Chapter News 8 (No. 6, June 1992): 1–4.

Insurance Issues

Today there are reports about uninsured and underinsured small businesses being wiped out as a result of the uprising. Similarly, there are reports about insurance companies being reluctant to process legitimate claims. Despite the fact that since 1965, the voters of California have created the office of State Insurance Commissioner, complaints about insurance companies persist. In 1965, it was the insurance companies that insisted what happened was not a riot but an "insurrection." This was not necessarily a political commentary seeking to provide context for the horrible conditions that led to the turmoil; it was simply that the typical byzantine insurance contracts contained clauses "exempting coverage in the event of an insurrection."[19]

By 1967, reports were trickling in indicating that the insurance industry had fled en masse from South Central, a development that contributed to urban blight and decay. The Times reported, "Fire insurance rates in Watts are three to five times what they were before the riot . . . the pool companies refuse to write policies covering theft, vandalism or malicious mischief . . . insurance losses in the Bel-Air fire of 1961 were spread statewide, so Watts helped pay for them, but that Watts business . . . must absorb the high cost of its own risk through escalated premiums . . . "[20]

The U.S. ruling elite seeks to foil the organizing of militant groupings pursing a redistributive agenda. Thus, the Black Panther Party, which arose from the ashes of South Central,

19   *Los Angeles Times*, 17 August 1965.
20   *Los Angeles Times*, 18 July 1967.

was battered out of existence. However, this destabilizing of organizations means that grievances have no channel for resolution and the only outlets become inchoate, spontaneous uprisings as in 1965 and 1992. Such uprisings come at great cost: 34 perished in 1965 and over 50 in 1992.

There Have Been Some Benefits

Nonetheless, it should be noted that these explosions do bring some benefit. After 1965, for example, Martin Luther King Hospital was built in the heart of the former "curfew zone."[21] A California State University campus that was sited originally for affluent Palos Verdes, was instead constructed at Dominguez Hills as "several trustees have expressed enthusiasm for this location, because it would bring the State College system into closer communication with the Negro community in South Los Angeles."[22] Months after August 1965, the Southwest Branch of the Los Angeles Realty Board voted 50–13 "to change their by-laws, liberalizing a rule which had permitted a small minority to block membership by Negro realtors . . . The change is a direct result of a secret U.S. Justice Department investigation . . . working under the theory that racial discrimination is a violation of federal anti-trust laws because it restrains trade . . ."[23] On the twentieth anniversary of the 1965 uprising, the Times reported that "since the riots, more than 500 housing units have been built, along with a health center, facilities for community action groups and most recently, two neighborhood shopping centers. "There was also a cultural renaissance

21   *Los Angeles Times*, 17 August 1980.
22   *Los Angeles Times*, 21 October 1965.
23   *Los Angeles Times*, 3 February 1966.

of sorts after 1965; e.g., the Watts Writers Workshop and other activities supported by foundations and creative artists like Budd Schulberg.

Hence, it may be said that the lives lost in 1965 were not necessarily lost in vain. Still, the fact remains that the building of organizations with a progressive outlook is the most reliable guarantee that even more gains can be made for national minorities and the working class generally in Los Angeles. The receding role of the U.S. in the global economy suggests that the types of concessions won after 1965 may not flow as readily today. In any case, 27 years from now when we look back on the events of 1992, it is to be hoped that we will have made considerably more substantial progress than we made during the period following the tumultuous developments of August 1965.

RACE BACKWARDS: GENES, VIOLENCE, RACE, AND GENOCIDE

Covert Action, Winter 1992–93

With a deteriorating economy and the concomitant rise in unemployment, along with spiralling racism, the notion inevitably bubbles to the surface that incarceration may not be sufficient to deal with widespread crime and violence; perhaps, more punitive measures are needed. Rather than confront the racism, unemployment, and poverty that have left millions without hope—or the means of subsistence—the government and many social scientists continue to direct research toward finding a genetic explanation or a medical "solution" for those who do not docilely accept their fate. The long history of "scientific racism" in the U.S. helps provide a rationale for this potentially genocidal approach and creates the context for the National Violence Initiative and the intemperate remarks of Dr. Frederick Goodwin.

When he took the podium to address the National Health Advisory Council on February 11, 1992, Dr. Frederick Goodwin, then head of the Alcohol, Drug Abuse and Mental Health Administration (ADAMHA), did not know he was about to ignite a major crisis. By the time he finished his remarks, he was embroiled in a raging controversy that has raised profound questions about efforts to deal with escalating problems in urban areas. Goodwin told his audience:

If you look, for example, at male monkeys, especially in the wild, roughly half of them survive to adulthood. The other half die by violence. That is the natural way of it for males, to knock each other off and, in fact, there are some interesting evolutionary implications of that because the same hyperaggressive monkeys who kill each other are also hypersexual, so they copulate more and therefore they reproduce more to offset the fact that half of them are dying. Now, one could say that if some of the loss of social structure in this society, and particularly within the high impact inner city areas, has removed some of the civilizing evolutionary things that we have built up and that maybe it isn't just the careless use of the word when people call certain areas of certain cities jungles, that we may have gone back to what might be more natural, without all of the social controls that we have imposed upon ourselves as a civilization over thousands of years in our own evolution . . . [1]

By associating African Americans with monkeys and "hypersexuality," Goodwin tapped into a wellspring of racist sentiment. He also provoked anti-racist anger. Rep. John Conyers (D-Mich.), a leading member of the Congressional Black Caucus (CBC), objected strenuously to Goodwin's

[1]   Warren Leary, "Struggle Continues Over Remarks by Mental Health Official," New York Times, March 8, 1992, p. 34.; partial transcript of the February 11,1992 meeting of the National Health Advisory Council is available, as are most items cited here, from Center for the Study of Psychiatry, Inc., 4628 Chestnut Street, Bethesda, MD 20814, 301-652-5580.

remarks and helped draft a letter signed by all 26 CBC members. It raised the issue of whether Dr. Goodwin had the necessary sensitivity and approach to continue heading a major government agency. Conyers asserted that Goodwin's dangerous and simplistic explanation for the violence in our cities evokes a type of social Darwinism that has long been discredited and continues to function as a smoke screen for the separate and discriminatory treatment of African Americans. It ignores a complex set of root causes of drug use and violence in our society.[2]

The CBC was joined in its denunciation by Senator Edward Kennedy (D-Mass.) and Congressman John Dingell (D-Mich.)[3] as well as the 114,000-member American Psychological Association and the 137,000-member National Association of Social Workers.[4]

Administration and most of the media reactions were more supportive of Goodwin. The Wall Street Journal invoked the specter of the "speech-police" and rushed to Goodwin's defense.[5] Although Health and Human Services Secretary Dr. Louis Sullivan criticized the remarks, he in effect rewarded Goodwin by appointing him head of the similarly influential National Institute of Mental Health—a post not requiring Senate approval or presidential appointment.[6]

2   Letter to the Editor, Wall Street Journal, April 1, 1992.
3   Editorial, "The Fred Goodwin Case," Washington Post, March 21, 1992.
4   Leary, op. cit.
5   Editorial, "The Speech Police," Wall Street Journal, March 9, 1992.
6   Leary, op. cit.

The Violence Initiative

And if the "monkey" remarks were not bad enough, Goodwin, during his notorious February 11 speech, casually revealed plans for a new National Violence Initiative. This proposal was slated to become the number one funding priority for the National Institute of Mental Health by 1994—the agency Goodwin would soon head. HHS has since declined to clarify the current status of the Initiative except to deny that it includes genetic research. Covert Action learned that the General Accounting Office "is looking into the entire research portfolio."

The initiative came as a surprise to many in Congress. Rep. Conyers was upset not only with the proposal, but with the lack of public disclosure surrounding it. Health and Human Services, he charged, had not been able to "supply us with the paperwork on this initiative and the two African-American members of the Mental Health Advisory Panel were unfamiliar with the program."[7]

Under the Initiative, researchers will use alleged genetic and biochemical markers to identify potentially violent minority children as young as five for biological and behavioral interventions—including drug therapy and possibly psychosurgery—purportedly aimed at preventing later adult violence.

The Initiative specifically rejects any examination of social, economic, or political questions, such as racism, poverty, or unemployment. Instead, this bio-medical approach focuses heavily on the alleged role of the brain neurotransmitter,

---

7   Letter, Wall Street Journal, op. cit.

serotonin, in violence. Not coincidentally, this approach is favored by many in the medical industry.

As Dr. Peter Breggin, the leading analyst in the field has observed, this [approach] corresponds with the current financial interests of the pharmaceutical industry, since several drugs affecting serotonin neurotransmission have been submitted for approval to the Food and Drug Administration.

The controversial antidepressant, Prozac, is the first of these serotonergic drugs, and it has become the largest money-maker in the pharmaceutical industry.[8] Against this backdrop, NIH provided a hefty $100,000 grant for a conference entitled "Genetic Factors in Crime: Findings, Uses and Implications." It was to be sponsored by the Institute for Philosophy and Public Policy at the University of Maryland and slated for October 1992. The promotional brochure promised that genetic research holds out the prospect of identifying individuals who may be predisposed to certain kinds of criminal conduct, of isolating environmental features which trigger those predispositions, and of treating some predispositions with drugs and unintrusive therapies.[9] . . . Genetic research also gains impetus from the apparent failure of environmental approaches to crime— deterrence, diversion and rehabilitation.[10]

With this last statement, the conference planners appeared to write off an entire generation, and focus exclusively on

8 Peter Breggin, "The Violence Initiative — A Racist Biomedical Program for Social Control," The Rights Tenet, (Center for the Study of Psychiatry) Summer 1992.

9 Christopher Anderson, "NIH, Under Fire . . . ," Nature, July 30, 1992, p. 357.

10 Vince Bielski, "Hunting the Crime Gene," San Francisco Weekly, July 15, 1992.

various genetic and medical solutions. The ensuing protest caused NIH to freeze conference funding—temporarily. The objections were led by enraged African Americans concerned that, in these dangerous times, such a project could easily be transformed into directed genocide. Their concern was not assuaged when it was revealed that Reagan appointee Marianne Mele Hall proclaimed that black and brown people are culturally or even genetically inferior. They have been conditioned, she said, "by 10,000 years of selective breeding for personal combat and the anti-work ethic of jungle freedoms" and were therefore unfit for civic life. Great Society programs just "spoiled" them, she argued, encouraging a sense of entitlement that led to laziness, drug use, and crime, particularly crime against whites.[11] Despite the fear that such a conference would encourage racism and broaden the path for potentially genocidal efforts, the NIH revealed recently that it was considering unfreezing the funds so that the conference may go forward in 1993.[12]

The Disease Model

The last time such an initiative was proposed, a firestorm of protest erupted. The context, not unlike today, was rising unemployment and poverty in the euphemistically termed "inner cities." Neurosurgeon William Sweet testified in 1968 before the New York state legislature that those participating in urban uprisings were suffering from brain disease (psychomotor

---

11 Micaela di Leonardo, "White Lies: Rape, Race and the Myth of the Black Underclass," Village Voice, September 22, 1992.

12 David L. Wheeler, "Genetic-in-Crime Meeting May Get Funds From NIH," Chronicle of Higher Education, September 30, 1992, p. A14.

epilepsy); i.e., blacks who rebelled against their plight could be "cured" by carving their brains or drugging them.[13]

That same year "successful" psychosurgery was performed on California prisoners[14] and other "undesirables."[15] Dr. Jewell Osterholm and his associate, Dr. David Matthews, confessed to performing psychosurgery, or cingulotomies, on drug addicts, alcoholics, and "neurotics." According to Dr. Peter Breggin, "a cingulotomy is nothing more than the newest version of lobotomy. It can turn a person into a zombie. It makes the patient docile, subdued and easy to manage."[16] This latter description was precisely what certain U.S. elites desired for often-rebellious blacks.

Perhaps Sweet and his colleagues, Dr. Frank Ervin and Dr. Vernon Mark, were inspired by these programs. In any case, they went directly to Congress for funding and in 1971, the NIMH awarded them a $500,000 contract, with the Justice Department kicking in a supplemental grant. Their mission was to research the causes of violence, with particular attention to possible genetic factors and to investigate treatments, including

13 David Bird, "More Stress Urged on Cause of Civil Disorders," *New York Times*, August 14, 1968, p. 19.

14 Leroy F. Aarons, "Brain Surgery Is Tested on Three California Convicts," *Washington Post*, February 25, 1972, pp. Al, 20; Peter Breggin, "Psycho- surgery for Political Purposes," *Duquesne Law Review*, vol. 13, no. 1, 1975, pp. 841–62.

15 Larry Fields, "Addict Who Died Had Brain Surgery to Fight Habit," *Philadelphia Daily News*, March 13, 1972; Breggin, "Psychosurgery." op. cit., p. 855.

16 B.J. Mason, "Brain Surgery to Control Behavior: Controversial Options Are Coming Back as Violence Curbs," *Ebony*, February 1973, p. 68.

psychosurgery and amygdalotomy.[17] Although public pressure eventually caused them to lose their funding, the effort to disguise racism as objective research and the search for a medical "cure" for socioeconomic problems did not die.

In 1972, the state of Michigan moved forward with funding for research into controlling violence through psychosurgery and chemical castration. Fortunately this project, too, was aborted in the face of public protest. In light of similar approaches today, the words of the neurologist in charge of this 1972 project, Ernest Rodin, remain relevant. Children of "limited intelligence" tend to become violent, he suggested, when treated as "equals," and were better brought up in an "authoritarian lifestyle." Much violence could be avoided by castrating "dumb young males. . . . It is also well known," he went on, "that human eunuchs, although at times quite scheming entrepreneurs, are not given to physical violence."[18]

The next year, the popular African American monthly, Ebony reported a disturbing story about Dr. O.J. Andy, a neurosurgeon at the University of Mississippi Medical Center, who had been performing psychosurgery, or thalamotomies. Dr. Andy revealed that the kind of brain damage that could necessitate such radical surgery might be manifested by participation in the Watts Uprising. Such people, he diagnosed, "could have abnormal pathologic brains." In addition to inducing

---

17   Breggin, "Psychosurgery . . . ," op. cit.

18   Ibid., p. 853; and Ernest Rodin, "A Neurological Appraisal of Some Episodic Behavioral Disturbances with Special Emphasis on Aggressive Out-bursts, Exhibit 3" for American Orthopsychiatric Association; and *Kaimowitz* v. *Department of Mental Health*, Civil No. 73-19, 434-AW (Circuit Court, Wayne Co., Michigan, July 10, 1973).

docility, side effects to such surgery could include loss of memory, dreams and daydreams, intellectual emptiness, lack of awareness, lack of creativity and loss of the ability to get angry. The desired result was enforced passivity for black and other communities perceived as dissident.[19]

Fortunately, the scientific community did not rest supine in the face of this atrocity. Dr. Seymour Pollack, among others, challenged sharply the idea that participating in a civil insurrection was a sign of mental disorder.[20] A remarkably diverse coalition sprang up in Congress to stymie the original violence initiative 20 years ago.

Roots of the Eugenic Solution

The historical roots of viewing rebellion against intolerable conditions as symptoms of disease go back more than a century. In the early years of the 19th century, Samuel Cartwright, a physician, argued that particular forms of mental illness caused by nerve disorders, were prevalent among slaves. Drapetomania, for example, could be diagnosed by a single symptom: the uncontrollable urge to escape from slavery. The symptoms exhibited by slaves who "suffered" from dysathesia aethiopica were more complex and included destroying plantation property, disobedience, talking back, fighting with their masters, or refusing to work. Despite the aura of expertise and the Latin terms, Dr. Cartwright and his 19th and 20th century counterparts were not practicing neutral science. Rather, they were providing

19   Mason, op. cit.
20   Letter, *Journal of the American Medical Association*, November 13, 1967.

convenient explanations that served to justify and rationalize the systemic exploitation practiced by their paymasters.[21]

" . . . *instead of waiting to execute degenerate offspring for crime . . . , society can prevent those who are manifestly unfit from continuing their kind."* —*U.S. Supreme Court, 1927*

In addition to blaming disease, some scientists and social scientists have concocted a genetic model to explain their own presumed racial superiority and justify exploitation and repression of their "inferiors." Such structured, organized disinformation has been part of social science since the "Age of Enlightenment." Sir Francis Galton, a cousin of Charles Darwin, coined the term eugenics for his study of how humans inherit physical and behavioral traits.[22]

Proponents of genetically based inferiority hold that a whole race is biologically, irredeemably inferior. The endemic nature of this racism tells less about the individuals who promote it than about the society that fosters their rise to positions of power. Remarks like Goodwin's, comparing blacks with monkeys, are not isolated. In the wake of the 1965 Watts uprising,

---

21   Carol Tavris, *The Mismeasure of Woman* (New York: Simon and Schuster, 1992), pp. 176–77.

22   Daniel Coleman, "New Storm Brews on Whether Crime Has Roots in Genes," *New York Times*, September 15, 1992, p. B5; and James Lawler, *IQ, Heritability and Racism* (New York: International, 1978), p. 39.

ultra-right Los Angeles Police Chief William Parker anticipated Goodwin's analysis by comparing African Americans to "monkeys in a zoo."[23] The L.A. police who beat Rodney King echoed the slur when they used the term "gorillas in the mist."

The genetic model has endured not because it has any scientific basis, but because it is useful. Around the turn of the century, eugenics took the ethnically diverse U.S. by storm. It provided a "scientific" justification for stigmatizing African Americans, Asians, and Eastern and Southern European immigrants and forcing them to work for less.

Theories of genetically determined inferiority also legitimated calls for forced sterilization. Theodore Roosevelt was not alone in calling for this radical solution to social problems.[24] In 1907, Indiana passed the first law allowing involuntary sterilization of "confirmed criminals, idiots, imbeciles and rapists."

A 1937 survey found that compulsory sterilization of so-called habitual criminals was supported strongly by "progressive" intellectuals and policymakers who were keen on applying social science to society. In 1939, the prominent Harvard anthropologist, E.A. Hooten, advocated "ruthless elimination of inferior types" and "biological housecleaning." By 1940, 30 states had sterilization laws, often for such vaguely defined "crimes" as "moral degeneracy"; 22 states continue to have such laws on the books.[25]

---

23 "Races," *Time*, August 27, 1965, p. 11.

24 Thomas Dyer, *Theodore Roosevelt and the Idea of Race* (Baton Rouge: LSU Press, 1980). Like many of the U.S. elite at the beginning of the 20th century, Roosevelt held firm views about the inferiority of certain racial and ethnic groups.

25 Letter to the Editor, *New York Times*, September 18, 1992, p. 34.

The legal basis in the U.S. had been established by a 1927 Supreme Court decision: "[It] is far better for all the world," proclaimed Justice Oliver Wendell Holmes on the constitutionality of sterilization, "if instead of waiting to execute degenerate offspring for crime . . . , society can prevent those who are manifestly unfit from continuing their kind."[26]

Thus, chillingly, the U.S. preceded the Nazis down this genocidal path. It was not until 1933, that Germany approved the Nazi Eugenics Sterilization Law. It was, noted New York University Prof. Norman Finkelstein, "the first fateful step toward the final solution."[27]

The misuse of social science to justify racism had deep roots in Europe. French research in 1857 "demonstrated" that criminality was hereditary. In 1874, Richard Dugdale published a study of an Irish family he called Jukes in which he purported to trace their hereditary tendency toward crime. In Italy in 1876, in his study, L'LJomo Delinquente, Cesare Lombroso asserted that criminals were the products of heredity and could be recognized by features such as small restless eyes (thieves) or bright eyes and cracked voices (sex criminals). Sadly, he did not leave us with a reliable method by which a robber baron could be recognized.

Quaint and vicious as that 19th century research now appears, it differs little from the intellectual offspring it has spawned in the last years of the 20th century. Contemporary "scientists" have simply become more sophisticated in delineating alleged "markers" that predict who will become a "criminal." In the 1970s, for example, the XYY chromosomal configuration

26   *Buck v. Bell*, 274 U.S. 207 (1927).
27   Letter to the Editor, *New York Times*, September 18, 1992, p. 34.

was said to be associated with crime and violence.[28] And as the 1992 Violence Initiative and the proposed Maryland conference demonstrate, the misbegotten search continues. Like Dracula, "scientific racism" continues to rise from the dead to stalk black America, in particular.

Deja Vu All Over Again

Not only science and government, but the media have been complicit in perpetuating the mythological link between genes and crime. Shortly before Goodwin's remarks to the advisory council, the New York Times gave front-page coverage to a modern Jukes study. "More than half of all juvenile delinquents imprisoned in state institutions and more than a third of adult criminals in local jails and state prisons have immediate family members who have also been incarcerated according to figures compiled by the Justice Department."[29] Backing up the article were predictable quotes from Harvard Professor Richard Herrnstein, who has been attacked in the past for taking stands on genes and crime perceived widely as racist. "These are stunning statistics," he said, accepting the unproven innuendo of genetic causality.

Some of the studies to determine "markers" for crime are stunning. In Nebraska, seven genetic marker systems were analyzed from liquid blood and dried bloodstain specimens and submitted from various law enforcement agencies throughout the state to the Nebraska State Patrol Crime Laboratory.

28 Coleman, "New Storm Brews . . . , op. cit., p. B5.
29 Fox Butterfield, "Study Finds a Family Link to Criminality," *New York Times*, January 31, 1992, p. A1.

The reported results indicated that criminal facial and body types correlated with crime statistics.[30]

Thus, it could be concluded easily, darker peoples may be committing more crime not necessarily because of socioeconomic conditions but because of genetic predisposition.

And if bad genes are the cause, the cure is certainly not education, jobs, equality of opportunity, decent health care, and an end to racism. Rather the solution is that people of color must reproduce less, be pharmacologically or surgically "repaired," or incarcerated.

The Media and the Myth of Neutral Science

Given the present climate, exploring the nature side of the nature-nurture controversy relating to crime and race is, in principle, objectionable. In the context of a declining capitalist economy suffused with racism, such research could be transmuted easily into a bludgeon wielded especially against people of color.[31]

---

30   "Distributions of Genetic Markers in a Nebraska Population," *Journal of Forensic Science*, vol. 35, no. 5, September 1990, pp. 1207–10.

31   It would be a mistake to suggest that all current research is "Jukes revisited." To get an idea of contemporary research, e.g., Adrian Raine and Jennifer Dunkin, "The Genetic and Psychophysiological Basis of Antisocial Behavior: Implications for Counseling and Therapy," *Journal of Counseling and Development*, vol. 68, no. 6, July-August 1990, p. 637; Jennifer White, et al., "How Early Can We Tell? Predictors of Childhood Conduct Disorder and Adolescent Delinquency," *Criminology*, vol. 28, no. 4, November 1990, pp. 507–33; Diana H. Fishbein, "Biological Perspectives in Criminology," *Criminology*, vol. 28, no. 1, February 1990, pp. 27–72; Glenn Walters and Thomas White, "Heredity and Crime: Bad Genes or Bad Research?" *Criminology*, vol. 27, no. 3, August 1989, pp. 455–85; Margaret A. Jackson, "The Clinical Assessment and Prediction of

Research is never "neutral." Who asks the questions, what questions are asked and what ones ignored, who pays for the research, who interprets the results are all subjective decisions outside the realm of "pure science." The bias is built in.

It is not only the kind of research which is problematic, but how the elite media choose to report it that promotes and perpetuates those biases. The New York Times, as noted, placed on the front page a pedestrian—at best—study suggesting genetic links between race and crime. In contrast, in 1988, Prof. Delbert Elliott of the University of Colorado Boulder published the results of his 10-year study demonstrating that black youth from poor sections of cities are only slightly more likely to commit crimes than are white youths from affluent neighborhoods. He factored in that the latter are more likely to have connections allowing them to escape punishment. Prof. Elliott was correct in his euphoric assertion that, "These findings have really challenged the old concepts about crime." Perhaps that is why the study received little attention.[32]

Target: Black and Brown Youth

Science which seeks explanations for crime and violence without carefully factoring in socioeconomic conditions is of special concern to those who see black youth as a targeted and endangered population. Inevitably, as the U.S. economy continues to

Violent Behavior: Toward a Scientific Analysis," *Criminal Justice and Behavior*, vol. 16, no. 1, March 1989, pp. 114–31; Lawrence Cohen and Richard Machalek, "A General Theory of Expropriative Crime: An Evolutionary Ecological Approach," *American Journal of Sociology*, vol. 94, no. 3, November 1988, p. 465.

32 Boyce Rensberger, "Study Discounts Race, Class as Studies in Youth Crime," *Washington Post*, August 15, 1988, p. A3.

deteriorate, the country will increasingly face organized challenges such as the Black Panthers and inchoate uprisings such as the one that shook Los Angeles in spring 1992.

Inevitably, the government will respond. Even without a formal violence initiative, other, similarly odious initiatives have already been implemented to control young urban blacks. Despite Jesse Jackson's admonition that it is more expensive to send a youth to jail than to Yale, to the state pen than to Penn State, incarceration has become the government's option of choice. In Baltimore, for example, on any given day in 1991, 56 percent of the city's African American men ages 18–35 were in jail or in prison, on probation or parole, awaiting trial or sentencing, or being sought on warrants for their arrest. That year, of nearly 13,000 individuals arrested on drug charges in Baltimore, more than 11,000 were African Americans. An African American youth was 100 times more likely to be charged with the sale of drugs in Baltimore than a Euro-American youth.[33]

California, the most populous state, reflects the national picture. The state's prison population has more than quadrupled from 22,500 inmates at the beginning of the 1980s, to over 100,000 eleven years later. In the decade ending in 1991, California had imprisoned seven times more people than during the 30 years between 1950 and 1980. Since 1985, California prisons added more prisoners each year than they added in each average decade between 1950 and 1980. There are 40,000 more inmates in California than in all of Great Britain or Germany. A disproportionate percentage of California's inmates are

---

33   National Center on Institutions and Alternatives, *Hobbling a Generation: Young African American Males in the Criminal Justice System of America's Cities: Baltimore, Maryland* (Alexandria, Va., 1992).

African American and Latino.[34] In short, rather than attacking the roots of crime by addressing socioeconomic questions, the authorities have chosen to lock up a generation and throw away the key.

Mass imprisonment is supplemented by another disquieting example of institutionalizing those who cannot be controlled. Southern Exposure documented the disproportionate number of blacks involuntarily committed to state-run mental hospitals in the southern U.S. In 1987, nearly 37 percent of those committed against their will were black. Consistently diagnosed with more severe mental illnesses than whites, they have been subjected to heavier doses of drugs and longer hospital stays as well as (in a number of southern states), indefinite commitment without judicial review. The pattern of over-institutionalizing and over-medicating blacks, the article suggests, may not be confined to the South.[35]

Nor—despite the fact that the greatest weight of overt repression falls on young minority males—do women escape society's "remedies." In late 1990, an editorial in the Philadelphia Inquirer suggested the ghastly scenario that the 5-year contraceptive, Norplant, be implanted in black women so that what was seen as their excessive number of babies would not swell the welfare rolls. Although the editors were sufficiently squeamish to acknowledge, "All right, the subject makes us uncomfortable, too," they did not jettison the macabre idea.[36]

---

34 Franklin Zimring and Gordon Hawkins, "Prison Population and Criminal Justice Policy in California," *California Policy Seminar Brief*, vol. 4, no. 8, August 1992, pp. 1–7.

35 David Ramm, "Over Committed," *Southern Exposure*, Fall 1989, pp. 14–17.

36 "Norplant and Poverty," December 12, 1990, p. A18.

Preventing Genocide

The U.S. faces stiffer challenges abroad not only from the so-called Third World but also from erstwhile allies in Western Europe and Japan. Simultaneously, restive minorities at home have made clear—through the fires of spring in L.A.—that they will not be recumbent in the face of massive unemployment, increased homelessness, and draconian cuts in education. Norplant, ethnic weapons, psychosurgery and the Violence Initiative are sophisticated stratagems designed to deal with these festering problems. As has happened often in the past, fundamental socioeconomic questions are redefined as biomedical problems, and these in turn are redefined as stemming from defective and possibly sub-human individuals. Hence, Goodwin's references to urban youth as "monkeys."

Rather than attacking the roots of crime by addressing socio-economic questions, the authorities have chosen to lock up a generation and throw away the key.

It is not enough for the targets to be viewed as less than human. Children as young as five years old—some of the most defenseless members of this society—are singled out for intervention. And, it is not enough for the targets to be young, they must also come from the ranks of despised and persecuted minorities. It will only be enough when minorities offer no more resistance and simply do as they are told.

That option is as unlikely as it is intolerable. So, unless dramatic intervention by the progressive movement occurs, genocidal measures will be moved a step closer. The Violence Initiative and its progeny must be rejected, and the movement to create a more humane society must be accelerated.

"MYTH" AND THE MAKING OF "MALCOLM X"

The American Historical Review, April 1993,
Volume 98, No.2

IN COMMON ORDINARY USAGE, to engage in myth mak-
ing suggests falsification, factual inaccuracies, and the like.
However, from another vantage point, myths are not necessarily lies, they are explications. These narratives extracted from
history perform a symbolic function essential to the culture
that produced them. Myths, in this sense, are useful parables
and allegories containing lessons for today. They help to explain
the world.

That is the good news. The bad news is that myths, at times,
can be misleading, not so much for mangling the facts but for
neglecting certain facts or distorting the relationship between
facts. As we have been reminded repeatedly and accurately, the
negative value of myth is reflected in the traditional story of the
"Old West." And Hollywood, the anchor of the West, has been
a major producer of myths.[1]

---

1   Richard White, "It's Your Misfortune and None of My Own": A History of
    the American West (Norman, Okla., 1991); Richard Slotkin, The Fatal
    Environment: The Myth of the Frontier in the Age of Industrialization,
    1800–1890 (New York, 1985); Patricia Nelson Limerick, et al.,
    eds., Trails: Toward a New Western History (Lawrence, Kan., 1991);

What is called the civil rights movement or the post-World
War II trajectory of African American history has developed a
certain mythology that Spike Lee's estimable and worthy epic,
Malcolm X, seeks to replace with an alternative mythology. The
traditional myth is centered on Martin Luther King, Jr., with Rosa
Parks and the Student Non-Violent Coordinating Committee
(SNCC) playing pivotal supporting roles. All of a sudden, in
the mid-1950s—during a period, we are told, for some reason
otherwise somnolent—Negroes, led by Dr. King and assisted by
brilliant attorneys and related law enforcement personnel, not
to mention sympathetic white elites, started marching and getting their rights.[2] The U.S. film industry, in *Mississippi Burning*,
The Long Walk Home, and other films, has presented a variation
of this theme, featuring ever-pious, long-suffering blacks and

Patricia Nelson Limerick, *The Legacy of Conquest: The Unbroken
Past of the American West* (New York, 1987); Arna Bontemps and
Langston Hughes, eds., *The Book of Negro Folklore* (New York, 1958);
Alan Dundes, comp., *Mother Wit from the Laughing Barrel: Readings
in the Interpretation of Afro-American Folklore* (Englewood Cliffs,
N.J., 1972). Myth making is not peripheral; it can be central. See
Dan Moldea, *Dark Victory: Ronald Reagan, MCA, and the Mob* (New
York, 1986).

2   Richard Kluger, *Simple Justice: The History of Brown v.Board of
Education and Black America's Struggle for Equality* (New York,
1976); David J. Garrow, *Bearing the Cross: Martin Luther King, Jr.,
and the Southern Christian Leadership Conference* (New York, 1986);
Taylor Branch, *Parting the Waters: America in the King Years, 1954–63*
(New York, 1988); Clayborne Carson, *In Struggle: SNCC and
the Black Awakening of the 1960s* (Cambridge, Mass., 1981); Fred
Powledge, *Free at Last? The Civil Rights Movement and the People
Who Made It* (New York, 1992); Peter B. Levy, ed., *Let Freedom Ring:
A Documentary History of the Modern Civil Rights Movement* (New
York, 1992); Carl T. Rowan, *Dream Makers, Dream Breakers: The
World of Justice Thurgood Marshall* (Boston, 1993); Kay Mills, *This
Little Light of Mine: The Life of Fannie Lou Hamer* (New York, 1993).

heroic whites, in a fashion not unlike anti-apartheid epics such as *Cry Freedom* and *A Dry White Season*. During these seasons of racial strife and conflagrations in Los Angeles, such images can be quite soothing and reassuring.

With his usual audacity, Spike Lee has dared to create a competing myth, akin to what Oliver Stone attempted in his alternative myth of Camelot, *JFK*. *Malcolm X* presents angry, not meek blacks. It suggests that Jim Crow violence and exploitation were eroded not only by smart lawyers and adroit FBI agents but by angry black Muslims and nationalists as well. In this alternative view, the nonviolence and passive resistance of Dr. King is juxtaposed with Malcolm X's language of militant self-defense. The narrative focuses on the many transformations of Malcolm, from terrorized child to hustler to prisoner to narrow nationalist to progressive nationalist.

Neither the King nor the Malcolm myth is an outright falsification (although some of the celluloid versions of the former come perilously close to this shifting border). However, both neglect highly relevant and persuasive evidence because it does not necessarily comport with the contemporary lessons that one is to draw from these myths. For example, in a nation where the Cold War and the Red Scare have been the defining postwar paradigms, the attacks on the civil liberties of black leftists— which were taking place as civil rights for blacks generally were being expanded—are not part of either myth. It is as if W. E. B. Du Bois, Paul Robeson, Ben Davis, Claudia Jones, and William Patterson did not exist. That Spike Lee, a filmmaker, could not transcend in *Malcolm X limits* that have ensnared many historians and activists should not come as a surprise.

JUST BEFORE THANKSGIVING DAY in 1948, the man who was to become Malcolm X sent a form letter to Elijah

Muhammad of the Nation of Islam seeking to join this religious sect. At that juncture, membership was relatively small and the Nation's fiery anti-white rhetoric had failed to strike much of a chord.[3] W. E. B. Du Bois had just been ousted from the leadership of the NAACP because of his refusal to go along with accommodation to the gathering Cold War consensus. He was still playing a key role in the Council on African Affairs, the leading organization in the United States involved in seeking to critique and alter U.S. policy toward colonialism and apartheid.[4] Ben Davis, a top black Communist, was still a member of the New York City Council, with substantial support from the Harlem community that was to cheer Malcolm X a few years later. Claudia Jones, an Afro-Trinidadian Communist leader in New York City, was becoming increasingly concerned about being deported, and William Patterson was just assuming leadership of the Civil Rights Congress (CRC), which was to defend Du Bois, Davis, Jones, Robeson, and the numerous other black leftists who were prosecuted, jailed, or harassed in the post-1948 era. At this juncture, the CRC was well

3   Karl Evanzz, *The Judas Factor: The Plot to Kill Malcolm X* (New York, 1992). Evanzz, a reporter for the Washington Post, has written the most informative book on Malcolm X and the Nation of Islam to date. For a sampling of the literature, see Bruce Perry, *Malcolm: The Life of a Man Who Changed Black America* (Barrytown, N.Y., 1991). For my critical review of this book, see *New York Amsterdam News*, November 30, 1991; Joe Wood, ed., *Malcolm: In Our Own Image* (New York, 1992); James Cone, *Martin and Malcolm and America: A Dream of a Nightmare* (Maryknoll, N.Y., 199 1); Peter Goldman, *The Death and Life of Malcolm X* (New York, 1974); C. Eric Lincoln, *The Black Muslims in America* (Boston, 1973).

4   Gerald Horne, *Black and Red: W. E. B. Du Bois and the Afro-American Response to the Cold War, 1944–1963* (Albany, N.Y., 1985).

respected and was collaborating with the NAACP and other centrist formations.[5]

By 1958, Malcolm X was attracting throngs to the Nation of Islam, especially in New York City, headquarters of the black Left. His ideas of "white devils," the tale of Yakub, and the evils of melanin-deficient people drew a generally favorable response in areas where, less than a decade earlier, disputed heirs of the Enlightenment—black Marxists and radicals—were attracting adherents with a narrative that did not stint on identification with Africa but did not embrace anti-white rhetoric, either. What had happened?

What had happened was something that neither the King myth nor its alternative presented in *Malcolm X* confronts. How could the United States dare to posture as the paragon of human rights locked in Cold War competition for "hearts and minds" with Moscow, when African Americans were treated like third-class citizens? Jim Crow had to go.[6] But an obstacle was the presence of this militant and leftist black leadership, who were all too friendly to Moscow. They had to go, too.

---

5   Gerald Horne, *Communist Front? The Civil Rights Congress, 1946–1956* (Rutherford, N.J., 1988); Gerald Horne, "The Case of the Civil Rights Congress: Anti-Communism as an Instrument of Social Repression," in Judith Joel and Gerald M. Erickson, eds., *Anti-Communism. The Politics of Manipulation* (Minneapolis, Minn., 1987); Gerald Horne, "William Patterson, 1891–1980," in *Research Guide to American Historical Biography*, vol. 5 (Washington, D.C., 199 l); Gerald Horne, "Ben Davis, 1904–1964," in *Research Guide to American Historical Biography* (Washington, D.C., 1991); Martin Bauml Duberman, *Paul Robeson* (New York, 1988).

6   Gerald Horne, "The Bolshevik Revolution and Afro-American Liberation," in Marilyn Bechtel and Daniel Rosenberg, eds., *Nations and Peoples: The Soviet Experience* (New York, 1984); Gerald Horne, "Civil Rights/Cold War," *Guild Practitioner*, 48 (Fall 1991): 109–15.

The attack on Du Bois and the undermining of black radicalism generally, not unlike the pattern now obtaining in Eastern Europe, created favorable conditions for the rise of various forms of nationalism, some progressive and some xenophobic; it is ironic indeed that many who cheered the demise of the Left are now acting as if its defeat had nothing to do with the rise of nationalism.[7] The assault on Left-led CIO unions served to undermine their tradition of militant, interracial struggle.[8] As unions condoned or promoted racism, the Nation's message about starting businesses—not working for someone else—began to make more sense. When televised violence erupted, featuring white racists beating black protesters, the black Left

7   Gerald Horne, "Re-educating the US Working Class on Race and Class," in Joseph F. Wilson, *et al.*, eds., *The Re-education of the American Working Class* (Westport, Conn., 1990); Gerald Horne, *Studies in Black: Progressive Views and Reviews of the African-American Experience* (Dubuque, Iowa, 1992); Robert M. Hayden, "Yugoslavia: Where Self-Determination Meets Ethnic Cleansing," *New Perspectives Quarterly*, 9 (Fall 1992): 41–46. A variation of this trend arose recently when the eminent anthropologist and president of Spelman College in Atlanta, Dr. Johnetta Cole was criticized sharply by certain forces within the Jewish community after her name was mentioned as a possible secretary of education in the cabinet of President Bill Clinton. Attacked were her alleged ties to specific left-wing organizations critical of U.S. foreign policy. (I should add that I had or have actual ties to the groupings in question.) Although there is much hand-wringing in New York City about the state of Jewish and Afro-American relations, Dr. Cole, a black woman, was also assailed for speaking in praise of a Jewish man—Herbert Aptheker. *Forward*, December 11, 1992; *Washington Post*, December 14, 1992; *New York Times*, December 17, 1992.

8   James J. Matles and James Higgins, *Them and Us: Struggles of a Rank-and-File Union* (Englewood Cliffs, N.J., 1974); Charles P. Larrowe, Harry Bridges: *The Rise and Fall of Radical Labor in the United States* (Westport, Conn., 1972); Philip S. Foner, *Organized Labor and the Black Worker, 1619–1981* (New York, 1982).

narrative that sought to explain such bestiality in terms of class, race, and capitalism was barely visible. A competing narrative that featured denunciations of "white devils" could be received more readily in the absence of the black Left narrative. The anti-white rhetoric had an obvious downside for U.S. elites, but, considering the alternative of challenges to property spearheaded by an exceedingly competent black Left, this rhetoric was deemed tolerable and acceptable. It had the added advantage of allowing black youth to blow off militant steam, without unduly jeopardizing property relations.

Spike Lee deftly portrays the avid reception of Malcolm's anti-white language, but, like most, he does not provide a proper context that might help to explain why the black leader's words fell on such receptive ears.

WHEN THE LENGTHENED SHADOW OF THE BLACK LEFT reappeared in the 1960s in the Black Panther Party, which was aided in its formation by William Patterson, it, too, had to go.[9] When Malcolm X turned away from narrow nationalism to embrace a more progressive form of nationalism—when he followed in Patterson's footsteps by seeking to take the Black Question to the United Nations—he was killed by narrow nationalists who may have been manipulated by others.

---

9   Huey P. Newton, "War against the Panthers: A Study of Repression in America" (Ph.D. dissertation, University of California, Santa Cruz, 1980); Bobby Seale, *A Lonely Rage: The Autobiography of Bobby Seale* (New York, 1978); Elaine Brown, *A Taste of Power: A Black Woman's Story* (New York, 1992); David Hilliard and Lewis Cole, *This Side of Glory: The Autobiography of David Hilliard and the Story of the Black Panther Party* (Boston, 1993); William L. Van Deburg, *New Day in Babylon: The Black Power Movement and American Culture, 1965–1975* (Chicago, 1992); Kenneth O'Reilly, *Racial Matters: The FBI's Secret File on Black America, 1960–1972* (New York, 1989).

Malcolm and a number of Panthers were murdered by narrow nationalists who today—according to the newspapers—have ideological hegemony among black youth.[10] In other words, progressive nationalist forces in the black community were liquidated by narrow nationalists (possibly in league with others), who now hold sway. It may be fair to conclude that the life expectancy of narrow nationalists is and has been longer than that of the progressive nationalists. At present, this relevant fact is absent from most discourses, narratives, and myths in the African American community.

That is not all. Black youth, in their myth making, have decided that the ideological descendants of the revered Malcolm X are those same forces who worked to kill him. I had a firsthand experience with this belief on September 9, 1992, when I interviewed Preston Holmes, a producer of the *Malcolm X* film, on my radio program on the Pacifica station in Los Angeles; repeatedly, I was instructed by callers and other participants that Malcolm X and the Nation of Islam leadership, including Louis Farrakhan, were about to reconcile just before Malcolm X was murdered in February 1965. The truth is, during a radio interview on February 18, 1965, on WINS-AM in New York, days before he was killed, Malcolm assailed his former comrades in the Nation of Islam in harsh terms, more than once. This story of reconciliation is part of a myth that

10   *New York Times*, January 18, 1993: "Their perception that [Martin Luther] King was a sellout is rooted in two factors. First, it reflects the continued influence of certain varieties of 1960's black power and black nationalist rhetoric, which often cast the debate about race in narrow, dualistic terms. Either one was for black separatist racial strategies or one was a pawn of white America." See also *In These Times*, January 25, 1993: "Among black students on college campuses no black person is more popular than [Louis] Farrakhan."

promotes a form of contemporary black unity. But it happens to be inaccurate.[11]

In his memoir detailing his construction of *Malcolm X*, Spike Lee concedes that he approached the question of Louis Farrakhan and the minister's mentor, Elijah Muhammad, gingerly. Tampering with the myth that Farrakhan is the ideological descendant of Malcolm X could conceivably upset the core audience for his film, black youth. So Minister Farrakahn is the unseen but looming presence in this film. He is absent because to include him would have been too difficult to explain and would have disturbed a major myth.

Despite the involvement of Nation of Islam members in Malcolm X's murder, the sect was a beneficiary of his legacy. For example, when Watts exploded in rebellion in August 1965, the authorities had difficulty blaming the "Red Scare" or Communist agitators—too good a job had been done in eliminating them—so the "Black Scare," or the Nation of Islam, was blamed. The murder of Malcolm had settled a major issue: it was determined that the Nation would not become involved in secular politics. But the incessant effort by local and national elites to point to anything but the deteriorating socioeconomic climate in south-central Los Angeles as a cause for the revolt led them to blame the Nation of Islam. In turn, this increased the sect's visibility and boosted its ideology and religion. Watts 1965 not only featured random "anti-white violence," or, more precisely, attacks on the melanin deficient (since lighter-skinned blacks such as H. Claude Hudson of the NAACP and Congressman Augustus Hawkins were also apprehensive about being in the

11   Malcolm X, *February 1965, The Final Speeches*, Steve Clark, ed. (New York, 1992); Bruce Perry, ed., *Malcolm X: The Last Speeches* (New York, 1989).

streets at that time), but the concern caused as a result of this fracture in the black community also presumably helped to forge a black unity that many felt a besieged minority could not live without.[12]

SPIKE LEE'S UNWILLINGNESS TO EXPLORE THE NUANCES of Malcolm's story did not assuage some critics. Yusef Salaam, writing in the December 5, 1992, edition of the *New York Amsterdam News*, the black-oriented weekly, condemned Lee for suggesting in an interview that "the Hon. Elijah Muhammad and Minister Louis Farrakhan had something to do with the death of Malcolm." In the November 21, 1992, edition of the same paper, Farrakhan himself is reported to have alleged that the film may be part of an effort to destroy him and the sect he leads.

Because the Lee film tracks so faithfully Malcolm X's duly praised autobiography, one might have expected certain black critics to have applauded this movie. Instead, former SNCC leader Stokely Carmichael, speaking from West Africa, condemned the film and Lee personally in incendiary language.[13] Armond White, writing in the Brooklyn-based black weekly, the *City Sun*, of December 2–8, 1992, was equally unkind. In New York City, where Lee resides, where Malcolm lived, and

---

12   12 Spike Lee with Ralph Wiley, By Any Means Necessary: The Trials and Tribulations of the Making of Malcolm X (New York, 1992), 50–58; Gerald Horne, "Hell in the City of Angels: 1965–1992," Guild Practitioner, 49 (Summer 1992): 65–72; Gerald Horne, "African-Americans 'Riot' in Watts," in Frank N. Magill, ed., Great Events from History II (Pasadena, Calif., 1992), 1301–04; see also Gerald Horne, Fire This Time: The Watts Uprising and the Meaning of the 1960s (forthcoming); Gerald Horne, "1965–1992: No Leap Forward," Crossroads, 1 (June 1992): 15.

13   *Los Angeles Times*, January 1, 1993.

where knowledge of him is at its zenith, a number of forums were held in which the speakers heaped vitriolic criticism on the film.[14]

A repeated complaint about the film is reflected in the words of Maulana Karenga, a founder of the African American holiday Kwanza, a popular speaker on college campuses, and whose organization, US, was implicated in the murder of Black Panthers. The December 26, 1992, edition of the *New York Amsterdam News* quoted him as saying, "Nowhere in the movie did Lee show Malcolm meeting with world leaders, especially on the African continent." This complaint happens to be valid. Karl Evanzz reveals, and FBI documents, show that during the last months of his life, Malcolm was meeting repeatedly with African leaders and diplomats. Even before then, Malcolm was interpreting the heralded 1955 Bandung conference of African and Asian leaders as spelling doom for the "white devils." This is a glaring omission in the film, but the critics apparently forget that neither the dominant King-driven myth nor the alternative Malcolm myth gives a proper account of the play of international forces. Lee's flaw is not his alone.[15]

---

14 *New York Amsterdam News*, December 5, 1992; *New York Amsterdam News*, December 12, 1992. This sensitivity about discussing difficult issues in the black community also was manifested during my 7 p.m. (PST) Pacifica Radio show in Los Angeles on January 20, 1993. I was interviewing Professor Bruce Tyler of the University of Louisville, who is writing a book that concerns in part the sharp conflict that erupted in the 1960s between the Panthers and the black "cultural nationalists" of the United States. A number of callers instructed us that this was not a worthy subject for discussion and that it threatened to disrupt black unity.

15 See Merton L. Dillon, *Slavery Attacked: Southern Slates and Their Allies, 1619–1865* (Baton Rouge, La., 1990). From the beginning of their presence on these shores, it was feared that blacks would

Indeed, with the dawning of the Cold War, the preeminent civil rights organization, the NAACP, drifted inexorably away from the international arena; since the eclipsing of Du Bois and the demise of the Black Panther Party, few African American organizations, activists, or intellectuals work consistently with and write critically about international affairs, although the country from which they hail plays an outsized and frequently negative role in the global arena.[16]

ally with the enemies of prevailing Euro-American elites, be they in Madrid, Paris, Port-an-Prince, Mexico City, or elsewhere. See also Alexander DeConde, *Ethnicity, Race, and American Foreign Policy: A History* (Boston, 1992); Alexander DeConde, *The Quasi-War: The Politics and Diplomacy of the Undeclared War with France, 1797–1801* (New York, 1966); Alfred N. Hunt, *Haiti's Influence on Antebellum America: Slumbering Volcano in the Caribbean* (Baton Rouge, La., 1988); Benjamin Quarles, *The Negro in the American Revolution* (Chapel Hill, N.C., 1961); James W. St.G. Walker, *The Black Loyalists: The Search for a Promised Land in Nova Scotia and Sierra Leone, 1783– 1870* (London, 1976). The subsequent fear that Du Bois, Robeson, *et al.* would align with Moscow should be viewed in this overall context of insecurity about the real loyalties of African Americans.

16   Gerald Horne, "Racism and the New World Order" in Stephanie Baker, ed., *New Walls in Europe: Nationalism and Racism—Civic Solutions* (Prague, 1992), 31–35; Gerald Horne, "Hands across the Water: Afro-American Lawyers and the Decolonization of Southern Africa," *Guild Practitioner*, 45 (Fall 1988): 110–28. There are exceptions, for instance, Congressman Ronald Dellums of Berkeley, Samori Marksman of Pacifica Radio, Don Rojas, editor of the *New York Amsterdam News* and former press secretary to slain Grenadian Prime Minister Maurice Bishop. Admittedly, there has been activity on certain "black" issues: apartheid, Haitian refugees, etc. But my opinion is that the response has not been commensurate to the challenge. Where was the response to Star Wars, the B-1 bomber, the U.S.-backed coup in Chile in 1973, tacit support for the genocidal Khmer Rouge in Cambodia? The list is long.

Having said that, however, there is little question that the film could have been enhanced immeasurably if more attention had been paid to the global dimension. Karl Evanzz argues provocatively that the Black Dragon Society of Japan had a hand in the founding of the Nation of Islam in the 1930s and influenced its line of anti-white rhetoric.[17] One scene framing this explosive connection with its manifold contemporary resonances would have greatly added to the drama of the film and the understanding of the Nation of Islam itself. Now it seems that the forthcoming filmed version of Michael Crichton's novel *Rising Sun* will touch on this question of anti-whiteness. This dark story about U.S.-Japan relations features the popular black actor Wesley Snipes in a crucial role, one in which he is opposed to Tokyo; interestingly, this black character is absent from the novel.[18]

Other scenes detailing Malcolm's meetings with leaders in Egypt, Tanzania, Ghana, and elsewhere would have given a fuller understanding of the slain martyr and his times. Dramatizing Malcolm's meeting with Fidel Castro in Harlem

17 Evanzz, *Judas Factor,* 138; A recent study disputes the widely held belief that during this century blacks closed ranks with Washington against Tokyo. Reginald Kearney, "Afro-American Views of the Japanese, 1900–1945" (Ph.D. dissertation, Kent State University, 1991); John Dower, *War without Mercy: Race and Power in the Pacific War* (New York, 1986); Gerald Horne, "Imperialist Rivalries," *Political Affairs,* 71 (November 1992): 9–15; Gerald Horne, "The Thomas-Hill Hearings and the Nexus of Race, Gender and Nationalism," in Robert Allen and Robert Chrisman, *Court of Appeal: The Black Community S peaks Out on the Racial and Sexual Politics of Clarence Thomas us. Anita Hill* (New York, 1992), 92–95.

18 Michael Crichton, *Rising Sun: A Novel* (New York; 1992); *Los Angeles Times,* January 24, 1993.

in 1960 would have been worthwhile.[19] The construction of the Malcolm myth—and it is heavily influenced by a pervasive narrow nationalism quite different from internationalism—is still in process, but as of now, like the King myth, it has not encompassed the international dimension. To do so might necessitate encompassing a now taboo history involving the Council on African Affairs and the black Left; and, unfortunately, this important history has yet to be subjected to the systematic inquiry it deserves.

There is another complex political question involving internecine conflict between Malcolm X and the Nation of Islam that the myth Lee weaves does not embrace. His final speeches are a reflection of the fact that Malcolm to his last days appeared frequently on "white-owned" television and radio denouncing the Nation of Islam. Speaking personally, as a longtime political activist in the African American community, I can attest that part of the protocol for at least the past two decades is that when one leaves an organization, one may try to organize to dislodge the leadership, but going public in the mainstream media is considered a gross error. Malcolm X, with his rapid-fire speech, biting humor, and quick mind, was a master of the electronic media; this was part of his appeal. But his media appearances inflamed the followers of Elijah Muhammad and fueled the perception that Malcolm was a traitor.

This level of conflict does not, however, fit the developing myth. The rift between Malcolm and the Nation of Islam is not given the sort of all-sided scrutiny it needs because raising the issue is perceived as tearing at some form of black unity;

---

19 Rosemari Mealy, *Memories of a Meeting: Fidel and Malcolm X* (New York, 1992).

also absent are the distinctions drawn in Malcolm X's final speeches between Nation followers, whom he often describes as being not sufficiently concerned about domestic and international politics, and black nationalists, like himself, who are. On February 21, 1965, this clash reached a murderous end when Malcolm X was assassinated. Today, there has evolved a united front, a historic compromise, between followers of Farrakhan and black nationalists who reject vital aspects of the Chicago-based minister's outlook. The developing Malcolm X myth seeks to maintain this unity, and many critics are upset with Spike Lee precisely because his depiction of the murder of Malcolm X reflects a conflict that some would prefer to erase from the pages of history.

THE MOST SEVERE CRITICS of *Malcolm X* have to concede that the film does a marvelous job of depicting social and cultural questions. This is all the more striking since Lee has been criticized repeatedly for his drawing of women characters.[20] But even, and perhaps particularly, his staunchest feminist critics (and I am among that group) had to admire the scene featuring Denzel Washington, playing Malcolm Little, sticking his head in the toilet to douse his scalp, which was burning because of a botched effort to straighten his hair. Before the rise of the "black is beautiful" movement, which was anticipated by the post-Mecca Malcolm, this often painful process was devised in part to make the hair of blacks appear more like that of certain whites. As this event occurs, the police burst into his apartment to arrest Malcolm for various crimes. The

---

20   *Los Angeles Times*, June 23, 1991; Gerald Horne, Review of Spike Lee, *Five for Five: The Films of Spike Lee*, in *Wide Angle: A Quarterly Journal of Film History, Theory, Criticism and Practice*, 13 (July-October 1991): 140–42.

question of hair, which has been an essential though contradictory component of African American identity, helps to create a scene that is an instant classic of African American cinema. Many black men no longer press their hair, although many black women for various reasons find it necessary to do so. Lee's film forces the audience to contemplate these complexities of a gendered racial identity.[21]

This is part of the value of Malcolm X as a historical figure. He is an integral part of the scaffolding that supports a contemporary African American identity. His fascination with music and dance and night clubs undergirded his bond with blacks. A significant development that is accelerating in Afro-America in the postwar era is cool or hip philosophy. It involves a manner, a language, a mode of dress, and more. It is reflected in Malcolm's well-known fascination with what is called jazz music and that milieu. Quite properly, the figure of Billie Holliday is represented in Lee's film. There is substantial time spent on dance and music, though this is not unusual for Lee, whose father is a noted bassist. Lee also shows how the world of cool and hip can devolve. Malcolm Little's plight—he found it better to hustle, to engage in petty crimes than to work at low-paying jobs where crass exploitation is the watchword—resonates with many contemporary black youth in urban areas.[22]

21 Kobena Mercer, "Black Hair Style Politics," in Russell Ferguson, ed., *Out There: Marginalization and Contemporary Cultures* (Cambridge, Mass., 1990), 247–63; Gwendolyn Brooks, "Helen," in Margaret Busby, ed., *Daughters of Africa: An International Anthology of Words and Writings by Women of African Descent from the Ancient Egyptian to the Present* (New York, 1992), 269–71.

22 Douglas Henry Daniels, "Schooling Malcolm: Malcolm Little and Black Culture during the Golden Age of Jazz," in James Gwynne, ed.,

The problem with this cool or hip philosophy and its present-day descendant, hip-hop, is that the heavily male orientation can shade easily into misogyny or at least insensitivity on gender matters. Again, Spike Lee's flaws in drawing female characters in this film and in his other works are not his alone. It is the inevitable result of a philosophy that arises when the Left is weakened and various forms of narrow nationalism are ascendant.

IN 1993, MALCOLM X STANDS AS AN ICON; many believe that he stands in the pantheon with Martin Luther King, Jr., himself. His figure is so luminescent that he can inspire an alternative myth. A recent poll reported by the black press states that 84 percent of those African Americans between the ages of fifteen and twenty-four who were queried felt that he was "a hero for black Americans today." However, that same poll found that a substantially smaller percentage of that age cohort knew much about him. This circumstance presents both a situation ripe for myth making and an indictment of how history is taught in this nation. To the extent that accurate and comprehensive knowledge of the past is useful in formulating tactics and strategy for economic betterment, distorted aspects of the Malcolm myths and other myths can be seen as a co-factor in explicating the continuing economic decline among blacks particularly and the U.S. working class

<hr>

Malcolm X-Justice Seeker (New York, 1993), 45–58; John Horton, "Time and Cool People," in Thomas Kochman, ed., *Rappin' and Stylin' Out: Communication in Urban Black America* (Urbana, Ill., 1972), 19–31; Richard Majors and Janet Mancini Billson, *Cool Pose: The Dilemmas of Black Manhood in America* (New York, 1992).

generally.[23] It also presents a challenge that the film may not be able to overcome. Research conducted for Warner Brothers, the film's distributor, showed in December 1992 that three-fourths of the members of the audience for the Lee production were twenty-five or older.[24] Blacks and other youths may have been sporting Xs on their baseball caps and t-shirts, but apparently they were not streaming to view this 3-hour, 20-minute epic. And even though the film was doing reasonably well at the box office—it grossed a hefty $38 million in the first five weeks after release in mid-November 1992—it was lagging behind films as diverse as *A Few Good Men, Aladdin, Home Alone 2, The Bodyguard*—even *The Mighty Ducks*.[25] If the alternative myth of Malcolm is to have the "crossover appeal" of the traditional myth—which may mean appealing to a U.S. population with notoriously low levels of political and ideological acumen—sharper, more insightful, analysis of black nationalism and the Nation of Islam may be necessary. But such analysis may only serve to enrage the same influential black critics now criticizing Lee's handiwork.

I recall when I was interviewing the producer of *Malcolm X*, Preston Holmes, a caller joked about how the furor surrounding the film might lead to Lee being a "black Salman Rushdie." That has not happened, fortunately, but there have been incidents not typical for multi-million-dollar Hollywood

---

23   *Los Angeles Sentinel*, January 7, 1993; *City Sun*, November 1 1—17, 1992; Gerald Horne, "Race Backwards: Genes, Violence, Race and Genocide," *Covert Action Quarterly*, 1 (Winter 1992–93): 29–35.

24   *Los Angeles Times*, December 23, 1992.

25   *Daily Variety*, January 5, 1993; *Daily Variety*, January 6, 1993; *Hollywood Reporter*, January 4, 1993; *Hollywood Reporter*, January 5, 1993.

productions. A "powerful pipe bomb" was found under a seat in a Dallas movie theater in December 1992.[26] There have been other unusual incidents. Lee charged that some patrons who went to multiplex theaters to buy tickets to *Malcolm X* were being given tickets to other movies instead, thereby depriving his film of revenue.[27] The *New York Amsterdam News* of January 16, 1993, reported that "bootleg" video copies of the film were being sold in black communities such as Hempstead, Long Island.

Other profiteering is above board. Malcolm X's widow, Betty Shabazz, has signed an agreement with the Curtis Management Group of Indianapolis to capitalize on the now runaway merchandising of the slain martyr; Curtis is controlled by a staunch conservative with past ties to the South African government and hostility to the local African American community. Or so says *New York Newsday* of November 6, 1992. Despite its alternative status, the Malcolm X myth is as subject to that most traditional force of commodification as any other "alternative" phenomenon.

A suggestive trend in that regard is the black conservative idea that Malcom is one of them because of his "insistence on black self-sufficiency."[28] Such a conclusion on their part may help to explain the future course and present utility of the Malcolm X myth. The idea that blacks should pay taxes yet not argue about the distribution of these funds but instead pay twice by then starting separate institutions should appeal to a deficit-ridden government and powerful elites with designs on

26 *Los Angeles Times*, January 3, 1992.
27 *Jet*, January 11, 1993.
28 *New York Times*, January 6, 1993.

this tax booty themselves. Xenophobic nationalism of various sorts can be useful to various elites in both south-central L.A. and South-Central Europe. Other trends seem more heartening. Black booksellers in New York City are arguing that the Lee film has spurred a number of families and children to purchase books about Malcolm X.[29] The relentless study and pursuit of history may prove to be the best guarantee that the magnificent Spike Lee film does not generate yet another empty myth but instead inspires a search for a full and complete history.

29   *New York Amsterdam News*, January 2, 1993.

WHO LOST THE COLD WAR? AFRICANS AND AFRICAN AMERICANS

Diplomatic History, Fall 1996, Vol. 20, No. 4

The story is well known about the man who jumps off the Empire State Building in New York City and as he passes the thirtieth-floor shouts, "So far, so good."

This story comes to mind when considering the linked themes of race and foreign policy raised in these three arresting articles. For the fact is that the Cold War did play a substantial role in eroding the formidable barriers of Jim Crow and colonialism in Africa. How could Washington credibly charge Moscow with human rights violations when African Americans in this nation and Africans in their own land—at the behest of U.S. allies in Western Europe—were treated like third-class citizens? In turn, newly enfranchised African Americans could more effectively trumpet the cause of their brethren in Africa languishing under colonial rule—and vice versa. "So far, so good." However, an essential component of this process was an international and domestic left that championed the basic rights of Africans and African Americans particularly.[1] The weakening of this left—a

---

1   Allison Blakely, *Russia and the Negro: Blacks in Russian History and Thought* (Washington, 1986); Jane Degras, ed. *The Communist*

result of how the Cold War concluded—has done more than contribute to a situation where Africa is largely thought to be marginalized: Sierra Leone, Rwanda, Burundi, and Liberia are just
the most extreme examples of a catastrophe that has befallen a
continent that could once court East and West to its advantage.[2]
The decline of a secular left also has prompted the rise of various forms of a religious "fundamentalism" that plays no small
role in the tearing apart of Sudan, Nigeria, Uganda, and a good
deal of North Africa.[3] Strikingly, this same phenomenon also has
afflicted African Americans, reeling from skyrocketing rates in
incarceration, attacks on the Voting Rights Act and affirmative
action, and stagnant wages that haste impacted them disproportionately.[4] Yes, "we all lost the Cold War" but some—who had
further to fall—lost more than others.

International, 1919–1943, Documents (London, 1971); Gerald
Horne, *Black Liberation/Red Scare: Ben Davis and the Communist
Party* (London, 1994); James Goodman, *Stories of Scottsboro* (New
York, 1999); Philip S. Foner and James S. Allen, eds. *American
Communism and Black Americans: A Documentary Histo*ry, *1919–
1929* (Philadelphia, 1987); Robert Hill, ed., *The Crusader*, 6 vols.
(New York, 1987); W. Alphaeus Hunton, *Decision in Africa. Sources
of Current Conflict (*(New York, 1960); Ronald Kasrils, *"Armed and
Dangerous": My Undercover Struggle against Apartheid* (Oxford, 1993).

2   Howard Adelman and John Sorenson, eds., *African Refugees:
Development Aid and Repatriation* (Boulder, 1994); Anton
Andereggen, *France's Relationship with Sub Saharan Africa* (Westport,
1994); Mohamed Sahnoun, *Somalia: The Missed Opportunities*
(Washington, 1994).

3   Mark Juergensmeyer, *The New Cold War? Religious Nationalism
Confronts the Secular State* (Berkeley, 1993); Said Adejumobi and
Abubakar Momoh, eds., *The Political Economy of Nigeria under
Military Rule: 1984–1993* (Harare, 1995).

4   Gerald Horne, "'Myth' and the Making of 'Malcolm X'", *American
Historical Review* 98 (April 1993): 440–50; idem, "Blowback: Playing

Only in Southern Africa—South Africa in particular—does it appear that Africans of whatever continent have emerged from the post-Cold War rubble with improved prospects. And, most revealing, it is here that the South African Communist Party rules in alliance with the African National Congress and the Congress of South African Trade Unions in the kind of left-labor alliance spurned by the NAACP when it fatefully threw in its lot with the Truman White House and joined the anti-Communist crusade.[5] In 1948, such an alliance may have seemed like the only viable alternative. But as the NAACP lies in tatters in the 1990s, along with the community it purports to represent, the time is long past due for historians to evaluate fateful historical decisions not only with keen hindsight but with keen foresight as well.

Meanwhile, the "liberation" of what was the Soviet Union has brought in its wake rapidly declining living standards, genocidal war in the Caucasus, and the rise of a Mafia class that has spread its tentacles to our shores.[6] The expenditures

the Nationalist Card Backfires," in *After Political Correctness: The Humanities and Society in the 1990s*, ed. Christopher Newfield and Ronald Strickland (Boulder, 1995), 79–89.

5   Fatima Meer, *Higher than Hope: A Biography of Nelson Mandela* (London, 1990); Basil Davidson, Joe Slovo and Anthony R. Wilkinson, Southern Africa: *The New Politics of Revolution* (Harmondsworth, 1976); Austin M. Chakaodza, *International Diplomacy in Southern Africa: From Reagan to Mandela* (London, 1990)' Allister Sparks, *Tomorrow is Another Country: The Inside Story of South Africa's Road to Change* (New York, 1995); Alex Boraine, Janet Levy and Ronel Scheffer, *Dealing with the Past: Truth and Reconciliation in South Africa* (Cape Town, 1994).

6   Stephen Handelman, *Comrade Criminal: Russia's New Mafia* (New Haven, 1994); Claire Sterling, *Thieves' World: The Threat of the New Global Network of Organized Crime* (New York, 1994); Suzanne

necessary to accomplish this "victory" haste helped to create a multi-trillion-dollar debt for the nation, while building up now-formidable rivals in Beijing, Tokyo, and Seoul who will continue to present substantial challenges to U.S. foreign policy well into the next century—and beyond.[7]

It simply will not do—even for a historian—to suggest that Edith Sampson and the NAACP took the proper course when they joined the anti-Communist crusade while ignoring the "downstream" consequences such a decision has had. Shouting "so far, so good" at the thirtieth-floor is insufficient.

Laville and Lucas refer to a "national interest" during the Cold War. But the question must be asked, "whose national interest?" I understand fully why certain Wall Street investors—or more precisely, Berlin speculators—may celebrate the opportunity to exploit new labor markets and mineral resources in Eastern Europe, while picking up privatized enterprises on the cheap; I am less sure about why an African American community that is predominantly working class and whose jobs now

Goldenberg, *Pride of Small Nations: The Caucasus and Post-Soviet Disorder* (Atlantic Highlands, NJ, 1994); Charles Undeland and Nicholas Platt, *The Central Asian Republics: Fragments of Empire, Magnets of Wealth* (New York, 1994). For a prescient view of the post-1989 events see Jonathan Boe, "American Business: The Response to the Soviet Union, 1933–1947" (Ph.D. diss., Stanford University, 1979).

7   Eamonn Fingleton, "Japan's Invisible Leviathan," *Foreign Affairs* 74 (March/April 1995): 69–85; Frank McNeil, *Democracy in Japan: The Emerging Global Concern* (New York, 1994); Lillian Craig Harris, *China Considers the Middle East* (New York, 1993); Young Whan Kihl, ed., *Korea and the World: Beyond the Cold War* (Boulder, 1994); Robert E. Bedeski, *The Transformation of South Korea: Reform and Reconstitution in the Sixth Republic under Rob Tae Woo, 1987–1992* (New York, 1994).

have yet another site to be shipped to overseas should celebrate. The disintegration of the Soviet Union has not so much lessened the so-called nuclear threat as it has widened it, as crucial technologies are now subject to a gigantic and chaotic yard-sale.

Indeed, the fundamental question that Laville and Lucas and Anderson, to an extent, must confront is this: Presumably "Stalinism" was sufficient reason for African Americans to join Washington's Cold War, while looking the other way as stalwarts like W. E. B. Du Bois and Paul Robeson were persecuted for their refusal to participate. Fine. But if "Stalinism" discredited socialism, why did slavery, the slave trade, and racism not discredit capitalism?[8] If Soviet intervention in Eastern Europe discredited socialism, then why did U.S. backing of apartheid South Africa not discredit capitalism?[9]

8   Peter Kolchin, *American Slavery: 1619–1877* (New York, 1993); Theodore Dwight Weld, *American Slavery As It Is: Testimony of a Thousand Witnesses* (New York, 1968); Eric Williams, *Capitalism and Slavery* (Chapel Hill, 1944); Maurice Glele-Ahanhanzo, *Report on Contemporary Forms of Racism, Racial Discrimination, Xenophobia, and Related Intolerance on His Mission to the United States of America from 9 to 22 October 1994* (New York, 1995); Civil Rights Congress, *We Charge Genocide! The Historical Petition to the United Nations for Relief from a Crime of the United States Government against the Negro People* (New York, 1951). Anderson refers to "cynical and opportunistic Soviet support" as a rationale for the NAACP failing to press the United Nations about human rights claims of African Americans. However, if blacks were to subject real or potential allies to a test of purity before collaborating, then they would have refused no doubt to join the North – which countenanced racism and segregation and worse – during the Civil War; or perhaps they should have reconsidered the decision to collaborate with the Dixiecrat Secretary of State Jams Byrnes or his boss, the descendant of slaveowners – Harry S. Truman – who occupied the White House.

9   Thomas Borstelmann, *Apartheid's Reluctant Uncle: The United States and Southern Africa in the Early Cold War* (New York, 1993);

Are we saying that what happens to Africans can be rationalized away, but that what happens to Europeans must be held to a higher standard? Are we saying that the enslavement and persecution of Africans is less important than what occurred in Eastern Europe? Are we saying that it is justifiable for Edith Sampson and the NAACP to collaborate with a U.S. government that retarded African freedom but inappropriate for a Du Bois or Robeson to collaborate with a Soviet government that was supporting Africans fighting apartheid and colonialism? Are African interests so unimportant, so trivial? Does being African and "American" involve a process of self-abnegation not required of others in this nation? If so, it is little wonder that a Louis Farrakhan can lead a march on Washington that dwarfs the procession led by Martin Luther King, Jr., thirty odd years earlier.[10]

Although these articles are concerned with the link between race and foreign policy during the Cold War, this epochal conflict was not the first time that African Americans sought to influence U.S. foreign policy. Indeed, the Cold War did not present the first time that African Americans found themselves in conflict with U.S. foreign policy.[11] Anderson and Laville and Lucas particularly should consider that it may inhere in the nature of being an oppressed nationality to adopt viewpoints

Thomas J. Noer, *Cold War and Black Liberation: The United States and White Rule in Africa, 1948–1968* (Columbia, MO, 1985); George M. Frederickson, *Black Liberation: A Comparative History of Black Ideologies in the United States and South Africa* (New York, 1995); Penny Marie Von Eschen, "African-Americans and Anti-Colonialism, 1937–1957; The Rise and Fall of the Politics of the African Diaspora" (Ph.D. diss., Columbia University, 1994).

10   *New York Times*, 17 October 1995; Washington Post, 17 October 1995.

11   Gerald Horne, "Race for the Planet: African-Americans and U.S. Foreign Policy Reconsidered," *Diplomatic History* 19 (Winter 1995): 159–65.

that are considered to be beyond the mainstream. Should it be deemed surprising, for example, that Africans and Indians in South Africa diverged from the views of their Afrikaner counterparts on the late-nineteenth-century war with Great Britain or World War I?[12] What would be the reason for Africans in North America to support Washington's effort to seize Native American land and drive them all into poverty, so this land could be stocked further with African slaves? Indeed, what would be the reason for Native Americans or Africans to back the Yankees during the 1776 revolution when it was clear that the rebels were bent on further land seizures and enslavement? In fact, just as it can be questioned whether the Cold War "victory" was a triumph for Africans and African Americans, it is not far-fetched to suggest that the interests of darker peoples in North America may have been better served had London been able to defeat the rebels. If, as Edmund Morgan has reminded us, "American Freedom" is grounded in African slavery, then this conclusion is not at all far-fetched. It is mandated.[13]

While conservatives flinched in the face of the revolutions of 1848 that swept Europe, Africans in North America cheered;

12   Albert Grundlingh, *Fighting Their Own War: South African Blacks and the First World War* (Johannesburg, 1987); Surendra Bhana and Bridglal Pachai, eds., *A Documentary History of Indian South Africans* (Stanford, 1984).

13   Edmund Morgan, *American Slavery/American Freedom: The Ordeal of Colonial Virginia* (New York, 1975); Colin G. Calloway, *The American Revolution in Indian Country: Crisis and Diversity in Native American Communities* (New York, 1995); Graham Hodges, ed., *The Black Loyalist Directory: African-Americans in Exile after the American Revolution* (New York, 1995); Robert M. Calhoon, Timothy M. Barnes, and George A. Rawlyk, eds., *Loyalists and Community in North America* (Westport, 1994); Sylvia R. Frey, *Water from the Rock: Black Resistance in a Revolutionary Age* (Princeton, 1991).

comparisons were drawn between freedom of slaves and freedom for serfs.[14] Naturally, after being accorded formal citizenship after the Civil War, it became easier for African Americans to speak with a louder voice on diplomatic matters. This was particularly true after the founding of the NAACP in 1909 with Du Bois as its essential operative. In 1910 the association harshly condemned the czar's expulsion of the Jewish population of Kiev.[15] At a two-day conference sponsored by the NAACP in Washington in May 1917, the assembled delegates drafted resolutions attributing the cause of World War I to racism and profit seeking.[16] Basically, they accepted the argument that Germany's aggression was sparked by its dearth of colonies in Africa.

The point is that it was difficult—in any historical era—for an organization that purported to speak on behalf of African Americans to take positions on the global scene that were not viewed by some as radical or left wing or beyond the mainstream. It has been difficult for African Americans to align internationally with those same elites that have been responsible domestically for their plight—in 1776, 1848, 1917, 1946, or, dare I say, 1996.

14   Philip S. Foner and George E. Walker, eds., *Proceedings of the Black State Conventions, 1840–1865*, 2 vols. (Philadelphia, 1979–80).

15   See generally Gerald Horne, *Black and Red: W. E. B. Du Bois and the Afro-American Response to the Cold War, 1944–1963* (Albany, 1986); Charles Kellogg, *NAACP* (Baltimore, 1967), 44, 250; and Arnold Shankman, "Brothers across the Sea: Afro-Americans on the Persecution of Russian Jews, Jewish Social Studies 37 (Spring 1975): 14.

16   Horne, *Black and Red*; James Ivy, "Traditional NAACP Interest in Africa (as reflected in the pages of Crisis)," in *Africa as Seen by American Negro Scholars*, ed. American Society of African Culture (New York, 1963); W. E. B. Du Bois, *Color and Democracy: Colonies and Peace* (Millwood, NY, 1975).

What Anderson needs to consider is that when Walter White in 1948 maneuvered to dump Du Bois from the NAACP and retreated from pressing the plight of African Americans at the United Nations because of fear of being associated with the domestic and international left, his actions may have pleased the White House and brought temporary concessions but they contradicted the historic and long-term interests of his constituency, which before and since has found it necessary to adopt unpopular diplomatic stances.

In discussing the NAACP, neither Anderson nor Laville and Lucas adequately sketch how this organization's positions changed so dramatically after the Cold War was launched, when compared to its viewpoints before this conflict. During World War II, the NAACP leadership particularly adopted positions that were to be deemed radical or left wing during the Cold War. These authors should explain how and why this reversal took place and what it signifies. If they were to do so, they would notice that this reversal was not solely voluntary—which suggests further that endorsing the Cold War agenda contradicted the historic and contemporary interests of African Americans.

Richard Dalfiume has commented that World War II "stimulated the race consciousness and the desire for change among Negroes. The hypocrisy and paradox involved in fighting a world war for the four freedoms and against aggression by an enemy preaching a master race ideology, while at the same time upholding racial segregation and white supremacy were too obvious. "[17]

17 Richard Dalfiume, "The Forgotten Years of the Negro Revolution," in *The Negro in Depression and War: Prelude to Revolution, 1930–1945*, ed. Bernard Sternsher (Chicago, 1969), 298–316; Richard M.

As in past wars, the United States needed African American labor in order to defeat the hated foe, which set the stage for wartime concessions; however, in this case, the foe—Nazi Germany—was the embodiment of racialism and reactionary politics. The combination of these elements—along with an alliance with the once-reviled Moscow—at once put the domestic right wing on the defensive, while elevating the left, which, as noted, had been the major predominantly Euro-American force championing the rights of blacks.[18] Simultaneously, U.S. elites had to be concerned with the special problem of Japan, which had played no small role in the formation of the Nation of Islam and whose attempt to portray itself as champion of the "darker races" had resonated among African Americans from the time this island nation had defeated Russia in 1905.[19]

The confluence of these elements—the retreat of the right, the rise of the left, the necessity to defuse Tokyo's special appeal to the "darker races"—is reflected in the 1944 "Declaration of Negro Voters," whose rhetoric and thrust sounds as if it were a document of the left-led National Negro Congress when, in fact, it was endorsed by the NAACP, along with other major black sororities and fraternities, professional organizations, etc. "We are concerned that this war bring to an end imperialism and colonial exploitation. We believe that political

Dalfiume, *Desegregation of the U.S. Armed Forces: Fighting on Two Fronts, 1939–1953* (Columbia, MO, 1969).

18   Ralph B. Levering, *American Opinion and The Russian Alliance, 1939–1945* (Chapel Hill, 1976).

19   Ernest Allen Jnr. "When Japan was 'Champion of the Darker Races': Satokata Takahashi and the Flowering of Black Messianic Nationalism," *Black Scholar: Journal of Black Studies and Research* 24:1 (1994): 23–46; Richard Storry, *Japan and the Decline of the West in Asia, 1894–1943* (New York, 1979).

and economic democracy must displace the present system of exploitation in Africa, the West Indies, India and other colonial areas."[20] This approach is reflected in the NAACP's own major resolution of 1944 which too reflects the influence of the left: "In common with progressive workers in all lands and from all groups we seek the ending of imperialism both as a matter of justice to the victims of imperialist exploitation and in order to remove a cause for war. The NAACP has a special stake in the abolition of imperialism because the members of the various colored races constitute most though not all of the victims of imperialist exploitation."[21]

It was not a Communist who castigated Winston Churchill "and his class who would perpetuate imperialism for the benefit of the few." It was not a Communist who favored "alliance with a steadily powerful Russia [rather] than further [reliance] on an Anglo-Saxon capitalist world." It was Walter White of the NAACP.[22]

It is with this background firmly in mind that one should assess the NAACP's subsequent Cold War "alliance" with the "Anglo-Saxon capitalist world." It is sometimes said of Palestinian leader Yasir Arafat that he plays a weak hand strongly. The opposite can be said of the post-World War II African American leadership: They played a strong hand weakly. For it was clear that World War II already had begun to erode the rationale and sinews of formal Jim Crow. The leadership did not have to sign on to the Cold War agenda—which ultimately was harmful to

20   Horne, *Black and Red*, 21–22.
21   *Ibid.*, 22–23.
22   *Ibid.*, 23.

their interests—in order to receive civil rights concessions that already were in the pipeline.

Certainly, it was not their constituency that impelled the NAACP to endorse the Cold War agenda. It has long been known that anticommunism, the wars in Korea and Vietnam, and the like were much less popular among African Americans than others.[23] When World War II discredited outright racialism as a rationale for subordinating African Americans, the Dixiecrats who held sway within the Democratic party quickly shifted ground and began scoring black activists as "Red." This slowed down the granting of civil rights concessions and gave racism a new lease of life; when the NAACP capitulated to the Red Scare, it hastened this process. Similarly, as World War II closed, white supremacists shifted from suggesting that colonialism was a boon for "inferior" Africans to suggesting that "premature independence" for the colonized would leave them vulnerable to the Soviets. The result was the same: continued colonial exploitation.

Although it has not been noted sufficiently, African Americans were a disproportionate victim of McCarthyism. Philip S. Foner has observed that "the black tobacco workers were the first to feel the sting of the CIO's red-baiting drive"

23   *Ibid.*, 2; Alfred O. Hero, *American Religious Groups View Foreign Policy: Trends in Rank and File Opinion, 1937–1969* (Durham, 1973), 85, 90–91; idem, "American Negroes and U.S. Foreign Policy: 1937–1967," *Journal of Conflict Resolution* 8 (June 1969): 220–51; James L. Roark, "American Black Leaders: The Response to Colonialism and the Cold War, 1943–1953," *African Historical Studies* 4 (1971): 253–70. The instant debate makes the point: The debate on blacks and the Cold War is not between the center and the right, as so often happens when the East-West conflict is mooted; it is a debate between the left and the center.

and that 6 percent of those in the International Longshore-
men and Warehousemen's Union who were "screened" from
the waterfront for decidedly "pinkish tendencies" were African
American. Ferdinand Smith, a Jamaican American and
Communist leader of the National Mari time Union, was one
of the first victims of the Justice Department's effort to deport
"aliens" who were Cold War opponents. This "Red Tagging of
Negro Protest" was designed not only to scare blacks away from
their traditional allies of the domestic and international left but
also to ensure that protest would not veer from the narrow path
of civil rights toward the more perilous terrain of redistribution
of wealth and property.[24]

As I have noted recently, this weakening of black labor
particularly may have had the "advantage" of helping to deflect
African Americans from the international arena where their
often stinging opposition to the Cold War caused so much con-
sternation, but it also facilitated the rise of virulent "anti-white"
tendencies that were to explode in urban conflagrations in the
1960s and racial tensions that continue to exist in the 1990s.
When the inclusive and collective approach of black labor and
the left faltered, it was easier for African Americans to listen
to the once-tiny Nation of Islam and its mantra that one should
"do for self.[25]

---

24 Philip S. Foner, *Organized Labor and the Black Worker, 1619–1993*
    (New York, 1982), 282, 283, 286; Richard Freeland, *The Truman
    Doctrine and the Origins of McCarthyism: Foreign Policy, Domestic
    Politics, and Internal Security, 1946–1948* (New York, 1974); Jane
    Cassels Record, "The Red Tagging of Negro Protest," *American
    Scholar* 26 (Summer 1957): 325–33.
25 Gerald Horne, *Fire This Time: The Watts Uprising and the 1960s*
    (Charlottesville, 1995).

Laville and Lucas and Anderson—and other students of the intersection of race and the Cold War—should contemplate more carefully how, after World War II, the construction of "whiteness" merged with anticommunism as a defense of the status quo, property and privilege; a more candid and racialist defense of white supremacy became more difficult with the discrediting of Hitlerism.[26] Similarly, the links between racism and anticommunism globally await a detailed analysis. It may not be coincidental that Communist parties were ousted from power in Europe after 1989 but retained power in Asia (China, Vietnam, North Korea, Laos) and Latin America (Cuba, a nation with a significant percentage of citizens of African descent). It may not be coincidental that, perhaps, the most popular Communist party in the world today is in South Africa. This development is not a worrisome concern of the propertyless black majority; it is a worrisome concern for the privileged white minority.

By signing on to the Cold War agenda, the NAACP leadership served to weaken a domestic and international left that had been their prime champion at a time when the Democrats were influenced strongly by Dixiecrats and Republicans were

26 David R. Roediger, *The Wages of Whiteness: Race and the Making of the American Working Class* (New York, 1991); Eric Lott, *Love and Theft: Blackface Minstrelsy and the American Working Class* (New York, 1993); Wayne Addison Clark, "An Analysis of the Relationship between Anti-Communism and Segregationist Thought in the Deep South" (Ph.D. diss., University of North Carolina, 1976); David Jacob Group, "The Legal Repression of the American Communist Party, 1946–1951" (Ph.D. diss., University of Massachusetts, 1979); Rubin F. Weston, *Racism in U.S. Imperialism: The Influence of Racial Assumptions on American Foreign Policy, 1893–1946* (Columbia, SC, 1972); Michael H. Hunt, *Ideology and U.S. Foreign Policy* (New Haven, 1987).

continuing their quest to become "lily-white."[27] The domestic assault on the left helped to set the stage for the coming of a war in Vietnam—the ultimate expression of the Cold War agenda—that drained tax dollars that could better have been spent on pressing domestic needs.[28] By casting leaders like Du Bois into purgatory because of failure to endorse the Cold War agenda, the NAACP leadership prompted the rise of a resurgent right wing that by the 1990s would cast into doubt basic civil rights guarantees.[29]

27 Donald J. Lisio, *Hoover, Blacks, and Lily-Whites: A Study of Southern Strategies* (Chapel Hill, 1985); Allen J. Lichtman, *Prejudice and the Old Politics: The Presidential Election of 1928* (Chapel Hill, 1979); Ralph J. Bunche, *The Political Status of the Negro in the Age of FDR* (Chicago, 1973); Thomas and Mary D. Edsall, *Chain Reaction: The Impact of Race, Rights, and Taxes on American Politics* (New York, 1991); Donald R. McCoy and Richard T. Ruetten, *Quest and Response: Minority Rights and the Truman Administration* (Lawrence, 1973); William C. Berman, *The Politics of Civil Rights in the Truman Administration* (Columbus, OH, 1970).

28 Seymour Melman, *Pentagon Capitalism: The Political Economy of War* (New York, 1970); Roger W. Lotchin, *Fortress California, 1910–1961: From Warfare to Welfare* (New York, 1992); Seymour Melman, *The Defense Economy: Conversion of Industries and Occupations to Civilian Needs* (New York, 1970).

29 Gerald Horne, *Reversing Discrimination: The Case for Affirmative Action* (New York, 1992); Douglas S. Massey and Nancy A. Denton, *American Apartheid: Segregation and the Making of the Underclass* (Cambridge, MA, 1993); Nijole V. Benokraitis, *Affirmative Action and Equal Opportunity: Action, Inaction, Reaction* (Boulder, 1978); Mel Laiman, *The Political Economy of Racism: A History* (Boulder, 1993). See also Herbert Haines, *Black Radicals and the Civil Rights Mainstream, 1954–1970* (Knoxville, 1988). As demonstrated here, when the left was weakened, civil rights concessions slowed down; thus, the actions of the NAACP leadership ultimately were self-defeating.

It is with this perspective firmly in mind that we can take a closer look at the NAACP and Edith Sampson. Sampson was not alone in her globetrotting on behalf of a State Department desperately seeking a black voice to reassure skeptical audiences that Jim Crow America was not all that bad. The writer J. Saunders Redding traveled to India for this purpose. Carl Rowan ventured to India, Pakistan, and Southeast Asia "to try to convince Asians that they should keep faith in democracy."[30] All faced doubting audiences who were quite familiar with the landmark petition to the United Nations of the left-led Civil Rights Congress—noted in passing by Anderson—which presented a devastating account of the "genocide" that was being visited upon African Americans.[31]

When Sampson traveled to India, she faced a barrage of embarrassing questions about the dire plight of African Americans. Said one, "We will believe in America's altruistic motives after we see the American government raise the living standard of the Negroes and extend to them full justice and equality." On one occasion, she was asked why she omitted the names of Du Bois and Robeson when she was listing noted African Americans.

Despite her exalted post, Sampson was not the most diplomatic of interlocutors. At one point she was quoted as saying that freeing "subject people before they are prepared . . . might result in their subjection to the 'new colonialism of the

30 Horne, *Black and Red*, 280; J. Saunders Redding, *An American in India: A Personal Report on the India Dilemma and the Nature of Her Conflicts* (Indianapolis, 1954); Carl Thomas Rowan, *The Pitiful and the Proud* (New York, 1956).

31 Gerald Horne, *Communist Front? The Civil Rights Congress, 1946– 1956* (Rutherford, NJ, 1988).

Soviet Union.'" This standard rationale for anticommunism might have warmed the cockles of her State Department sponsors, but it won her little credibility among Indians—a "subject people" for a good deal of the twentieth century. She was heckled in Vienna when she "denied that the color bar is typical in the U.S."[32]

The point is that for generations, blacks, like Frederick Douglass, had traveled abroad in order to rally support against racism and barbarism at home.[33] The Cold War junkets of Sampson, Redding, Rowan, et al. represented a relatively new development: blacks traveling abroad—on behalf of the U. S. government—to cover up racism and barbarism at home.

Although Laville and Lucas cite an early statement from Martin Luther King, Jr. , that seems to reflect anticommunism, they neglect to mention that the Nobel laureate's reluctance to dump alleged Communists like Jack O'Dell and Stanley Levison helps to account for the unremitting hostility he experienced at the hands of the FBI.[34] O'Dell got it right when he proclaimed—after King had moved to dismiss him because of

32   Horne, *Black and Red*, 280–81. Paul Robeson's paper, *Freedom*, expressed the sentiments of many of his compatriots when it editorialized that African American "leadership must decide whether its mission in life is to 'foil the Russians' or to free the Negroes." *Freedom*, July 1951.

33   R. J. M. Blackett, *Building an Antislavery Wall: Black Americans in the Atlantic Abolitionist Movement* (Baton Rouge, 1983); Waldo E. Martin, Jr., *The Mind of Frederick Douglass* (Chapel Hill, 1984); Philip S. Foner, ed., *The Life and Writings of Frederick Douglass*, 4 vols. (New York, 1950–55).

34   Stephen B. Oates, *Let the Trumpet Sound: The Life of Martin Luther King, Jr.* (New York, 1982); David Garrow, *Bearing the Cross: Martin Luther King, Jr., and the Southern Christian Leadership Conference, 1933–1968* (New York, 1986).

FBI pressure—"'I am not the issue!'" The real issue, as he told the writer Taylor Branch, was "control of the movement."[35] This point was lost on Walter White years earlier—and on Laville and Lucas today.

Laville and Lucas claim that "Sampson had become an essential part of the counterattack against Soviet criticism of racial discrimination." However, as Michael Krenn notes sagely, when U.S. elites were plotting a "counterattack against Soviet criticism" at an important juncture, "nothing in the papers of groups such as the NAACP or individuals such as Ralph Bunche indicates they were ever consulted during this matter. Even after the controversy over the [1958 World's Fair] exhibit broke out, nothing was done to contact black leaders." Like most African Americans who have collaborated with U.S. elites on diplomatic affairs, Sampson was kept distant from important matters like policymaking; she was a hired gun (is the term "stooge" too harsh?) useful for a specific question—that inevitably involved race—but not deemed essential when the heavy lifting was to be done.

Sampson campaigned for prisoners of war from Nazi Germany captured by the Soviets, sang the praises of "American democracy" (though most African Americans in the Deep South still could not vote), denied that Jim Crow existed on "street cars in . . . Chicago" (while disingenuously omitting Montgomery, perhaps because she "had not visited" the Deep South in the 1950s), and worse. She had "little contact" with the civil rights movement, though it could have used her legal skills to rescue activists from Deep South dungeons. Yet, for all

35   Taylor Branch, *Parting the Waters: America in the King Years, 1934–1963* (New York, 1988), 845; Kenneth O' Reilly and David Gallen, ed., *Black Americans: The FBI Files* (New York, 1994), 28.

that, she was still dumped by U.S. elites when she had outlived her usefulness.

Laville and Lucas tell us much about Truman's words in favor of civil rights but much less about his deeds. They ignore the fact that the war in Korea where black soldiers complained mightily about racial discrimination derailed whatever civil rights plans Truman may have developed in 1948 in order to ensure that Henry Wallace would not garner the black vote. "Abolition of poll taxes" did not occur until the King-led movement, which facilitated passage of the Voting Rights Act of 1965; "desegregation of interstate transportation" did not occur until the "Freedom Rides" of the 1960s; "discrimination in the federal government and the armed forces" continues to exist. Laville and Lucas deny Du Bois's allegation that the NAACP was "tied in 'with the reactionary, war-mongering colonial imperialism of the present administration'" but say nothing about how its denial corresponds with the NAACP leadership's backing of war in Korea and NAACP inactivity about Truman's support for the apartheid regime in South Africa—whose soldiers fought on the same side as the United States during this war. There is much said about paper resolutions of the NAACP board; much less about what they actually did in the way of petitions, marches, conferences, or demonstrations in support of, say, Mandela's African National Congress. But, of course, since the ANC was in alliance with South African Communists, it would have been unwise for the NAACP to be vocal in support—if it wished to retain the goodwill of U.S. elites.

Laville and Lucas hail NAACP support for the Marshall Plan but say nothing about how aid to colonial powers like fascist Portugal helped this NATO ally repress further Angolans

and Mozambicans; nor do they discuss how aid to France facilitated Paris's wars of aggression against Algeria and Madagascar,
not to mention Indochina. Laville and Lucas should ask why
the NAACP leadership did not press for Marshall Plan aid to
the victims of colonialism, as opposed to the perpetrators.
Was not their mission designed to propel the "advancement of
colored people"?

It was bad enough for the NAACP leadership to provide aid
and succor to a U.S. foreign policy that supported apartheid;
but worse perhaps, as Kenneth O'Reilly has pointed out, was
this leadership's abject and direct collaboration with the FBI in
order to isolate and root out those not willing to go along with
their policy.[36]

I am afraid that Anderson as well stumbles on this FBI issue.
She relies heavily on their agents' accounts to describe the motives
and doings of the National Negro Congress, which is akin to citing Birmingham police chief "Bull" Connor as the chief witness
for the motives and doings of King's movement. Perhaps this is
why in one sentence she has the Communists ditching the NNC
in favor of "infiltrating" the NAACP (query: When Republicans,
Democrats, and Catholics "join" the NAACP, should they be
described as "infiltrating" too?) and in the very next sentence she
describes the reality, which is that the NNC was folded into the
Civil Rights Congress, which continued its work.

These are not trivial matters. Although Anderson suggests
skepticism, or at least no backing, of the anti-Communist claims
that undergirded the Truman administration's intervention in
Greece, like most U.S. historians, she is much more accepting

36   Kenneth O'Reilly, *"Racial Matters": The FBI's Secret File on Black
     America, 1960–1972* (New York, 1989); O'Reilly and Gallen, *Black
     Americans*, 21, 25; Horne, *Communist Front?* 140, 246.

about domestic anti-Communist claims, presumably because of U.S. Communists' alleged "slavish" devotion to Moscow. But why? Vietnamese Communists received more support from Soviet Communists—and for a while, Chinese Communists—than U.S. Communists did; with such reasoning this should have been sufficient reason to back the U.S. war in Vietnam. And, of course, such reasoning did lead to support for this disastrous conflict. Opponents of progress from Vietnam to South Africa charged local Communists with "slavish" devotion to Moscow; Fidel Castro had a point when he reputedly complained after the collapse of the Soviet Union that first Washington disliked him because he was supposedly a Moscow puppet, now they hate him because he is not.

Walter White retreated from the international arena rather than face the same allegation of being accused of such "slavish" devotion. It is high time to challenge positions on their merit—or lack thereof— rather than resorting to the intellectually lazy charge of "slavish" devotion to Moscow, and this should be the case whether Vietnam, South Africa, Cuba, Greece, or the United States is involved. At least since the dissolution of the Communist International during World II, Belgrade's break with Moscow a few years later, and China's rupture with the Soviet Union a few years after that, the notion of an "international Communist conspiracy" that could justify a global war because of local Communists' "slavish" devotion has been a dangerous illusion. More recent studies have suggested that this illusion is no less misleading when applied to the United States.[37]

37   Robin D. G. Kelley, *Hammer and Hoe: Alabama Communists during the Great Depression* (Chapel Hill, 1990); Mark Naison, *Communists in Harlem during the Depression* (Urbana, 1983). Interestingly, those who have subscribed to overheated "conspiracy theory" when discussing

In any event, using FBI documents to score points on the left is a perilous business, not only because these agents often had an incentive to distort and inflate in order to satisfy the anti-Communist impulses of J. Edgar Hoover.[38] Then as now, those truly concerned about the fate—and history—of African Americans should be more concerned about their leadership's "slavish"—here this adjective is all too appropriate—devotion to the predilections of U.S. elites.

This brings us to a major point: These articles—particularly Michael Krenn's superb effort—suggest that we can learn more about the all-important topic of race and foreign policy by examining the archives of U.S. elites, rather than the files of Edith Sampson, the NAACP leadership, and other centrists. As Krenn has observed, these centrists were on the periphery, and by 1948 were firmly within the Cold War camp—end of story, except for a few details, perhaps, about collaboration with the CIA abroad, sabotaging of the ANC and other anti-colonial movements, etc. As Krenn has done, we need an investigation of the archives of key government agencies; we need a close examination of the cable traffic between U.S. embassies and the State Department and the holdings of presidential libraries from Hoover to Reagan. We need excavation in archives abroad, particularly in Moscow, so we can establish definitively whether

the links between Moscow and U.S. Communists have neglected fundamentally the question of black radicals and radicalism, which-along with labor-was the central domestic preoccupation of the Reds; similarly, they have hardly touched the post-World War II era. See Harvey Klehr, John Earl Haynes, and Fridrikh Igorevich Firsov, *The Secret World of American Communism* (New Haven, 1995).

38   David Garrow, "FBI Political Harassment and FBI Historiography: Analyzing Information and Measuring the Effects," *Public Historian* 10 (Fall 1988): 5–18. See also Horne, *Communist Front?*

Du Bois, Robeson, and other dissenters were being directed by those ultimate "outside agitators"—the ever-busy inhabitants of the Kremlin, efficiently fomenting subversion from South Africa to the South Bronx on behalf of blacks too unenlightened to be aware of their true interests.

We need detailed examinations of race and foreign policy from the colonial era to the present. For the post-World War II era, we need to know more about, for example, the Black Panthers' relationship to Cuba, China, and Algeria; Malcolm X's ties to independent Africa; Dr. King's relationship with the peace and antiwar movements; the Nation of Islam's evolving relationship with Japan.

When this examination is done, it needs to be placed in a larger context: For example, African American ties to London, Mexico City, and Moscow should be compared with, say, Ireland's centuries-old effort to build an alliance with France against their mutual antagonist in England. Likewise, those wondering why various ethnic and religious groups in Bosnia are reluctant to become a "minority"—a motive force for "ethnic cleansing"—might understand why if they understood better the "minority" experience in the United States.[39]

The comedian Richard Pryor once joked that blacks should keep quiet about their association with the "Buffalo Soldiers," those U.S. army men who were so essential in routing and displacing Native Americans in the Far West. "You want them to hate us too?" he remarked.[40] African Americans should claim

---

39   David Rieff, *Slaughterhouse: Bosnia and the Failure of the West* (New York, 1995); Robert J. Donia and John V. A. Fine, Jr., *Bosnia and Hercegovina: A Tradition Betrayed* (New York, 1994).

40   John A. and Dennis A. Williams, *If I Stop I'll Die: The Comedy and Tragedy of Richard Pryor* (New York, 1991); Mel Watkins, *On the*

no credit for a Cold War "triumph" that the twenty-first century will reveal was costly indeed. In retrospect, Du Bois was right. Sampson and the NAACP leadership were wrong in endorsing the Cold War agenda—if the principal criterion for judging is what has been in the best interests of Africans and African Americans. More to the point, we do not need to create what could well be called a "Richard Pryor School of History" that causes us to celebrate what should be mourned. Laville and Lucas and Anderson, to an extent, should digest this sober.

Real Side: Laughing, Lying, and Signifying-The Underground Tradition of African-American Humor that Transformed American Culture from Slavery to Richard Pryor (New York, 1994).

THE DAWNING OF THE APOCALYPSE: THE ROOTS OF SLAVERY, WHITE SUPREMACY, SETTLER COLONIALISM, AND CAPITALISM IN THE LONG SIXTEENTH CENTURY

Monthly Review, 2020

It should not have been deemed surprising when in 1977 Washington's ambassador to the United Nations—Andrew Young, a former chief aide to Dr. Martin Luther King, Jr.—asserted audaciously that London "invented" racism. Instead, the pastor-cum-diplomat was pelted ferociously in a hailstorm of invective,[1] as he backpedaled rapidly. Actually, London had a point it did not articulate: if anything, its bastard offspring in Washington, in the government the envoy represented, was probably more culpable for the continuation of this pestilence,[2] as it lurched into incipient being in the 1580s in what is now North Carolina and gravitated toward a model of development

---

1   *New York Times*, 8 April 1977.
2   Cf. Ivan Van Sertima, *They Came Before Columbus: The African Presence in Ancient America* (New York: Random House, 1976), 130: Here the scholar speaks broadly of the "unconscious racial reflex of British scholars."

that diverged from those spurred by the Ottomans and Madrid, then rebelled in 1776 to ensure this putridness would endure.[3] How and why this deadly process unfolded in its earliest stage rests near the heart of this book.

Still, Ambassador Young, an ordained Protestant minister, would have better served historical understanding (besides providing useful instruction to predominantly Protestant London) if he had reflected on the point that the rise of this once dissident and besieged sect in the North American settlements led to the supplanting of religion as an animating factor of society with "race,"[4] a major theme to be explored in the pages that follow.[5] Certainly "whiteness"—effectively, Pan-Europeanism—

---

3   Gerald Horne, *The Counter-Revolution of 1776: Slave Resistance and the Origins of the United States of America* (New York: New York University Press, 2014).

4   Gerald Horne, *The Apocalypse of Settler Colonialism: The Roots of Slavery, White Supremacy and Capitalism in Seventeenth Century North America and the Caribbean* (New York: Monthly Review Press, 2018). B.M.S. Campbell, *Transition: Climate, Disease and Society in the Late Medieval World* (New York: Cambridge University Press, 2016).

5   C.f. Frank Tannenbaum, *Slave and Citizen: The Negro in the Americas* (New York: Knopf, 1947): The point argued in these pages is not that Catholicism was more progressive than Protestantism in handling slavery but that the nation where the latter prevailed – that is, England – as an underdog felt compelled to move away from religious sectarianism to confront the primary foe in Madrid by allying with, for example, the Ottoman Turks and Morocco (predominantly Muslim nations); as an underdog moving away from religious sectarianism, London proved to be more flexible in forming settlements, for example, Maryland, where Catholics played a major role: likewise, Madrid was capable of embracing African conquistadors – Catholics certainly – whereas London, pressed to the wall, embraced a Pan-European project that generally was not able to make as much room for African conquerors in North America. This project

provided a broader base for colonialism than even the Catholicism that drove Madrid. Historian Donald Matthews has observed that white supremacy in any case—a ruling ethos in London's settlements, then the North American Republic— had a religious cast, indicative of its tangled roots, with lynchings of Negroes emerging as a kind of sacrament.[6]

continued for some time, for example, Stephen Conway, *Brittania's Auxiliaries: Continental Europeans and the British Empire, 1740–1800* (New York: Oxford University Press, 2017).

6   Donald Matthews, *At the Altar of Lynching: Burning Sam Hose in the American South* (New York: Cambridge University Press, 2017). Fortunately, some scholars of late have explored how religion helped to propel "race". See, for example, Terence Keel, *Divine Variations: How Christian Thought Became Racial Science* (Stanford: Stanford University Press, 2018); John Hayes, *Hard, Hard Religion: Interracial Faith in the Poor South* (Chapel Hill: University of North Carolina Press, 2017). Tisa Wenger, *Religious Freedom: The Contested History of an American Ideal* (Chapel Hill: University of North Carolina Press, 2017), 1, 3, 10–11: The author argues that religious liberty "helped define American whiteness and make the case for U.S. imperial rule." Thus, "religious freedom talk" became code for "white and Protestant", juxtaposed against "the supposed bondage of the pagan and the Catholic." This trope of religious liberty "served ad an imperial mechanism of classification and control, helping to define not only what counted as religion, but also the contours of the racial." Yes, the victims of this entrapment – especially African Americans – in a form of intellectual and theological judo, sought to deploy religion against the victimizer, but the halting nature of real progress today should suggest that this ideological grappling – turning the strength of the oppressor's tool back against him – may have reached the outer limits of its possibilities. See also Peter Kerry Powers, *Goodbye Christ? Christianity, Masculinity and the New Negro Renaissance* (Knoxville: University of Tennessee Press, 2017). Of course, the fifteenth century publication of the Gutenberg Bible and the technological innovation it represented marked a turning point in the rise of both literacy and dissidence within Christianity more generally. See Janet Ing Freeman, *Johann Gutenberg and His Bible: A Historical Study* (New York: Typophiles, 1990). See also Margaret

Ambassador Young would also have better served under-standing if he had had the foresight to reflect the penetrating view of the eminent scholar Geraldine Heng, who has argued that at least by the thirteenth century, England had become "The First Racial State in the West," referring to the pervasive anti-Judaism that then prevailed. And just as it became easier to impose an expansionist foreign policy that propelled colo-nialism, given the experience with the Crusades, likewise it became easier to impose the racism that underpinned settler colonialism and slavery, once anti-Judaism became official pol-icy in London. As U.S. Negroes were to be treated, the Jewish community in England was said to emit a "special fetid stench," while bearing "horns and tails" and engaging in "cannibalism." Religion was deployed "socio-culturally" and "bio-politically" to "racialize a human group" in England in a manner eerily sim-ilar to what was to unfold in North America. Certainly, there are differences that distinguish anti-Judaism from anti-Negro bias. The persecuted in England were "unable to own land in agricultural Europe," but in response, "Jews famously estab-lished themselves as financiers," a status generally unavailable to Negroes, though the ban on landowning was. Interestingly, though this murderous bigotry is understandably associated with Madrid, which dramatically expelled the Jewish commu-nity in the hinge year that was 1492, it was London that was the first European country to "stigmatize Jews" as "criminals"—another parallel to U.S. Negroes—and the "first to administer the badge" this community was forced to wear. England was the first to initiate "state-sponsored efforts at conversion" and,

Leslie Davis, *The Lost Gutenberg* (New York: TarcherPerigee, 2019) and Eric Marshall White, *Editio Princeps: A History of the Gutenberg Bible* (London: Miller, 2017).

more to the point vis-à-vis Spain: "the first to expel Jews from its national territory." Then it was the prevailing religion, says Heng, that "supplied the theory and the state and populace supplied the praxis" of bigotry, analogous to the deployment of the "Curse of Ham" and racism targeting U.S. Negroes. Fear of "interracial sexual relations" was then the praxis in London, just like it was subsequently in Washington.[7] Ironically and perversely, London's earlier bigotry positioned England to capitalize upon Madrid's later version, by appealing to Sephardim and the Jewish community more broadly that had been perniciously targeted by the Spanish Inquisition.

THIS IS A BOOK ABOUT the predicates of the rise of England, moving from the periphery to the center (and inferentially, this is a story about their revolting spawn in North America post-1776). This is also a book about the seeds of the apocalypse, which led to the foregoing—slavery, white supremacy, and settler colonialism (and the precursors of capitalism)—planted in the long sixteenth century (roughly 1492 to 1607),[8] which eventuated in what is euphemistically termed "modernity," a process that reached its apogee in North America, the essential locus of this work. In these pages I seek to explain the global forces that created this catastrophe—notably

7   Geraldine Heng, *England and the Jews: How Religious Violence Created the First Racial State in the West* (New York: Cambridge University Press, 2019), 11, 12, 14, 20, 48, 52, 70. Cf. David M. Whitford, *The Curse of Ham in the Early Modern Era: The Bible and the Justifications for Slavery* (Burlington, Vermont: Ashgate 2009) and David M. Goldenberg, *Black and Slave: The Origins and History of the Curse of Ham* (Boston: de Gruyter, 2017).

8   Frederick J. Baumgartner, *France in the Sixteenth Century* (New York: St. Martin's 1995), xi: "The Long Sixteenth Century" is referenced here.

for Africans and the indigenous of the Americas—and how the minor European archipelago on the fringes of the continent (the British isles) was poised to come from behind, surge ahead, and maneuver adeptly in the potent slipstream created by Spain, Portugal, the Ottomans, even the Dutch and the French, as this long century lurched to a turning point in Jamestown. Although, as noted, I posit that 1492 is the hinge moment in the rise of Western Europe, I also argue in these pages that it is important to sketch the years before this turning point especially since it was 1453—the Ottoman Turks seizing Constantinople (today's Istanbul)—that played a critical role in spurring Columbus's voyage and, of course, there were other trends that led to 1453, and so on, as we march backward in time.[9]

In brief, and as shall be outlined, the Ottomans enslaved Africans and Europeans, among others, as contemporary Albania and Bosnia suggest. The Spanish, the other sixteenth-century titan, created an escape hatch by spurring the creation of a "Free African" population, which could be armed. Moreover, for 150 years until the late seventeenth century, thousands of Filipinos were enslaved by Spaniards in Mexico,[10] suggesting an alternative to a bonded labor force comprised of Africans or even indigenes. That is, the substantial reliance on enslaved African labor in North America honed by London was hardly inevitable.

Florida's first slaves came from southern Spain, though admittedly an African population existed in that part of Europe and wound up in North America. Yet at this early

---

9   Marching forward in time, the white supremacist in 2019 who massacred Muslims in New Zealand earlier visited the Balkans to study the uprooting of Christians: *London Daily Mail*, 16 March 2019.

10   Taina Seijas, *Asian Slaves in Colonial Mexico: From Chinos to Indians* (New York: Cambridge University Press, 2014).

juncture, sixteenth-century Spanish law and custom afforded the enslaved rights not systematically enjoyed in what was to become Dixie. Moreover, Spain's shortage of soldiers and laborers, exacerbated by a fanatical Catholicism that often barred other Europeans under the guise of religiosity—a gambit London did not indulge to the same extent—provided Africans with leverage.[11]

However, as time passed, it was London's model, then accelerated by Washington, that prevailed,: focusing enslavement tightly on Africans and those of even partial African ancestry, then seeking to expel "Free Negroes" to Sierra Leone and Liberia. London and Washington created a broader base for settler colonialism by way of a "white" population, based in the first instance on once warring, then migrant English, Irish, Scots, and Welsh; then expanding to include other European immigrants mobilized to confront the immense challenge delivered by rambunctious and rebellious indigenous Americans and enslaved Africans. This approach over time also allowed Washington to have allies in important nations and even colonies, providing enormous political leverage.[12]

This approach also had the added "advantage" of dulling class antagonism among settlers, who, perhaps understandably, were concerned less about the cutthroat competition delivered by an enslaved labor force and more with the real prospect of

11 Larry Eugene Rivers, *Slavery in Florida: Territorial Days to Emancipation* (Tallahassee: University Press of Florida, 2000), 2.

12 Gerald Horne, *Race to Revolution: The U.S. and Cuba During Slavery and Jim Crow* (New York: Monthly Review Press, 2014); Gerald Horne, *White Supremacy Confronted: U.S. Imperialism and Anticommunism vs. the Liberation of Southern Africa, from Rhodes to Mandela* (New York: International Publishers, 2019).

having their throats cut in the middle of the night by those very same slaves. Among the diverse settlers—Protestant and Jewish; English and Irish et al.—there was a perverse mitosis at play as these fragments cohered into a formidable whole of "whiteness," then white supremacy, which involved class collaboration of the rankest sort between and among the wealthy and those not so endowed.

In a sense, as the Ottomans pressed westward, Madrid and Lisbon began to cross the Atlantic as a countermove by way of retreat or even as a way to gain leverage.[13] But with the "discovery" of the Americas, leading to the ravages of the African slave trade, the Iberians, especially Spain, accumulated sufficient wealth and resources to confront their Islamic foes more effectively.[14]

The toxicity of settler colonialism combined with white supremacy not only dulled class antagonism in the colonies. It also solved a domestic problem with the exporting of real and imagined dissidents. In 1549 England was rocked to its foundations by "Kett's Revolt," where land was at issue and warehouses were put to the torch and harbors destroyed. A result of this disorienting upheaval, according to one analysis, was to convince the yeomanry to ally with the gentry,[15] a class collaborationist ethos then exported to the settlements. Assuredly, this rebellion

13   Andrew C. Hess, *The Forgotten Frontier: A History of the Sixteenth Century Ibero-African Frontier* (Chicago: University of Chicago Press, 1979), 20.

14   One scholar has "estimated that the Spanish Crown's original investment in Columbus's first voyage provided a return of 1,733,000 per cent." See David Childs, *Invading America: The English Assault on the New World, 1497–1630* (Yorkshire: Seaforth, 2012), 278.

15   Andy Wood, *The 1549 Rebellion and the Making of Early Modern England* (New York: Cambridge University Press, 2007).

shook England to its foundations, forcing the ruling elite to consider alternatives to the status quo, facilitating the thrust across the Atlantic. It is evident that land enclosure in England was tumultuous, making land three times more profitable, as it created disaster for the poorest, providing an incentive for them to try their luck abroad. A plot of land that once employed one or two hundred persons would—after enclosure—serve only the owner and a few shepherds.[16]

This vociferation was unbridled as the unsustainability of the status quo became conspicuous. Palace intrigue, a dizzying array of wars, with allies becoming enemies in a blink of an eye, the sapping spread of diseases, mass death as a veritable norm, bloodthirstiness as a way of life—all this and worse became habitual. This convinced many that taking a gamble on pioneering in the Americas was the "least bad" alternative to the status quo. Indeed, the discrediting of the status quo that was feudalism provided favorable conditions for the rise of a new system: capitalism.

As I write in 2019, there is much discussion about the purported 400th anniversary of the arrival of Africans in what is now the United States, though Africans enslaved and otherwise were present in northern Florida as early as 1565 or the area due north as early as 1526. As the following paragraphs suggest, this 1619 date is notional at best or, alternatively, seeks to understand the man without understanding the child. In my book on the seventeenth century, noted above, I wrote of the mass enslavement and genocidal impulse that ravaged Africans and indigenous Americans. That book

16 John Butman and Simon Target, *New World Inc.: The Making of America by England's Merchant Adventurers* (New York: Little Brown, 2018), 10, 16.

detailed the arrival in full force of the apocalypse; the one at hand limns the precursor: the dawning of this annihilation. The sixteenth century meant the takeoff of the apocalypse, while the following century embodied the boost phase. In brief, this apocalypse spelled the devastation of multiple continents: the Americas, Australia,[17] and Africa not least, all for the ultimate benefit of a relatively tiny elite in London, then Washington.

Thus, for reasons that become clearer below, the enslavement of Africans got off to a relatively "slow" start. From 1501 to 1650, a period during which Portuguese elites, at least until about 1620, and then their Dutch peers, held a dominant position in delivering transatlantic imports of captives: 726,000 Africans were dragged to the Americas, essentially to Spanish settlements and Brazil. By way of contrast, from 1650 to 1775, during London's and Paris's ascendancy and the concomitant accelerated development of sugar and tobacco, about 4.8 million Africans were brought to the Americas. Then, for the next century or so, until 1866, almost 5.1 million manacled Africans were brought to the region, at a time when the republicans in North America played a preeminent role in this dirty business. Similarly, at the time of the European invasion of the Americas, there were many millions of inhabitants of these continents, but between 1520 and 1620 the Aztecs and Incas, two of the major indigenous groupings, lost about 90 percent of their populations. In short, the late seventeenth century marked the ascendancy of the apocalypse, and the late sixteenth century marked the time when apocalypse was

---

17   Gerald Horne, *The White Pacific: U.S. Imperialism and Black Slavery in the South Seas After the Civil War* (Honolulu: University of Hawaii Press, 2007).

approaching in seven-league boots.[18] Yet the holocaust did not conclude in the seventeenth century, as ghastly as it was. The writer Eduardo Galeano argues that in three centuries, beginning in the 1500s, the "Cerro Rico" alone, one region in South America, "consumed eight million lives."[19] Thus, due north in California, the indigenous population was about 150,000 in 1846 at the onset of the U.S. occupation, but it was a mere 16,000 by 1890,[20] a direct result of a policy that one scholar has termed "genocide."[21]

IN LATE 1526 IN WHAT is now South Carolina, perhaps closer to what is now Sapelo Island, Georgia, in what was to be the case for centuries to come, enslaved Africans were on the warpath, along with their indigenous comrades. The Africans had escaped from a Spanish settlement, which had endured for a scant three months before the uprising, and set it aflame, as they fled into the waiting arms of similarly rebellious indigenes—Guale—and put paid to Madrid's attempt to extend their tenuous remit beyond the territory to the south

18   Aline Helg, *Slave No More: Self-Liberation Before Abolition in the Americas* (Chapel Hill: University of North Carolina Press, 2019) , 18, 19, 21, 22.

19   Eduardo Galeano, *Open Veins of Latin America: Five Centuries of The Pillage of a Continent* (New York: Monthly Review Press, 1973), 50. See also Peter J. Blackwell, *Miners of the Red Mountains: Indian Labor in Potosi, 1545–1650* (Alberquerque: University of New Mexico Press, 1984).

20   D. Michael Bottoms, *An Aristocracy of Color: Race and Reconstruction in California and the West, 1850–1890*, (Norman: University of Oklahoma Press, 2013), 27.

21   Benjamin Madley, *An American Genocide: The United States and the California Indian Catastrophe, 1846–1873* (New Haven: Yale University Press, 2016).

they had named Florida.[22] In a sense, this was not a first for a
territory later to labor under the Stars and Stripes, for in 1514
scores of enslaved Africans revolted in Puerto Rico in what one
scholar has described as "the first African uprising known to
have taken place anywhere in the Indies."[23]

Evidently, Madrid's minions envisioned turning the southeast quadrant of North America into a feudal empire staffed by
indigenous workers and enslaved Africans, but the latter's joint
revolt buried yet another exploiter's dream. In the resultant chaos,
even some Europeans appeared to join the victors and deserted to
the Native American side.[24] Actually, if alert Spaniards had been
paying closer attention, they would not have been overly surprised
by this uprising and what it portended, for in 1527 in the region
stretching southward from Panama an African escaped from a
colonizer's vessel, swam ashore, and ensconced himself among
the indigenes, who he then proceeded to organize and lead so
thoroughly that this community became a continuing thorn in
the flesh of the would-be European usurpers.[25]

22 Susan Richburg Parker, "Slaves Flee St. Augustine – 1603," *El
    Escribano*, 41 (2004): 1–8, 1. For more on this revolt, see Paul E.
    Hoffman, *A New Andalucia and a Way to the Orient: The American
    Southeast During the Sixteenth Century* (Baton Rouge: Louisiana
    State University Press, 1990), 78. See also Jerald T. Milanich, *Florida
    Indians and the Invasion from Europe* (Gainesville: University Press of
    Florida, 1995), 13.

23 Casey Farnsworth, "The Revolt of the Augueybana II: Puerto Rico's
    Interisland Connections," in Ida Altman and David Wheat, eds.,
    *The Spanish Caribbean and the Atlantic World in the Long Sixteenth
    Century* (Lincoln: University of Nebraska Press, 2019), 25–45, 25.

24 Andrew Lawler, *The Secret Token: Myth, Obsession and the Search for
    the Lost Colony of Roanoke* (New York: Doubleday, 2018), 19–20.

25 Robert Cushman Murphy, "The Earliest Spanish Advances
    Southward from Panama Along the West Coast of South America",

Madrid was dimly aware of the dilemma it had created for itself. Enslaved Africans were being imported to the Americas by 1503, in part premised on the idea that—perhaps because of the disorientation delivered by dumping aliens in a foreign land—the labor of one of these imported workers was equal to or surpassed by that of four "Indians."[26] But as early as 1505, reconsideration was occurring, as there was a suspension, albeit temporary, of the importation of slaves into Hispaniola, as quite ominously, this would-be chattel had been fleeing and setting up outlaw settlements of their own in the mountains and forests and from there executing violent raids on Spanish towns and haciendas. Thus, by 1522, the first large-scale uprising of the enslaved occurred during the Christmas holiday (which was to become a prime time in following centuries to attack dulled and inebriated settlers), as a sugar mill belonging quite appropriately to the son of Columbus was victimized, with a number of his comrades slaughtered. That same year an enslaved man named Miguel led an army of 800 former chattel that forced the closing of profitable mines and delivered horror to the homes of settlers due south. By 1529, four years after being built, Santa Marta on the northern coast of South America was razed by rebellious Africans. In Mexico, there were slave insurrections in 1523, 1537, and 1546. Puerto Rico experienced severe trouble of this type in 1527, and by the 1540s it was again Hispaniola's turn as settlers were terrorized by maroons

Hispanic American Historical Review, 21 (Number 1, February 1941): 1–28, 16.

26 Lesley Byrd Simpson, *The Encomienda in New Spain: Forced Native Labor in the Spanish Colonies, 1492–1550* (Berkeley: University of California Press, 1929), 16.

or cimarrones.[27] Slave revolts hit Cuba in 1530, not to mention the capital along the coast of today's Colombia that same year, which was destroyed. Africans fled to today's Ecuador and formed an independent polity that Madrid was compelled to recognize in 1598.[28]

This earlier North American revolt of 1526 made it possible for Londoners, many decades later, to make their own claim to this vast territory, which was then inherited by their preening settler colony, now known as the United States of America. In other words, those who triumphed in what is now the United States had a kind of "second mover's advantage," advancing in the wake of Spanish retreat and, as shall be seen, learning lessons from this competitor's defeat that proved to be devastating to Africans particularly.

Today's Dixie is well aware of the debt owed to Madrid: the conquistador Hernando de Soto nowadays is venerated as the "first white hero" of the region; towns and cities annually hold parades, barbeques, and pageants in his honor, downplaying his conspicuous role as an enslaver and his catastrophic impact on indigenes, while pooh-poohing the massive evidence that depicts his savage quest as the handiwork of a psychopathic killer.[29]

Though often neglected, the contemporary United States remains ensconced in the shadow of the original colonizers.

---

27   Nick Hazlewood, *The Queen's Slave Trader: John Hawkyns [sic], Elizabeth I and the Trafficking in Human Souls* (New York: Morrow, 2004), 42, 43.

28   Kathleen Deagan and Darcie McMahon, *Fort Mose: Colonial America's Black Fortress of Freedom* (Tallahassee: University of Press of Florida, 1995), 13.

29   David Ewing Duncan, *Hernando De Soto: A Savage Quest in the Americas* (Norman: University of Oklahoma Press, 1996), xix.

Before the arrival of Spanish conquistadors in the 1500s, the population of the Caddo people in the southeastern quadrant of what is now the United States was an estimated 200,000, but by the eighteenth century, as the new nation was being launched, their population had shrunk reportedly to about 1,400, making the final ouster of indigenes more likely.[30] By the nineteenth century, the northern reaches of Mexico, soon to be incorporated into the United States, was regarded widely as the "land of war," indicative of how indigenous resistance had not only been longstanding but also had been weakening the original inhabitants of the land.[31] The genocide that was visited upon the indigenous of North America was a rolling process, with the republican knockout blow facilitated mightily by the preceding blows inflicted by Madrid.[32]

Thus, it was in the twentieth century that enraged settlers in the newly minted republican state New Mexico remained furious about the indigenous challenge to their alleged right to the land. The settler delegate returned to a 1551 decree by Charles V for justification supposedly sketching "separation of races" that was said to castigate "'Negroes, Mulattos and Mixed Bloods" who were said to "teach . . . evil ways" to indigenes. Then the

---

30 Charles C. Mann, 1491: *New Revelations of the Americas Before Columbus* (New York: Knopf, 2005), 99.

31 David J. Weber, "American Westward Expansion and the Breakdown of Relaitions Between Pobladores and 'Indios Barbaros' on Mexico's Far Northern Border", *New Mexico Historical Review*, 56 (Number 3, July 1981): 221–238.

32 Cf. Edward Westermann, *Hitler's Ostkrieg and the Indian Wars: Comparing Genocide and Conquest* (Norman: University of Oklahoma Press, 2016) and James Q. Whitman, *Hitler's American Model: The United States and the Making of Nazi Race Law* (Princeton: Princeton University Press, 2017).

rationalizer returned to Spanish law of 1513 for justification for what would have been deemed "Anglo" occupation of the land.[33]

Washington was even able to co-opt, to a degree, settlers dispatched by Spain. Recently, for example, the *New York Times* reported the story of Patricia Aragon Luczo, a retired flight attendant from New Mexico, who traced her Sephardic legacy to Juan de Vitoria Carvajal, a member of the Spanish expedition that sought to seize the area surrounding Santa Fe in 1598.[34]

TODAY A SELF-DESCRIBED "New Conquest History" has arisen that stresses the sixteenth-century presence of African maroons whose very existence called into question the purported control of Spain, even in Hispaniola, to the point where the notion of "maroons as conquerors" has to be taken seriously.[35] As events in 1526 in what is now South Carolina indicate, there

---

33   "Address of A.B. Renehan of Santa Fe"...at the Conference of the League of the Southwest, at Santa Barbara, California, June 9, 1923 on 'Laws and Equities Affecting the So-Called Settlers on Pueblo Indian Land Grants', *Huntington Library San Marino, California*. See also Geoffrey Parker, *Emperor: A New Life of Charles V* (New Haven: Yale University Press, 2019).

34   *New York Times*, 8 November 2019.

35   Robert C. Schwaller, "African Maroons and the Incomplete Conquest of Hispaniola," *The Americas*, 75 (Number 4, October 2018): 609–638, 611, 637. See also Matthew Restall, "Black Conquistadors: Armed Africans in Early Spanish America," *The Americas*, 57 (Number 2, 2000): 171–205; Ignacio Gallup-Diaz, "A Legacy of Strife: Rebellious Slaves in Sixteenth-Century Panama," *Colonial Latin America Review*, 19 (Number 3, December 2010): 417–435, 417, 423, 429, 430, 433: These Africans "wrecked the Isthmus of Panama in 1555–1556" in what was termed the "War of Vallano," named after the "rebellious slave Vallano." These Africans, it was reported, "had an army numbering more than 1200 men and women." By 1574 it was said that there were about "3000" maroons in that vicinity. As late as the 1580s, the marauding of "uncontrollable rebel slaves" remained a major force. Sir Francis Drake of England "coordinated his activities

was a kind of advantage of the latecomer, the tardy, enjoyed by London, which could profit as Africans and indigenes, on the one hand, pounded would-be conquistadors and, on the other hand, allowed Englishmen to administer knockout blows to the exhausted survivors in succeeding decades.

Debilitating blows were also unleashed by the initial invaders too. For the land upon which Dixie was built still groans from the excruciating dread delivered by the likes of de Soto and his comrades, groans that continue to resound in the form of dispossessed indigenes and severely oppressed Africans. These conquerors bulled their way into indigenous settlements, murdering all they encountered, including small children, old men, pregnant women—especially pregnant women. They hacked them mercilessly, slicing open their bulging bellies with their sharpened swords with macabre intensity. They grabbed suckling infants by the feet, ripping them from their mothers' breasts, dashing them headlong against the ground.[36]

There were "Holocaustic levels of slaughter and enslavement,"[37] asserts scholar Matthew Restall with accuracy, speaking of Mexico in words that are hardly unique to this territory.

The deadliness of the resultant apocalypse commenced virtually from the day Columbus reached terra firma in October

with a band of free blacks," weakening Madrid and allowing London to advance.

36 Kay Wright Lewis, *A Curse Upon the Nation: Race, Freedom and Extermination in America and the Atlantic World* (Athens: University of Georgia Press, 2017).

37 Matthew Restall, *When Montezuma Met Cortes: The True Story of the Meeting that Changed History* (New York: HarperCollins, 2018), 298.

1492.[38] In the decades immediately following, an estimated 650,000 indigenes were enslaved and by 1580, in Algiers, enslaved indigenes from the Americas were to be found.[39] In other words, it was not just European microbes that devastated indigenes, it was also a conscious strategy of naked profiteering from enslaving combined with a maniacal desire to remove the existing population, with enslaved Africans then arriving to develop the land. Thus, by 1530, 69 percent of the enslaved in Puerto Rico—now a U.S. "possession"—were African.[40] Simultaneously, a market in Europe quickly developed involving indigenous American women and children deployed as domestic or household slaves.[41]

For as early as 1514, a few decades after the epochal voyage of Christopher Columbus, Madrid was frightened by the rapid increase in the number of enslaved Africans in Hispaniola, their initial foothold, and as one twentieth-century observer put it, "By 1560 the natural increase of that prolific race," meaning Africans, "coupled with the constant inflow brought by the slave traders"—intoxicated by the maddening scent of profit—"had

---

38   Jerald T. Milanich and Susan Milbrath, eds., *First Encounters: Spanish Explorations in the Caribbean and the United States, 1492–1570* (Gainesvilles: University Press of Florida, 1989).

39   Nancy E. Van Deusen, *Global Indios: The Indigenous Struggle for Justice in Sixteenth Century Spain* (Durham: Duke University Press, 2015), 2, 247. See Matthew Restall, *When Montezuma Met Cortes*, 298: By the early sixteenth century there were more than 500,000 enslaves across the Caribbean, Mesoamerica and Central America. Cf. Nabil Matar, *British Captives in the Mediterranean and the Atlantic: 1563–1760* (Leiden: Brill, 2014).

40   Karen Anderson Cordova, *Surviving Spanish Conquest: Indian Flight and Cultural Transformation in Hispaniola and Puerto Rico* (Tuscaloosa: University of Alabama Press, 2017), 108.

41   Matthew Restall, *When Montezuma Met Cortes*, 304.

created a most alarming preponderance in their number" compared to the colonizers.[42]

As early as 1570, Africans in the Caribbean exceeded the number of Europeans and, after bloodily targeted violence, probably that of indigenes too; that year, there were an estimated 10 million indigenes, 250,000 Africans—"mulattos" or "mestizos"—and 140,000 "Europeans" in Iberian America. That first figure fell sharply in succeeding years, while that of Africans continued to rise relative to that of Europeans. By 1576 there were reportedly more Africans than colonizers in the important node that was Mexico City. Part of Madrid's problem was overweening ambition; more Spaniards reached Manila in 1580 than any other year of the sixteenth century, and it was near then that the grasping power began dreamily to contemplate an invasion of China, to then be followed by thrusts into India, Cochin China (or Vietnam), Siam, the Moluccas, Borneo, and Sumatra. Still, by 1600, Madrid controlled the largest collection of territories the world had seen since the fall of the Roman Empire and the heyday of Genghis Khan, as it also dominated Italy, southern Netherlands (the ancestor of modern Belgium), a good deal of the Americas, and its pioneering neighbor, Portugal. Yes, it was a Pan-European project, albeit with a Catholic tinge from the start; after all, Columbus's roots were in Genoa; there were Basques, of course, and Florentines and Frenchmen (Magellan was Portuguese), Greeks and Cordobans.[43] Yet, as the following pages suggest,

---

42 Woodbury Lowery, *The Spanish Settlements Within the Present Limits of the United States: Florida, 1562–1574* (New York: Putnam's, 1905), 14.

43 Hugh Thomas, *World Without End: Spain, Philip II and the First Global Empire* (New York: Random House, 2014), 230, 232, 260, 267, 279,

it was also a religious project, as signaled by the vanguard role played by Jesuits.[44]

Spain's vaulting ambition, according to one assayer, led to the commencement of the dominating process known as "globalization," in that in 1571 Manila was founded as a crucial entrepot linking the Americas and Asia in the trading of silver bullion between China and Spain, with knock-on effects worldwide, including in Africa, increasingly the favored source of labor supply. Silver traded for Chinese silk, tea, and porcelain fueled the rise of Madrid, facilitating the precipitous decline of indigenous Americans and their replacement by enslaved Africans.[45] After 1571, Chinese fabrics were arriving in substantial quantities in South America, as a result of the Manila galleon trade. This form of "globalization" is in a sense a euphemism for the roots of capitalism.[46]

By 1500, China accounted for an estimated 25 percent of the world's output of goods and services and England for about 1 percent, but by 1900 as an outgrowth of slavery and rapacious colonialism, those numbers had been virtually reversed.[47]

282, 289. Readers should note that for the sake of convenience I will at times refer to certain regions by their modern names – for example, Italy, Germany, New Mexico, etc. – though aware that these entities were not necessarily cognizable in the sixteenth century.

44   Christopher Hollis, *The Jesuits: A History* (New York: MacMillan, 1968).

45   Dennis O. Flynn, et,al., eds., *China and the Birth of Globalization in the 16th Century* (Aldershot: Ashgate 2010).

46   Kris Lane, Potosi: *The Silver City that Changed the World* (Oakland: University of California Press, 2019), 57, 69. See also Arturo Giraldez, *The Age of Trade: The Manila Galleons and the Dawn of the Global Economy* (Boulder: Rowman and Littlefield, 2015).

47   John Butman and Simon Target, *New World Inc.: The Making of America by England's Merchant Adventurers* (New York: Little Brown, 2018), 23.

We continue to reside in the shadow of this important century—the sixteenth—as globalization accelerated and the state was strengthened. Not accidentally, it was then that John Harrington, described recently as the "cynic-in-residence" in Queen Elizabeth's court, opined: "Treason doth never prosper: what's the reason? Why, if it prosper, none dare call it treason,"[48] a statement that also reflected the overthrow and weakening of various unsustainable polities in the name of the new force created by "globalization."

STILL, DESPITE THE ONRUSH of the global, the ruler in Madrid was not known as "His Catholic Majesty" by accident, for religion, or more precisely, Catholicism, was privileged. "Religious adherence was more important as a test of loyalty than ethnicity"—or race—according to an analysis of the Spanish settlement in St. Augustine, Florida: "Slaves, therefore, received different treatment here than in English or even other Spanish colonies" in part because protecting the wealth

---

48 *Washington Post*, 24 December 2018. See also John A. Stormer, *None Dare Call it Treason* (Florissant: Liberty Bell Press, 1964). That the sixteenth century continues to resonate today is reflected not only in the recent evocation of Harrington's evocative words but also in reference to the Pilgrimage of Grace, a revolt that threatened Henry VIII's England, until the conspirer's reach exceeded their grasp and they were crushed. "As in many Tudor risings," said the contemporary pundit, Robert Shrimsley, "public discontent over issues like food prices was [harnessed] until it morphed into a challenge to the Crown. By the time it was suppressed, few were fighting for the causes that initially drove them to action. It is a lesson Britain's Brexit hardliners should consider . . . " *Financial Times*, 5 March 2019. See also Michael Questier, *Dynastic Politics and the British Reformations, 1558–1630* (New York: Oxford University Press, 2019).

of Cuba and Mexico was the primary goal,[49] not least by dint of slave-constructed fortifications and in part because religion was overdetermined.

This telescoped disquisition about Florida brings into sharp relief major themes of this book: the firm implantation of settler colonialism in what is now the United States—including the enslavement of Africans—originated in today's "Sunshine State" and, as shall be seen, in New Mexico, the "Land of Enchantment." The history of Virginia and New England, which wrongly deems either or both to be the seedbed of settler colonialism in what is now the United States—and, in the long run, the United States itself has to be adjudged with this point firmly in mind. Thus, armed Africans in Spanish Florida played an expansive role, in a way that would have been difficult in Virginia or Massachusetts, for example.[50] London, the "second" colonizer and their republican successors, grappled assiduously with the formidable problem of how to defang embattled and armed Africans in Florida, leading to ruinous nineteenth-century wars.

Thus, the armed Africans of northern Florida were an obvious counterpoint to the enslaved Africans languishing across the border in what became London's settlements in Georgia and South Carolina, forcing Britain to expend blood and treasure to extirpate this "threat," which it did by about 1763, which was then followed by the rebellious settlers intervening

---

49   Christopher Putchinski Beats, "African Religious Integration in Florida During the First Spanish Period", M.A. Thesis (University of Central Florida, 2007), iii, 3.

50   Gerald Horne, *Negro Comrades of the Crown: African Americans and the British Empire Fight the U.S. Before Emancipation* (New York: New York University Press, 2012), 3, 46.

more forcefully in Florida over the next half-century or more, until the matter was resolved by the creation of the "Sunshine State" in the slaveholders' republic. London, then Washington, decided not to build on the "St. Augustine exception" created by Madrid but to strangle it instead. It was left to London, then Washington, to leapfrog Madrid altogether by developing a sturdier axis of colonialism, namely "whiteness," the privileging of "race" over religion, a process (again) extended by Britain's erstwhile stepchild in 1776, allowing for the incorporation more readily and easily of a growing number of European immigrants, with little room to compromise with a "Free Negro" population.[51]

THERE WAS A CONTRADICTORY APPROACH to Africans by Spanish colonizers. There were so-called Black Conquistadors, for example, Juan Garrido, instrumental in the creation of "New Spain" or Mexico, and Sebastian Toral, who obtained his freedom because of his role in the siege of Yucatan, and Juan Valiente, who helped to conquer Guatemala, then settled in Chile. On the other hand, there was a history congruent with subsequent slave revolts within the slaveholders' republic, for example, that of Miguel in 1553 in the gold-rich region of Venezuela; similar rebellions erupted in like gold mining regions in today's Colombia in the late sixteenth century.

---

51 On contestation between London and Madrid, particularly during the heralded revolt of the enslaved, encapsulated as "Stono's Revolt," see Gerald Horne, *The Counter-Revolution of 1776: Slave Resistance and the Origins of the United States of America* (New York: New York University Press, 2014). On the contestation between the slaveholders' republic and Florida before and after statehood, see Gerald Horne, *Negro Comrades of the Crown: African Americans and the British Empire Fight the U.S. Before Emancipation* (New York: New York University Press, 2012).

It is possible that thousands of the enslaved murdered their masters and foremen and hid in the mountains and forests, constructing palenques and various forms of marronage that proved difficult to eradicate. Near that same time, in Cuzco in Peru, enslaved Africans and indigenes—in contrast to the Black Conquistadors—formed a rebellious contingent led by an indigene, Francisco Chichima. Due north in Vera Cruz, a citadel was formed in the 1580s by Nanga (Yanga), possibly of Akan or West African origin. About three decades later, the settlers effectuated a kind of entente with these rebels. Perhaps as a partial result, legislation enacted by the monarchs in Madrid and Lisbon were more demanding of masters and more humane toward the enslaved than their peers in London, Paris, The Hague, and especially Washington.[52]

In a sense, Madrid took religion too seriously, seemingly oblivious to the rising notion that settler colonialism required "race" more than religion. Madrid assumed that it could both enslave and empower Africans, whereas the ultimately victorious republicans begged to differ. I argue that this difference between Madrid and London is to be found in religion, not necessarily because Catholicism was more "progressive" than Protestantism,[53] but more so because the former was a more centralized faith, better able to enact and enforce edicts, as opposed to the fissiparous latter. Decentralized Protestantism was a better fit than rigid Catholicism, perhaps by virtue of the fabled "absence of mind" in forging a settlement project that relied more heavily on a construction of "whiteness" or

52   Aline Helg, *Slave No More*, 77–78, 46–48.

53   Frank Tannenbaum, *Slave and Citizen: The Negro in America* (New York: Knopf, 1946).

the ingathering of various and disparate European ethnicities. Similarly, the heralded "religious liberty" that characterized the republican secession in the late eighteenth century coincidentally allowed for a Pan-European mobilization to crush rebellious Africans and indigenes alike.

AS THE TIME APPROACHED TO colonize what became St. Augustine in 1565, the monarch in Madrid was told that "there are many Negroes, mulattoes and people of evil inclination in the islands of Santo Domingo, Puerto Rico, Cuba, and others nearby. In each of these islands," said conquistador Pedro Menendez de Aviles disconsolately, "there are more than thirty of them to each Christian. It is a land where this generation multiplies rapidly," and, besides, "in possession of the French" most notably, "all of these slaves will be set free," since "to enjoy this freedom, the Negroes will help them against their own masters and rulers, for them to take over the land. It will be a very easy thing to do with the help of the Negroes."[54] This was perceptive, and combined with Madrid's self-defeating religious sectarianism, which hindered the necessity to build, à la London, a "whiteness" project, crossing theological borders, left few alternatives beyond seeking to co-opt Africans, creating a "Free African" population that could be armed, an endangering process that certain settlers may have deemed to be a cure worse than the illness.

This was part and parcel of the elongated process whereby religion was supplanted by "race" as the animating axis of society, which reached its zenith in the Americas, especially

54 Pedro Menendez de Aviles to King Philip II, February-March 1565, in Edward W. Lawson, editor and translator, *Letters of Pedro Menendez de Aviles and Other Documents Relative to His Career, 1555–1574* (St. Augustine Historical Society Florida).

Protestant-dominated North America. For as the late doyen of historians Herbert Bolton once averred, "In the English colonies the only good Indians were dead Indians."[55] But this induced morbidity did not occur to a similar degree in, for example, French settlements in North America. After all, London coveted the land of indigenes for settlement, while Paris was more intrigued by the trade in furs and a military alliance with the indigenes against other European powers such as London. Thus, says the scholar W. J. Eccles, Perfidious Albion "had to displace—that is destroy—the Indians" and France was more interested in seeking to "preserve them, in order to achieve their aims."[56] Furthermore, as a nineteenth century California leader put it, "the success of Britain as a colonizing power was ascribable to its strict policy of racial separation and that the failures of France and Spain"—and Portugal too, it might have been added—"were due to the absence of such a policy...."[57] And the hateful Jim Crow policy installed in the revolting spawn of London in Washington further bolstered this malignant analysis.

Paris was the wild card in terms of European powers, willing to work with indigenes—and Africans too—against their competitors. On 10 July 1555, Jacques de Sores (at times

55   Herbert Bolton, "The Mission as a Frontier Institution in the Spanish American Colonization," *American Historical Review*, 23 (Number 1, October 1917): 42–61, 61.

56   W.J. Eccles, *The French in North America, 1500–1783* (Markham, Ontario: Fitzhenry and Whiteside, 1998), 8. Cf. Suzannah Lipscomb, *The Voices of Nimes: Women, Sex, Marriage in Reformation Languedoc* (New York: Oxford University Press, 2019).

57   D. Michael Bottoms, *An Aristocracy of Color: Race and Reconstruction in California and the West, 1850–1890* (Norman: University of Oklahoma Press, 2014), 107.

known as Soria), described as "the most heretic Lutheran," attacked Havana, which was defended in turn by a force of 355, including 220 indigenes, 80 Africans, and only 35 Spaniards, the numbers a hint as to how dependent the colonizers were at fraught moments. This "heretic Lutheran" was a kind of John Brown of the Pan-Caribbean, threatening slave revolts in order to attain his sweeping goals,[58] and providing untold leverage to Africans and lessons for them too, in terms of aligning with one power against another. The Frenchman and his hearty crew of a mere 53 men had leveraged African disgruntlement when he freed the enslaved in attacking Margarita, Cabo de la Vela, La Burburata, Santa Maria, Cartagena, Santiago de Cuba, and Havana—and, for a while, captured all of these enriched sites.[59]

TO BE SURE, EVEN IF London were to surpass Madrid or Paris, it would not guarantee European supremacy, setting aside the ultimate goal of global dominance. For in the sixteenth century, in some ways the most fearsome of them all was the Ottoman Empire. The potency of the Ottomans was signaled when Christians, sensing the directions of the prevailing winds, began defecting to the Ottoman side.[60] Yes, some of these "defections" were coerced, but many were not. In any event,

---

58   Alejandro de la Fuente, *Havana and the Atlantic in the Sixteenth Century* (Chapel Hill: University of North Carolina Press, 2008), 1, 2.

59   Paul E. Hoffman, *A New Andalucia and a Way to the Orient: The American Southeast During the Sixteenth Century* (Baton Rouge: Louisiana State University Press, 1990), 225.

60   Tobias P. Graf, *The Sultan's Renegades: Christian Europe Converts to Islam and the Making of the Ottoman Elite, 1575–1610* (New York: Oxford University Press, 2017). See also Joshua M. White, *Piracy and Law in the Ottoman Mediterranean* (Stanford: Stanford University Press, 2018).

the formidable Ottoman fleet was a microcosm of the Ottoman Empire. Commanders tended to be Turks, but the oarsmen were Greeks and Bulgarians, and the specialists emerged from the heart of Christian Europe: Genoese, Catalans, Sicilians, Provençals, Venetians.[61]

So bolstered, as Madrid was seeking to repress Africans, Constantinople captured Belgrade in 1521, conquered Rhodes in 1522, destroyed the Hungarian army at Mohacs in 1526, and besieged Vienna with a massive army of 400,000 in 1529. On the western Mediterranean front, the Turks seized Tripoli from the Knights of Malta in 1551, destroyed a Spanish armada at the island of Djerba in 1560, and besieged Malta in 1561.[62] The Ottomans seemed to be soaring from strength to strength in the early sixteenth century, not only bombarding Serbia and Buda but more generally besieging eastern Europe too. Syria and Palestine were subjugated, along with Baghdad, Basra, Aden, and Cairo. Bases were established in Ethiopia and Algeria. In the prelude to 1492, the Ottomans were seeking to bolster their fellow Muslims in Andalusia. Ironically, as the Habsburgs, as well as Spain, expanded into the Americas, this made it easier for the Ottomans to expand into Europe and nearby regions. Ultimately, however, the wealth accumulated by Spaniards and other Western Europeans in the Americas allowed Madrid and

61   Stefan Stantchev, "Venice and the Ottoman Threat, 1381–1453," in Norman Housley, ed., *Reconfiguring the Fifteenth Century Crusade* (New York: Palgrave, 2017), 161–205, 181. See also Maria Fusaro, *Political Economies of Empire in the Early Modern Mediterranean: The Decline of Venice and the Rise of England, 1450–1700* (New York: Cambridge University Press, 2015).

62   Maria Antonio Garces, ed., *An Early Modern Dialogue with Islam: Antonio de Sosa's Topography of Algiers (1612)* (South Bend: University of Notre Dame Press, 2011), 27.

their immediate neighbors to reverse what appeared to be insuperable advantages enjoyed by the Ottomans.[63]

Yet, as matters evolved, 1516–17 was a critical time, not only because of the ascendancy of Martin Luther[64] and the expansion of the Ottomans into North Africa and beyond, but also because of the consolidation of Spain and the Habsburgs. The split among Christians appeared at first glance to provide an immense opportunity for the Ottomans, but instead, in the longer term it boosted Luther's heirs.

Western Europe's contestation with the Ottomans was a precondition of the rise of plundering of the Americas and Africa. The Iberians pirouetted deftly from the directive of Pope Nicholas V in 1452 sanctifying Lisbon's praxis of selling into slavery all "heathens" and "'Foes of Christ'"—principally Moslems—to the broader application in the Americas.[65] This fifteenth-century edict was an extension of the Crusades.[66] That is, a Pan-European Christian campaign against Islam extended to a campaign against non-European/non-Christians (especially in the Americas and Africa); arguably, this Pan-European

---

63 Thomas D. Goodrich, *The Ottoman Turks and the New World: A Study of Tarih-I Hind-I Garbi and Sixteenth Century Ottoman Americana* (Wiesbaden: Harrassowitz, 1990), 5, 9. See also Thomas A. Carlson, *Christianity in Fifteenth Century Iraq* (New York: Cambridge University Press, 2018).

64 Christopher Ocker, *Luther, Conflict and Christendom: Europe and Christianity in the West* (New York: Cambridge University Press, 2018).

65 L.R. Bailey, *Indian Slave Trade in the Southwest: A Study of Slave Taking and Traffic in Indian Captives* (Los Angeles: Western Lore, 1966), xii.

66 Cf. Steve Tibble, *The Crusader Armies, 1099–1187* (New Haven: Yale University Press, 2018). The author downplays the religious character of the crusades.

initiative was a prelude to the rise of the similarly devastating "whiteness" project. Thus, in fifteenth-century Valencia, Spain, captors sought to misrepresent what amounted to Senegalese and Gambians (West Africans) as Moors (North Africans) —religious-cum-political antagonists—so as to enslave them consistent with theological mores.[67]

As suggested earlier, with the taking of Constantinople in 1453, Christian Europe endured an existential crisis, a calamity that was seen as almost unprecedented in history. Unshackled ire was not caged when Ottomans began gifting Hungarian slaves to their North African allies.[68] Defeated Christians were forced into slavery, contributing to a growing sense of "Europe" against "Asia," a confrontation that was fungible and easily transferable to "America" and "Africa." The explosive charge was made that the 1453 setback meant "virgins prostituted, boys made to submit as women," garnished with the repeated use of the term "inhuman race" affixed to victorious Turks. By 1530 the eminent Dutch Christian philosopher Erasmus continued to charge that even God would sanction war against the Turks, this "race of barbarians," a fury then being transferred to Africans and "Americans" too.[69] "We are far inferior to the Turks unless Christian Kings should unite their forces," said

---

67 Debra Blumenthal, *Enemies and Familiars: Slavery and Mastery in Fifteenth Century Valencia* (Ithaca: Cornell University Press, 2009), 41.

68 Cihan Yujse Muslu, *The Ottomans and the Mamluks: Imperial Diplomacy and Warfare in the Islamic World* (London: Tauris, 2014), 295.

69 Nancy Bisaha, "Reactions to the Fall of Constantinople and the Concept of Human Rights," in Norman Housley, ed., *Reconfiguring the Fifteenth Century Crusade* (New York: Palgrave, 2017), 285–331, 297–300, 305, 310.

Pope Pius II in 1462,[70] a putative precondition for the racial vehemence—white supremacy, in other words—that was to be unleashed in the sixteenth century in the Atlantic corridor.

This was an era of an enslaving free-for-all in any case, one that ensnared others besides Africans; the Turks and those in their vicinity were preeminent in this regard but part of the diabolical "genius" of settler colonialism, notably as it matured in North America, was that those who had once been victimized by enslavers instead were invited to become enslavers themselves—or perfidious discriminators—in the new guise of "whiteness." About 2,000 Slavs yearly were enslaved by Crimean Tartars and sold to the Ottomans in the fourteenth century, with that figure rising in the fifteenth century; slave raiding into Muscovy reached crisis proportions after 1475 when the Ottomans took over the Black Sea trade from the Genoese, as the Crimeans were instigating industrial-scale enslaving, especially between 1514 and 1654.[71]

Indeed, it is easy to surmise that the impetus impelling Europeans westward—particularly the Spaniards who had endured the most bracing experience with Islam, arriving at a terminal point (ironically) in 1492—was the continued push westward of Islam, veritably chasing the Iberians in that direction too. Periodic defeats at the gates of Vienna failed to squelch fears altogether of being overrun, especially given that Islam long since had established a beachhead in North Africa, visible

70   Norman Housley, "Conclusion: The Future of Crusading in the Fifteenth Century," in *ibid.*, Housley, editor, 325–331, 325.

71   Allesandro Stanziani, "Slavery and Bondage in Central Adia and Europe: Fourteenth Nineteenth Century", in Christopher Witzenrath, ed., *Eurasian Slavery, Ransom and Abolition in World History* (Burlington, Vermont: Ashgate, 2015), 81–104, 97–98.

from Gibraltar. Algiers alone—whose very name sent frissons of nervousness coursing down the spines of Western Europeans—was said to have an enslaved population of at least 25,000 Christians by the late sixteenth century, many of whom were Spanish, Portuguese, and English.[72] These latter nations, particularly London, "won out" in the sixteenth century, replacing West Asia and Turkey as the core of the world system,[73] argues contemporary analyst, Bruno Macaes, though he could have added that this was done by way of imposing apocalyptic conditions on Africans and indigenes of the Americas.

Thus, a telling indicator is that from the sixteenth to the mid-seventeenth century, Russia's trade with the East was more profitable than European trade, but then, as the impact of slavery and settler colonialism in the Americas began to assert itself, this commerce with the Ottomans, Safavid Persia, Mughal India, and China began to decline,[74] then reawakened in the twenty-first century.

Yes, the Ottoman Turks also enslaved Africans: each year from the sixteenth century through the late nineteenth century thousands of slaves from Ethiopia, Nubia, and Southern Sudan arrived in the slave markets of Cairo—seized by the Ottomans in 1517, as post-1492 competition with the Habsburgs and Spain accelerated—then hundreds of these manacled workers made

72 Andrew C. Hess, *The Forgotten Frontier: A History of the Sixteenth Century Ibero-African Frontier* (Chicago: University of Chicago Press, 1978), 125, 175.

73 Bruno Macaes, *The Dawn of Eurasia: On the Trail of the New World Order* (New Haven: Yale University Press, 2018), 66.

74 Nancy Shields Kollman, *The Russian Empire, 1450–1801* (New York: Oxford University Press, 2017), 192. See also Parag Khanna, *The Future Is Asian: Commerce, Conflict, and Culture in 21ˢᵗ Century* (New York: Simon and Schuster, 2019).

their way to Istanbul and provincial capitals of the empire alike. Ironically, as embodied in the power and influence wielded by the eunuchs of African descent,[75] the Ottomans' designation of Africans differed from that created by London, then Washington, with the latter waiting until the twentieth century to create a virtual equivalent of the "Black Eunuch." Moreover, unlike the "whiteness" project captained by the slaveholders' republic that led to the creation of a powerful capitalist economy, the Ottomans deigned to enslave Europeans too.

There were a number of signposts on the road to Ottoman decline, a power that by the mid-sixteenth century seemed to be an unstoppable juggernaut with their equal-opportunity enslaving. But surely one of these emblazonments was their defeat at Lepanto in 1571 when the Christian, principally Catholic, powers ganged up and administered a withering setback on their foe to the east. No, the Ottomans did not sink into precipitous decline thereafter, but as the nineteenth-century historian Leopold Ranke put it succinctly, "The Turks lost all their old confidence after the Battle of Lepanto."[76]

A predicate to the rise of London was the deal that it brokered with the Ottomans, then the Moroccans, against Spain, not altogether unlike the deal brokered by China in the late twentieth century with those thought to be its capitalist antagonists, which has left this Asian giant in the passing lane.

---

75 Jane Hathaway, *The Chief Eunuch of the Ottoman Harem: From African Slave to Power Broker* (New York: Cambridge University Press, 2018), 29.

76 Leopold Ranke, *The Ottoman and the Spanish Empires in the Sixteenth and Seventeenth Centuries* (Philadelphia: Lea and Blanchard, 1845), 33.

London, in other words, which had been buying an alliance with the Ottomans to blunt its mutual Catholic antagonist in Madrid, could now calculate that this policy was less of a necessity after Lepanto and could then begin to turn its attention to weakening Spain at the source of its then immense wealth: the Americas. More to the point, all this set the stage for the eclipse of the Ottomans' equal-opportunity enslaving policy and the rise of London's—then Washington's—single-minded focus on bonding Africans and indigenes. A by-product of this lengthy process was the formation of today's "Latin America," characterized on this side of the border in a decidedly racialized manner,[77] a legacy of the continuing and defining stain of white supremacy in the North American republic.

Thus, a few years after Lepanto, the officially authorized pirate Francis Drake set sail and landed in what was said to be Spanish territory—California—where "New Albion" was declared, making the so-called Golden State, appropriately enough, the "founding site for the overseas British Empire," according to scholar Robert H. Power,[78] and today's citadel of republican and capitalist hegemony.

IT IS CRUCIAL TO ACKNOWLEDGE that not only did Western European nations, especially England, rise on the backs of enslaved Africans and dispossessed indigenes, but that this too arrested development on a continental scale.[79] The

---

77   Mauricio Tenorio-Trillo, *Latin America: The Allure and Power of an Idea* (Chicago: University of Chicago Press), 2017.

78   Robert H. Power, "Francis Drake and San Francisco Bay: A Beginning of the British Empire," Davis: Library Associates of the University of California Davis, 1974, Vertical File, San Francisco Public Library.

79   See e.g. Gerald Horne, *The Apocalypse of Settler Colonialism: The Roots of Slavery, White Supremacy and Capitalism in the 17th Century*

story of Mali's Mansa Musa is now well known, not least the immense wealth that obtained in his golden realm, where Islam prevailed. Actually, most of the gold then circulating in what amounted to global markets and providing currency for the silk and spice roads in antiquity and the Middle Ages came from West Africa, soon to decline vertiginously, as Western Europe rose at its expense.[80] The "fame" Musa and his polity generated, especially the gold there, "inundated the fourteenth century," says one leading scholar. This "left a deep impression," says François Xavier Fauvelle, to the point that "people were still talking about it half a century later."[81] For millennia, gold has been a means of exchange and a store of value,[82] making it hardly coincidental that a great swathe of Africa was pillaged to obtain this mineral.

Ironically, this religious inflected battle with Islam was accompanied by yet another bitterly sectarian conflict, that between Catholics and Protestants (with both having difficulty in overcoming deeply rooted anti-Semitism). This was not simply a theological difference. The Iberians' "first mover advantage" in looting the Americas, then sanctified by the Vatican in the Treaty of Tordesillas, dividing the world between Madrid and Portugal, provided London with disincentive to continue

North America and the Caribbean (New York: Monthly Review Press, 2018), passim.

80 Michael A. Gomez, *African Dominions: A New History of empire in Early and Medieval West Africa* (Princeton: Princeton University Press, 2018), 110.

81 Francois Xavier Fauvelle, *The Golden Rhinoceros: Histories of the African Middle Ages* (Princeton: Princeton University Press, 2018), 194.

82 Rebecca Zorach and Michael W. Phillips, Jr, *Gold* (London: Reaktion, 2016).

adherence to the One True Faith. When Henry VIII broke
bonds with Catholicism, ostensibly because of differences over
his divorce, this also meant the dissolution of monasteries,
an act that filled royal coffers and released timber, stone, and
bronze for national defense projects—precisely to challenge
Spain. Also empowered were ascending lawyers and merchants
who became influential stakeholders in the newer system, an
aristocracy that stood to lose all in a return to the old faith and
old relationships.[83]

The abject terror of the horrendous Protestant-Catholic
conflict in Europe was in a sense a dress rehearsal and precedent for what was visited upon indigenes in the Americas and
their African counterparts. As late as the twentieth century,
the lapsed populist turned demagogue Tom Watson of Jim
Crow Georgia continued to wallow in the rampant religiosity
run amok of the epoch-making St. Bartholomew's Massacre of
1570s France, when thousands of Protestants were liquidated
by genocidal Catholics. This bloodthirstiness was employed
as a rationale for the anti-Catholicism of a resurgent Ku Klux
Klan, illustrating once more the continuing potency of the sixteenth century.[84] The soon-to-be Senator Watson apparently
did not realize that a kind of reconciliation between once warring Protestants and Catholics on a common altar of "whiteness" and white supremacy was the essential epoxy that bound

83   Andrew Lambert, *Seapower States: Maritime Culture, Continental
     Empires and the Conflict that Made the Modern World* (New Haven:
     Yale University Press, 2018), 269.

84   Thomas E. Watson, *The Massacre of St. Bartholomew in Paris, France:
     Overwhelming Proof that it was the Result of the Teachings, the Law and
     the Practice of Popery* (Thomson, Georgia: Jeffersonian, 1914). See
     also C. Vann Woodward, *Tom Watson: Agrarian Rebel* (New York:
     Oxford University Press, 1963).

together those in his own former slaveholders' republic, a principle enunciated solemnly in the First Amendment to the U.S. Constitution that this attorney knew well.

Catholic Spain's military prowess was honed in a centuries-long battle with Arabs and Muslims, which was then exercised brutally not just against Protestants but indigenes in the Americas and Africans there too.

Protestant England evolved similarly. The costs of war were immense, exacting a heavy cost in lives and taxes alike. London's ill-fated French campaign of 1513–14 alone consumed a million pounds, equivalent to ten years' worth of ordinary revenue. Military expenses between 1539 and 1552 came to about 3.5 million pounds, a million of which was spent on campaigns in Scotland and keeping Boulogne. The 1513 initiative witnessed an English army of 28,000 men joined in France by around 7,000 German and Dutch mercenaries. Simultaneously, a force of more than 26,000 marched speedily to meet King James IV's army in Northumberland for the slaughter of Flodden. Campaigning on a similar scale took place in 1522, 1544, and 1545. Even the stupendous gain delivered by the liquidation of monasteries was insufficient to cover the expense of warmongering: more taxes were imposed. Thus, England contained a precursor of a military-industrial complex, as towns and parishes stored armor and weapons and coastal works—bulwarks, beacons, and bastions—were constructed for defense. As early as 1468 Southampton had a gun of about 1,000 pounds in weight. Landowners were expected to maintain an armory of sorts. The monarch had no standing army, but every able-bodied man was expected to fight, again making a venture into the wilderness of the Americas seem tame by comparison, a speculation reflected in the high level of desertion and mutiny. Certainly, military experience in Europe proved to be quite useful for London on the battlefields of the Caribbean, Africa, and North America.

London, during the tumultuous reign of Henry VIII in the sixteenth century, endured a much higher proportion of Englishmen than French or Spaniards serving as soldiers at some point during his reign. With regard to Paris alone, there were wars in 1475, 1489–1492, 1512–1514, 1522–1525, 1542–1546, 1549–1550, 1557–1559, 1562–1564, etc. In yet another sixteenth-century idea that has yet to dissipate, per Machiavelli, was that foreign wars defuse domestic conflict. In any case, European elites often sought to depend on mercenaries rather than domestic forces to suppress domestic dissent, with the resultant benefit flowing to these guns-for-hire, serving as yet another boost for a Pan-European identity that could easily morph into "whiteness"—a militarized identity politics, in other words. In any event, London had its hands full seeking to contain Wales, Ireland, and Scotland during the sixteenth century (and before) with settlements and wars in the Americas emerging as not only a safety valve relieving pressure on London but allowing often disgruntled "minorities," especially Catholics, to stake a claim on the fruits of Empire, thus diverting their anger away from England.[85]

Necessity is not only the mother of invention but the crucible of warfare is as well. The "discovery" of the Americas raised the stakes for sovereignty with Madrid's wealth and firepower seemingly threatening the existence of London itself. Coincidentally, post-1500 there was a much ballyhooed "Military Revolution," which transformed warfare on the old

85 Stephen J. Gunn, *The English People at War in the Age of Henry VII* (New York: Oxford University Press), 137, 284, 148, 150, 151.

continent, and had the added "benefit" of destabilizing Africa and the Americas. The invention, then proliferation, of gunpowder meant that old medieval city walls could no longer offer adequate protection. New fortifications also meant that wars became longer with many sieges lasting more than a year. The rise of firearms translated into a need to train soldiers. Armies became increasingly professionalized, evolving from bands of mercenaries. Armies expanded in size, meaning more men under arms and militarized societies, as well as militarized thinking, suitable for conquest abroad. Along with dispatching domestic foes to far-flung settlements as disposable colonizers, armies also facilitated the liquidation (or quieting) of domestic opponents. Government debt also rose coincidentally in the sixteenth century, enhancing the power of the state. Spain was an initial beneficiary here as their legendary ruler, Philip II, was at war in every single year of his long sixteenth-century reign.[86] But, again, London—then Washington—surpassed Madrid in virtually every one of these important categories.

The repeated attempted invasions of England by Spain— the late sixteenth century notwithstanding—culminated in the game-changing defeat of the Armada in 1588, with London maneuvering adroitly in the slipstream created by Madrid's propulsion. Certainly 1588 was a true sign of things to come. Historian Geoffrey Parker has argued that the failure of the Armada "laid the American continent open to invasion and colonization by northern Europeans and thus made possible

---

86 Mauricio Drelichman and Hans-Joachim Voth, *Lending to the Borrower from Hell: Debt, Taxes and Default in the Age of Philip II* (Princeton: Princeton University Press, 2014), 19, 23, 26, 29. Of course, today's United States makes this earlier "borrower from hell" seem like a minnow or pike by way of comparison.

the creation of the United States." The future, he asserts, "pivoted on a single evening—August 7, 1588," as "Spain began a slow decline and a new world order [began] its gradual ascendancy."[87]

Of course, alert Spaniards would have been wise to pay attention to Londoners within their ambit, prior to invading. There were English merchants resident in Andalusia from 1480 to 1532, a number of whom were slaveholders actively engaged in the transatlantic slave trade. One scholar argues, contrary to previous assessments, that 1489 marks the starting point in the English history of African slaveholding. "Englishmen of all social classes from low class to high class, and even to royalty … emerge[d] as slaveowners," asserts historian Gustav Ungerer, a trend that waxed and waned over the centuries but continued to carry sufficient strength to shed light on the prolonged existence of alliances across class lines among those defined as "white" that exerted itself most recently in the former slaveholders' republic in November 2016. There was also a goodly number of slaveholders who were Englishwomen too, which may shed light on their descendants' twenty-first-century voting habits in North America as well.[88]

YET ANOTHER CONDITION PRECEDENT for the rise of London and the simultaneous decline of Africa and the Americas took place a few years after the failed Armada,

---

87   Parker quoted in John Lewis Gaddis, *On Grand Strategy* (New York: Penguin, 2018), 152.

88   Gustav Ungerer, *The Mediterranean Apprenticeship of a British Slaver* (Madrid: Editorial Verbum, 2008), 15, 29, 72–74, 164. See also Heather Dalton, *Merchants and Explorers: Roger Barlow, Sebastian Cabot and Networks of Atlantic Exchange, 1500–1560* (New York: Oxford University Press, 2016). See, for example, *New York Times*, 9 November 2016: "White women helped elect Donald Trump."

in 1591. The site was north central Africa. Morocco, yet another predominantly Islamic nation courted by London, had invaded with England's assistance the once mighty Songhay Empire. This proved to be a double disaster, with both victor and vanquished emerging weaker, a boon to an ascending "Christian"—if not Protestant—Europe. By destroying the strongest centralized state in sub-Saharan Africa, the Moroccan conquest did irreparable harm to the trans-Saharan routes that had enriched both Morocco and West Africa, and this instability radiated to the aptly (and unfortunately) named Gold and Slave Coasts of Africa, indicative of what was soon to be plundered excessively on the beset continent.[89] Morocco's force of 5,000 was bolstered by Moriscos (Muslims expelled from Spain) and mercenaries, as they proceeded to Gao on the Niger River. Over 80,000 fighters with mere lances and javelins were mowed down systematically by weapons, an outgrowth of the aforementioned "Military Revolution." In a sad coda to a bygone era—and the commencement of a newer one—they reportedly cried, as they fell, "We are Muslims, we are your brothers in religion,"[90] apparently unaware that this newer era was in the long run to sideline religion in favor of

89 Stephen Charles Cory, *Reviving the Islamic Caliphate in Early Modern Morocco* (Burlington, Vermont: Ashgate, 2013), 199, 236. See also Jessica A. Coope, *The Most Noble of People: Religious, Ethnic and Gender Identity in Muslim Spain* (Ann Arbor: University of Michigan Press, 2017).

90 Jerry Brotton, *The Sultan and the Queen: The Untold Story of Elizabeth and Islam* (New York: Penguin, 2017), 171. Cf. Ruth Nisse, *Jacob's Shipwreck: Diaspora, Translation and Jewish-Christian Relation in Medieval England* (Ithaca: Cornell University Press, 2017), and Alan E. Bernstein, *Hell and Its Rivals: Death and Retribution Among Christians, Jews and Muslims in the Early Middle Ages* (Ithaca: Cornell University Press, 2017).

capitalism. Moroccans had been armed with English muskets in return for saltpeter for ammunition, then soon wielded in what was to be called Virginia in the early seventeenth century. The Moroccan envoy in London was quite close to Anthony Radcliffe, residing at his home for six months at one point; the latter's daughter, Anne, was a benefactor of what became Harvard University, which once housed a women's college named in her honor, continuing the resonances from the sixteenth century.[91] Relations between England and Morocco were so close—perhaps a key to understanding Shakespeare's *Othello*, for example—that less than a decade after the transformative 1591 vanquishing of the Songhay Empire, the two powers were huddling and discussing a joint invasion of their mutual foe, Spain, then followed by a joint ouster of the Spaniards from the Caribbean.[92]

The Moroccan-English collaboration was not the only factor contributing to the subjugation of Africa and the Americas. By 1420, Europe counted barely more than a third of the people it contained one hundred years before as a result of the disease known as the Black Death. Predictably, the Jewish minority was blamed, leading to terrible violence against them; thus, early in 1348 the rumor arose that this minority in northern Spain and southern France were poisoning Christian wells and thus disseminating the plague.[93] This served to lead

---

91   Miranda Kaufman, *Black Tudors: The Untold Story* (London: One World, 2017), 138.

92   Ibid., Stephen Charles Cory, 186. See also R.G. Howarth, "The Tragedy of Othello, the Moor of Venice," 20 April 1953, Huntington Library San Marino, California.

93   David Herlihy, *The Black Death and the Transformation of the West* (Cambridge: Harvard University Press, 1997), 17.

to the mass expulsion of this minority from Spain in 1492, and, in the longer run, their being incorporated with untoward consequences for Madrid in the Netherlands, Turkey, and, to a degree, in England too. In the shorter term, their diaspora networks proved to be essential to the new era that was arising, purportedly investing in Columbus's voyage and—perhaps absconding from inquisitorial Madrid—fleeing on his vessels. Some from this Iberian minority were present when São Tomé in West Africa was being subjected to enslavement and sugar production, a pestiferous process then exported to Brazil with devastating consequences for Africans and indigenous Americans both.[94] Other "New Christians," that is, those from the minority subject to an inauthentic conversion, wound up in Cape Verde and Congo with untoward consequences for Africans.[95]

Still, it was not just a more forthcoming approach to the Jewish community and Islam that served ultimately to catapult London into the first rank of nations. Protestants and their often bewildering array of sects and tendencies—Arminian, Calvinist, Lutherans, Presbyterians, Anabaptists, Antinomian, Socinian, Society of Friends (Quakers) et al.—jutted out of Europe, undermining existing beliefs and preparing the ground for a new kind of thinking: capitalism,

---

94 Eva Alexandra Uchmany, "The Participation of New Christians and Crypto-Jews in the Conquest, Colonization and Trade of Spanish America, 1521–1660," in Paolo Bernardini and Norman Fiering, eds., *The Jews and the Expansion of Europe to the West, 1450–1800* (New York: Berghahn, 2001), 186–202, 187 and in the same volume, Ernst Pijning, "New Christians and Sugar Cultivators and Traders in the Portuguese Atlantic, 1450–1800", 485–500, 486.

95 Toby Green, *The Rise of the Trans-Atlantic Slave Trade in Western Africa, 1300–1589* (New York: Cambridge University Press, 2012), 135.

white supremacy, and anti-Catholicism too, destabilizing the One True Faith—and "His Catholic Majesty" in the bargain, as a previously mighty Gulliver was tied down by an ant-like army of Lilliputians.[96]

In undermining existing beliefs, Protestants set the stage for the rise of others: racism, not least, a point that Ambassador Young could have mentioned in 1977. In short, the radical decentralization of Protestantism, as opposed to the hierarchical centralization of Catholicism, provided fertile soil for the rise of racism and other "faiths." Besides, as besieged underdogs in the midst of religious wars, Protestants were poised to make overtures to the Jewish community and Islam alike, as a matter of survival if nothing else but contrary to past praxis,[97] and, ultimately, Protestants and Catholics, then the Jewish, were rebranded as "white" republicans, curbing murderous interreligious conflict and ushering in an era of racialized conflict, victimizing Africans and indigenes alike.

Ambassador Young also could have noted that the evolution of settler colonialism in his homeland involved a religious compromise between Protestants and Catholics, then a transition to "race" as they were rebranded as "white" in North America, easing the path for racialized slavery and uprooting of indigenes, which in turn was disrupted by the Haitian Revolution,[98]

---

96 Victoria Freeman, *Distant Relations: How My Ancestors Colonized North America* (Toronto: McClelland and Stewart, 2000), 13.

97 Geraldine Heng, *England and the Jews: How Religion and Violence Created the First Racial State in the West* (New York: Cambridge University Press, 2019) and Geraldine Heng, *The Invention of Race in the European Middle Ages* (New York: Cambridge University Press, 2019).

98 Gerald Horne, *Confronting Black Jacobins: The U.S., the Haitian Revolution and the Origins of the Dominican Republic* (New York: Monthly Review Press, 2015).

which then gave rise to an emphasis on class as the animating axis of society with the rise of socialism and working-class movements.[99] He could have mentioned that English, Irish, and Scots warred against each other but then united as "white" in the colonies to fight "others." This book is about the earliest stage of this centuries-long process.

---

99 Gerald Horne, *Cold War in a Hot Zone: The U.S. Confront Labor and Independence Struggles in the British West Indies* (Philadelphia: Temple University Press, 2007); Gerald Horne, *Class Struggle in Hollywood, 1930–1950: Moguls, Mobsters, Stars, Reds and Trade Unionists* (Austin: University of Texas Press, 2001).

PART II:
INTERNATIONALISM

RETHINKING THE LUMPEN: GANGSTERS AND THE POLITICAL ECONOMY OF CAPITALISM

Nature, Society, and Thought,
Volume 10 (1–2): (1997)

In his classic Eighteenth Brumaire of Louis Bonaparte, Karl Marx provides a vivid description of what he calls the lumpen proletariat: "vagabonds, discharged soldiers, discharged jail-birds, escaped galley slaves, swindlers, mountebanks, lazzaroni, pickpockets, tricksters, gamblers, maquereaus [procurers], brothel keepers, porters, literati, organ-grinders, knife grinders, tinkers, beggars" (1979, 149; see also Engels 1975 and Winston 1973, 75).

This class—or stratum—is not to be confused with the unemployed, or with the proletariat itself; indeed, this grouping tends to prey on the working class. They are the detritus of capitalism and, in some ways, form a mirror image of the parasitical and exploitative practices of the bourgeoisie itself.

Class analysis is a staple of the Marxist method, and volumes have been devoted to various classes, ranging from the bourgeoisie to the petit bourgeoisie to the working class to the peasantry. Herbert Aptheker's work on slavery can also be seen in this context in that it focuses on the irreconcilable antagonism between one class, slaves, and another class, slaveholders.

The lumpen proletariat, however, has not received the kind of sustained attention it deserves in the analysis of capitalism. This is unfortunate, for the lumpen over time have come to play an increasingly outsized role in the evolution of exploitative societies. Indeed, as one examines the fate of the former Soviet Union, it is apparent that what has transpired over the past decade is the decline of working-class organization and ideology and the rise of the lumpen (Sterling 1994; Handelman 1995).

In the United States, the lumpen historically have played a large role. Just as England dumped lumpen elements in its colony of Australia, it did the same thing in Georgia and other colonies (Salgado 1982; Hughes 1987; Wood 1984; Galenson 1991; Asbury 1928). This served multiple purposes: it provided a safety valve for England itself, allowing the nation to rid itself of elements that might be disruptive and that were viewed as undesirable. Moreover, the kind of violence and subterfuge necessary to subdue indigenous peoples, whether they were in Australia or North America, was a particular specialty of "mountebanks . . . tricksters, . . . brothel keepers" and the like, acting at the behest of powerful elites.

What needs to be considered more carefully is that over time not only did lumpen elements, particularly in the United States, develop powerful syndicates or organized crime families but some lumpen elements also, like a caterpillar becoming a butterfly, became part of the bourgeoisie itself and came to influence the already degraded culture of the bourgeoisie. Indeed, scholars and activists need to pay more attention to the role that organized crime has played in the evolution of the vaunted U.S. economy (Johnson 1995a; Browning and Gerassi

1980). Seeing imperialism itself as a form of organized crime tells us quite a bit, but not enough.

In the United States, the lumpen have come to dominate entire sectors of the economy and have attained particular influence within an industry that garners enormous profits while shaping consciousness—the entertainment industry. The images flowing from this industry have blanketed the planet and helped to inject the culture of U.S. imperialism into the four corners of the globe. Again, the import of this development needs to be considered more carefully, if we are ever to understand and subvert imperialism itself.

Of all of the crimes perpetrated by colonialism and imperialism in Africa, one of the most dastardly has been the dumping of lumpen elements in colonized lands. In 1961, the Bureau of African Affairs in Kwame Nkrumah's Ghana, quoting Sir Cornwall Lewis, sadly reflected on the social costs of this practice: "The scum of England is poured into the colonies, briefless barristers, broken-down merchants, ruined debauchees, the offal of every calling and profession are crammed into colonial places." Citing the author Mabel Jackson, the report continued, "Each year a shipload of human flotsam and jetsam is sent to Angola and Mozambique from Portugal. Beggars embittered by hardship, thieves, assassins, incorrigible soldiers and sailors, together with a sprinkling of political exiles are dumped into the colonies. She tells us that sometimes these men are called degradados—[and] are accompanied by their wives who are girls from orphanages or reformatory schools whom they marry at the moment of embarkation from Europe" (Voice of Africa 1961).

These declassed elements took quite quickly to the reigning philosophy of white supremacy, as this new racial status of "whiteness" rescued them from their declining class status (see, for example, Roediger 1991, Ignatiev 1995, and Saxton 1991). Over time they helped to introduce and fortify a lumpen culture that is bedeviling independent Africa to this day.

Lumpen elements also have played a key role in another phenomenon that has plagued Africa over the years: mercenaries. Of course, the deployment of European mercenaries was not unique to Africa. For years the Swiss developed a notorious reputation as suppliers of mercenary forces to various regimes in Europe; these regiments were heavily lumpen (McCormack 1993, 80; see also Langley and Schoonover 1995). The promiscuous use of mercenaries was a close cousin to the deployment of pirates, buccaneers, and soldiers of fortune, whose bloodthirsty escapades often were the basis of the primitive accumulation of capital itself. One scholar has observed that the concept of "plausible deniability," which has served imperialism so well in episodes ranging from Watergate to the Iran-Contra scandal, was actually invented by rulers in the early seventeenth century as a spur to mercenarism and piracy: thus, if these bandits obtained the necessary booty—fine—and if they did not or were apprehended, then responsibility for their activity could be denied (Thomson 1994; Tilly 1990).

These freebooters were a useful adjunct to U.S. foreign policy, as this young nation in the nineteenth century sought to seize territory throughout the hemisphere and beyond and to circumvent the ban on the slave trade (Brown 1980; Smith 1978; Krasner 1978). When the Civil War began, many of these forces joined with the Confederacy and terrorized entire states, particularly Kansas. A noteworthy band of thugs, Quantrill's Raiders, spawned the notorious outlaws Jesse and Frank James, Cole Younger, and a generation of cutthroats, providing a vivid example of the connections between the lumpen, racism, and war (Schultz 1996).

Nevertheless, the impact of what the Portuguese call the degradados has been most dramatic in the continent that Western Europe has specialized in degrading—Africa. The dumping of these forces in Africa continues to resonate, even though European colonialism has been uprooted. For example, in South Africa, the apartheid authorities concentrated more on fighting political dissent than crime. As a result, independent South Africa is faced with a staggering crime problem, fueled by what one newspaper there has called "state sponsored gangs who used government patronage to build criminal business empires." In the province of Mpumulanga they are called "businessmen's gangs" and were known to have worked with the Zulu chauvinist Inkatha Freedom Party; one gang was "run by five heavyweight black businessmen" (Weekly Mail and Guardian, 6–12 September 1996). An estimated 278 organized crime syndicates in South Africa are involved in drug-dealing, car-jacking, and worse (Zimbabwe Herald, 15 February 1996). Then there are the firms of mercenaries, such as Executive Outcomes, that sell their services to governments in exchange for diamond concessions (Horne 1995).

Of course, the lumpen are far from being unique to Africa. In Japan, the highly influential Yakuza—gangsters known for their tattooed bodies and amputated fingers—are quite close to certain financial elites. They pioneered in running movie houses, strip shows, prostitution, and gambling (Saga 1991, 195). In China, before the advent of Communist Party rule, the nationalist forces under Chiang Kai-shek collaborated with racketeers like Du Yuesheng of the notorious Green Gang; these thugs acted as labor bosses and plant managers and helped the nationalists break workers' power in 1927 (Wakeman 1994; see also Emsley and Knafla 1996).

Even today, according to the Far Eastern Economic Review (1 May 1997), it is estimated conservatively that about 10 percent of the elected officials in the legislature and National Assembly of Taiwan had gang affiliations. Taiwan's most well-known gang-affiliated politician, Luo Fu-tsu, "has identified himself as the 'spiritual leader' of one of Taiwan's largest gangs, the Heavenly Way Alliance." He is also "chairman of the legislature's judiciary committee," which formulates the basic laws of this rebel province of China.

Ascertaining the influence of this pervasive lumpen culture on the political culture of China—including the culture of the Communist Party—is a task worthy of consideration. In any event, these racketeers flourish during times of unrest and war, when normal channels of production are disrupted, as was the case, for example, in London during World War II (Murphy 1993, 81).

It is clear that the lumpen have not always had an entirely baneful impact. The role of "social bandits" is well known (Perez 1989; Schwartz 1989). Just as one distinguishes between big and small peasants and between workers who make $1 million a year and those who earn less than $10,000, one must make distinctions among various types of lumpen in their sociopolitical impact and potential. Still, as Alisse Waterston has pointed out, what must be carefully scrutinized is the rampant notion that gangsters represent some sort of culture of resistance to capitalism. There may be a scintilla of evidence imbedded in this idea but often ignored is the salient point that gangsters in the United States most notably have been highly accommodating to larger cultural norms and to the requisites of social production.

Ultimately their defiance is limited to symbolic suggestion and often remains on the level of appearance. Indeed, the experience of most gangsters in this nation suggests that their goals are congruent with and help to sustain the goals of capitalism itself. The heralding of the alleged resistance represented by gangsters obscures their true role in social reproduction, subverts actual resistance, and helps to suppress alternatives—particularly those of the working-class variety (Waterston 1994).

In the United States, organized crime is reported to have significant influence in the construction industry, the vending machine industry, waste removal, and the usual staples of gambling, drugs, prostitution, and the like. Gangsters also have influence in areas where their presence has not attracted attention. For example, much attention is devoted to the pornography industry, particularly the issue of whether it is misogynist and should be restrained or, as some would have it, not to be tampered with because it is the truest expression of free speech (Kipnis 1996; Hunt 1991; Dworkin 1989). What is rarely mentioned—though highly relevant—is that this is one of many industries where racketeers wield hegemony; similarly, at least before the 1960s, the same could be said about so-called "adult bookstores" and gay clubs (Potter 1986; Washington Post, 12 April 1979).

The failure to divine the role of organized crime makes it difficult to analyze complex phenomena fully. For example, the music industry is one of the few industries where African Americans have played a central role. Here they have encountered the pervasive role of mobsters, some of whom were Jewish and Italian Americans. Because of a failure to examine a particularly vile form of class exploitation, this antagonism has often been expressed in racial and ethnoreligious terms.

Thus, legendary music critic and producer John Hammond estimated that at one time "no fewer than three in every four jazz clubs and cabarets . . . were either fronted, backed, or in some way managed by Jewish and Sicilian mobsters" (Morris 1980, 4). Morris Levy, who owned the famous club Birdland, "never made any secret of his connections with the New York Mafia . . . Many have speculated that it was the Mob who put Levy in business and that he is beholden to gangsters to this day" (Picardie and Wade 1990, 53, 57). Crass exploitation of musicians—particularly African American musicians—is widespread. Sadly, when objection was made to those of Levy's ilk, more attention was at times paid to his ethnoreligious, rather than class, background.

Unfortunately, U.S. popular culture—and not just "gangsta rap"—is suffused with the influence of lumpen elements, which is one reason why it has been so stiffly resisted worldwide. This has not only been true of music and, as will be shown shortly, film, but literature as well. Herbert Huncke, described by the New York Times (9 August 1996) as a prostitute, "street hustler, petty thief and perennial drug addict," was better known as the man "who enthralled and inspired a galaxy of acclaimed writers and gave the Beat Generation its name"; he was a former "runner for the Capone" gang and spent eleven years in prison, "including almost all of the 1950s." He was featured in works by writers ranging from William Burroughs (1966) to Allen Ginsberg (1956) to Jack Kerouac (1957). This beat generation played a major role in shaping a U.S. youth culture of the 1960s that has had global influence.

What is most revealing about the role of gangsters in the political economy is their historic function as a disruptive force within the trade-union movement. Here their role as accomplice of the bourgeoisie and parasite is exposed crudely. In his analysis of the Fur and Leather Workers Union, Philip S. Foner limned "the vast chain that connected anti-labor employers, right-wing Socialist union chiefs and the most notorious of all gangs of underworld criminals," referring to Louis (Lepke) Buchalter and Jacob (Gurrah) Shapiro (1950, 396). Sidney Lens reported that "Lepke and Gurrah at one time had two hundred and fifty thugs on their payroll to help run the New York painter's union." Congressional hearings during the 1930s investigated what Leo Huberman termed the "labor spy racket," an entire industry that did the dirty work of disrupting unions on behalf of corporate elites (Huberman 1937; Howard 1924).

In his analysis of Ford Motor Company's use of mobsters, Stephen Norwood has observed that the United States is "the only advanced industrial country where business corporations wielded coercive military power." Harry Bennett, Henry Ford's top aide, was close to "Detroit's underworld," which was pivotal in the "violence and espionage" that animated "management's campaign to disrupt union organizing and break strikes" (1996, 367, 391). Indeed, in comprehending the weakness of the Left and the ascendancy of the Right in the United States, progressive forces have paid insufficient attention to the totality of the opposition faced by the working class.

The Teamsters, for decades one of the largest unions in the capitalist world, has been known as a union where mobsters held great influence. Union officials who opposed their rule were killed, and business at times was complicit in this effort (Witwer 1994, 175, 233). In Las Vegas, where mob dominated unions have been prevalent, financiers like George Wingfield—a patron of the Republican Party—employed unsavory characters to keep unions out of the state and keep quiescent those who were not chased away (Raymond 1993, 79).

Organized crime—the "big lumpen"—historically has been one of the bourgeoisie's chief allies in this nation in maintaining its hegemony. In return, gangsters have been allowed, in some instances, to evolve "respectably" to bourgeois status themselves. In any case, mobsters in this nation have enjoyed a form of enrichment that the bourgeoisie in many nations will never see. This has added a level of coarseness and lack of principle to the otherwise crude and unprincipled rule of the bourgeoisie.

An examination of the memoirs and biographies of top U.S. mobsters is quite instructive in revealing their close ties with the state and the bourgeoisie, their ethnocentrism, and their ties to the entertainment industry. Arnold Rothstein, for example, has been given credit for bribing members of the Chicago White Sox to lose intentionally in the 1919 "World Series" of baseball. In his hometown of New York City there was an "alliance between [the] political machine [Tammany] and crime"; moreover, "much of Rothstein's bankroll came from Wall Street." In fact, Rothstein was one of the earliest investors in "Loew's Inc., parent company of MGM," the film company. Rothstein acted as "middle man in the deal whereby [Horace] Stoneham, John McGraw and Judge McQuade purchased the New York Giants baseball team" (Katcher 1994, 73, 165, 192).

Meyer Lansky, a top mobster for decades, had business relationships with the Bronfman family, who started Seagram's, and with Lewis Rosensteil of Schenley's, who was close to FBI head J. Edgar Hoover. Lansky discussed international politics constantly and sensed earlier than most the triumph of the Cuban revolution, an event that led to substantial business losses for him and other mobsters; this event helped to spur an alliance between mobsters and the U.S. government to oust the Castro regime. Early on, Lansky contributed heavily to Zionist causes and later in life, because of perceived anti-Semitism on the part of his Italian American colleagues—and in a transparent attempt to escape the long arm of the law—went to live in Israel; his effort to avoid deportation was backed by the Ultraright there. Lansky invested heavily in Las Vegas and felt that "the WASPS couldn't have it . . . that a bunch of Jewish and Italian street boys could make so much money in Vegas and other places. They wanted to drive us out and finally they succeeded" (Lacey 1991, 55, 80, 255, 291, 337).

Sam Giancana, who shared a mistress with John F. Kennedy, bragged that organized crime sponsored stars, including "the Marx brothers, George Raft, Jimmy Durante, Marie McDonald, Clark Gable, Gary Cooper, Jean Harlow, Cary Grant and Wendy Barrie." He said that then President Harry Truman was "their boy" and added that the mob in "Chicago used its money and influence to try and get close to everybody from Ronald Reagan to Ed Sullivan." Mobster Diamond Joe Esposito:

> " . . . routinely boasted of meeting with Calvin Coolidge and dispensing votes and favors at the President's request." Giancana "often conducted business with producer Harry Cohn" of Hollywood and proved helpful to him in his conflicts with unions. Indeed, the mob wanted a "takeover of unions, coast to coast... By threatening union members with loss of work, the gangsters could marshal the efforts of husbands, wives, sons, and daughters in support of virtually any scam the gang could dream up, including swinging an election" (Giancana 1992, 34, 105, 107, 158, 409).

Mickey Cohen, the top mobster in Los Angeles during the 1940s and 1950s, raised large sums for the Irgun in Israel. He was not alone in exploiting consciousness; Jack Dragna, another top mobster in Los Angeles, also was the head of a leading Italian American civil rights organization in the city of stars. Like Lansky, Cohen was quite sensitive to real and imagined anti-Semitism at the hands of his Italian American colleagues and others. Cohen also was close to studio boss Harry Cohn, but refused his request to murder Sammy Davis Jr. after the African-American star created a controversy because of his intimate relationship with actress Kim Novak. Like many other top mobsters, Cohen was close to Frank Sinatra, who once aligned with the Left but later became a top supporter of the Republican Party. Cohen too had political connections, claiming that "at one point during the 1940s and 1950s I had the police commission in Los Angeles going for me. A lot of the commissioners didn't have any choice. Either they would go along with the program, or they would be pushed out of sight." He funneled money to the political campaigns of Mayor Fletcher Bowron and added, "I had the private number in his office and the private number in his home." He also raised funds for the early political campaigns of Richard M. Nixon. He was grateful to the press controlled by William Randolph Hearst, which portrayed him as "sort of like a Robin Hood" and ordered his press organs to refer to the mobster as a "gambler" not a "hoodlum" (Cohen 1975, 43, 83 91, 95, 106, 232; see also Reid 1973, 110, 171).

Abner "Longy" Zillman, a top hoodlum from New Jersey, also felt that "most of the Italian gangsters in New York were anti-Semites"; he too was close to Harry Cohn of Columbia Pictures and the Schenck Brothers of MGM, not to mention

Dore Schary, "a boyhood friend" and yet another key movie executive. He too took a decided interest in unions though "this stemmed . . . from a need to find jobs for his army of relatives." Like Cohen and Lanksy, he had widespread interests, including steel mills, Kinney Parking Systems (eventually absorbed by Time-Warner), jukeboxes, hotels, clubs, etc. (Stuart 1985, 50, 188, 88–89, 97).

An examination of the lives of mobsters raises intriguing questions worthy of investigation, even if one does not accept every aspect of their stories. If one examines "ethnic cleansing" in the Balkans, for example, it is apparent that organized crime figures like Arkan, who happen to be ultranationalists, basically plunder and loot other nationalities and hand over the booty to their "blood brothers" who join them; lumpen activity makes use of ethnicity for its own purposes (Rieff 1995; CNN 1997). Organized crime "families" have operated on a similar principle, insofar as they have tended toward ethnocentrism and have spread their plunder among members of the "family." This raises the question of the extent to which the resurgence of nationalism nowadays has a distinctly lumpen flavor. As noted, the construction of "white" identity in colonized Africa was based predominantly on a shared melanin deficiency and the sharing of booty looted from the Africans.

Then there is the mobsters' distinct view of "sex." Homosexual rape has been a staple of punishment preferred by gangsters and, unfortunately, has become part of the culture of some prisons where they enjoy hegemony. Like its heterosexual counterpart, homosexual rape is more a crime of violence and subordination than a sexual act. Thus, a favored tactic of punishment by Giancana was shoving a poker "right up [the] ass of opponents"; Giancana once threatened to put a gun "up [the] ass" of an opponent and pull the trigger. When William Jackson was murdered by the mob, they "rammed an electric prod up his rectum" (Giancana 1992, 100, 148, 397).

The mob in pre-1959 Cuba specialized in holding sex shows, featuring live sex acts, particularly "lesbian acts" (Ragano and Raab, 1994, 46). Cohen bragged about owning "gay places," though he quickly added, "I never had to go into them" (1975, 223). It is recorded that pirates, the precursors of organized crime, at times tended toward similar views of sexuality (Burg 1982). What needs to be interrogated more systematically is the influence of the lumpen—beyond male and female prostitution—on the sexual culture of the United States, particularly the linkages between sex and violence (Chauncy 1994; Faderman 1991; Duberman 1991). Such interrogations are necessary, for it is apparent that progressive forces may have underestimated the pervasive influence of organized crime on U.S. culture, despite its obvious role in assassination plots here and abroad. This is a shame, for as the United States spreads its tentacles of influence to Russia, the Balkans, and other parts of the globe, there has been an inevitable and not coincidental rise in organized crime. The influence of the mob has been hidden in plain view—its very prominence in the headlines and on the silver screen has dulled our sensitivity to its impact. New York Times investigative journalist Jeff Gerth is not far from the mark when he suggests that organized crime has quietly entrenched itself within all levels of the social structure, leading Donald Cressey, consultant to the President's Commission on Violence, to conclude: "The penetration of business and government by organized crime has been so complete that it is no longer possible to differentiate 'underworld' gangsters from 'upperworld' businessmen and government officials." (1976, 132).

These connections have been particularly evident in California and most notable in the careers of two of this state's favorite sons, Richard Nixon and Ronald Reagan. California, the "last frontier," within the past century was involved in an event that called for the bloodthirsty tactics that the lumpen have specialized in—the expropriation of the Native Americans. Here on the frontier, as Mickey Cohen has detailed, mobsters openly consorted with elected officials and otherwise "respectable" business figures. To cite one instance: Guy McAfee, chief of the vice squad of the Los Angeles Police Department in the 1930s, built a career in bookmaking and casino operations in league with mob figures; he helped build the Golden Nugget in Las Vegas, for example (Johnson 1975b, 55).

What is fascinating is that few of these relationships were shrouded in secrecy. Michael Denning has noted that "the pulp magazines were full of gangster stories; by the early 1930s, there were entire magazines devoted to 'Gangster Stories,' 'Racketeer Stories,' and 'Gangland Detective Stories'" (1997, 254). Strikingly, the narrative that focused on the expropriation of the land of the Native Americans—the "western"—was supplanted in Hollywood by the gangster movie, which simply updated the story of plunder and politics (Dargis 1996).

Those who played gangsters on the silver screen, like George Raft, were close to real-life gangsters like Bugsy Siegel and Owney Madden. Howard Hughes, the industrialist, was a partner with Siegel in the Flamingo of Las Vegas. The director Howard Hawks was buddy-buddy with Al Capone. The movie Scarface included scenes from gangster life, such as Raft and Paul Muni bringing flowers to a rival gangster in a hospital, then pulling a gun out of the flowers and shooting him (Munn 1993,

32, 89, 204). Indeed, Meyer Lansky suggests, real mobsters learned from Raft styles of dress and mannerisms that came to define the gangster mode (Lacey 1991, 148).

Los Angeles and its primary industry, Hollywood, became an enormous source of profit for gangsters and, in turn, a massive recruiting broadside and image polisher for the gangster life. F. Scott Fitzgerald hinted at this dark alliance in his novel about Hollywood, The Last Tycoon (1969). This alliance deepened during the Depression of the 1930s when, according to one analyst, the studios were strapped for cash and mobsters like Longy Zwillman, who had preexisting relationships with Hollywood executives, provided an infusion of capital. This analyst, Hank Messick, has charged further that as a result of this alliance and "under the pressure of gangsters, art was being abandoned in favor of fast-buck productions designed to appeal to the largest common denominator of society" (1973, ix, 51–52).

Still, the major import of this alliance was not solely relevant to the state of cinema art. No, this alliance aided mobsters in spreading their influence among unions, particularly unions in Hollywood—Teamsters, painters, and the like—and increased their influence in society at large. Again, this relationship was no secret. Early on, Orson Welles sensed the deeper implications of this when he observed,

A group of industrialists finance a group of gangsters to break trade unionism, to check the threat of socialism, the menace of socialism or the possibility of democracy... When the gangsters succeed at what they were paid to do, they turn on the men who paid them . . . The puppet masters find their creatures taking on a terrible life of their own. (Denning 1997, 375)

Whether one accepts the analysis of Messick or Welles, the point is that there was a clear and open relationship between mobsters and one of the most profitable industries in the nation.

Thus the Washington Times-Herald complained on 26 September 1947 that most of the "California gangsters . . . either have social entree among the parvenus or themselves rank as the Astors and Vanderbilts of their time and place." It was not accidental that this comment was made during a year when the postwar upsurge of strikes presented a direct and per-ceived threat to the hegemony of the bourgeoisie, which looked to the muscle of the mob to crush this insurgency. At the same time the infamous Merchants and Manufacturers Association of Los Angeles formed a Citizens Law and Order Committee to back up the Los Angeles Police Department in confronting strikers (Labor Herald, 15 February 1946).

Hollywood itself was being confronted with militant strikers in the wake of the dislodging of mob dominated union leadership of the International Alliance of Theatrical Stage Employees (IATSE) and the rise of a militant Left-led Conference of Studio Unions.

The story actually begins in the 1930s when the studios became heavily dependent on mob money. At this juncture, Al Capone managed to install two of his cronies, Willie Bioff and George Browne, as leaders of the key film union, IATSE. The two quickly became comfortable with the allures of Southern California. Bioff, a convicted pimp who boasted of drinking one hundred bottles of beer in one sitting, came to own stock in Fox and became friendly with Harry Warner. He owned eighty lush acres in the San Fernando Valley "hard by the estates of Tyrone Power and Annabella, Clark Gable and Carole Lombard"; his estate included "$600 olive trees, the biggest and oldest in

California" (Muir 1940, 11; Chicago Daily News, 19 July 1935; Chicago Tribune, 12 June 1935).

As World War II approached, however, the enthusiasm for the mobsters, many of whom were sympathetic to Mussolini, began to crumble. The studios admittedly had been paying Bioff and Browne handsomely to maintain labor peace; however, an indictment of the labor leaders charged that this was not bribery but extortion. Capone's chief lieutenant, Frank Nitti, committed suicide after his indictment—at least he was found with a bullet in his skull (New York Times, 20 March 1943; 5 November 1943; 28 October 1941).

Bioff and Browne wound up turning on their mob partners and testifying against them. Among those convicted as a result was Johnny Roselli, the mob's key operative in Southern California. Born Filippo Sacco in Esteria, Italy, in 1905, he came to the United States in 1911 and quickly became involved in criminal activity. He rose to a position of authority among mobsters, became the "mafia's bridge" to Mayor Frank Shaw of Los Angeles, and was the chief "labor enforcer" for the film industry. As his biographers put it,

> The sudden and enormous success of the movies spawned an orgy of vice that threatened to shatter the industry. Drug use was widespread, including cocaine, heroin and illegal alcohol. Sexual favors were demanded by casting directors and became a sort of alternative currency. Mack Sennett's Keystone Studios had to be tented and fumigated of venereal crabs.

Gambling was rife and controlled by the mob, with studio executives dropping as much as $15,000 in one evening. Roselli was "instrumental" in the success of Harry Cohn and

Columbia Studios; they lived in the same apartment building and exchanged rings. The "closest friend" of MGM's Louis B. Mayer was Roselli's mob comrade, Frank Orsatti (Rappley and Becker 1991, 75, 54, 60, 62).

But all of his elevated connections did not prevent Roselli from being convicted and sentenced in 1944. In 1945 the Conference of Studio Unions (CSU) led a bitter and acrimonious eight-month strike. When the studio retaliated by locking them out in 1946, picket lines were once more punctuated with regular scenes of violence. In 1947 Roselli was surprisingly released from prison, with some suggesting that his studio friends required the muscle he could muster in order to squash the CSU once and for all. His parole caused a "national scandal"; his attorney, Paul Dillon, had served as Harry S. Truman's senatorial campaign manager, and these connections were seen as important in gaining his premature release (Johnson 1950, 30; Los Angeles Times, 5 July 1987).

The CSU was squashed, and Roselli reentered the film industry, this time as a producer. Among his works were T-Men, Canon City, and He Walked by Night. These films were "popular with critics and fans and became a major influence on early radio and television shows such as Dragnet." He also became involved in business dealings with the Guatemalan military in the early 1950s, reputedly participating in the overthrow of Jacobo Arbenz in 1954, and he developed close ties to the Teamsters, Joseph Kennedy, and Las Vegas casinos. He was recruited by the Central Intelligence Agency to murder Fidel Castro. In the mid-1970s his torso was found in an oil drum floating off Miami Bay as a congressional committee called him as a witness in an investigation of his more nefarious activities. Bioff changed his name and moved to Phoenix, where he became friendly with Senator Barry Goldwater; his luck ran out in the mid-fifties when he was killed by a car bomb (Rappley 1991, 155, 202; Clarens 1980, 167; Los Angeles Times, 28 July 1948; Los Angeles Examiner, 26 August 1948).

Meanwhile, as they were going down to defeat, the CSU proclaimed that the "gangsters are coming. . . . The pay-off boys, slot machine kings, brothel keepers and underworld characters kicked out of town when the people recalled Mayor Frank Shaw" are back; "the movie magnates have allied themselves in the underworld … as they did in the days of Shaw" (CSU ca. 1945/1946).

The odyssey of Johnny Roselli was not the only intriguing aspect of the aftermath of the crushing of the CSU. Ronald Reagan, the former liberal leader of the Screen Actors Guild, aligned with the studios during this labor unrest; as a result he developed relationships with corporate leaders that were to prove essential in his subsequent races for elective office.

Sidney Korshak, a lawyer during Roselli's trial who had once served as counsel to Capone, went on to become, in the words of one FBI official, the "primary link between big business and organized crime." Lew Wasserman, formerly Reagan's agent, called Korshak "a very good personal friend." Korshak also had Hilton Hotels, MGM Hotel, Paramount, and General Dynamics as clients; he was friendly with J. Edgar Hoover. Wasserman had reason to be grateful to Reagan since Reagan (when head of the Screen Actors Guild) allowed Wasserman to serve as both agent for actors and as their employer (Wasserman was head of MCA Universal studio). This circumvented antitrust guidelines. Wasserman also was a major donor to the Democratic Party. Korshak was also quite close to the producer of the Godfather saga, Robert Evans, illustrating once again the close link between screen representations and reality (New

York Times, 22 January 1996; Hollywood Reporter, 19 August 1994; Moldea 1986; U.S. Congress 1951).

The crushing of the Conference of Studio Unions after World War II was an essential element in cementing the ongoing trend of the increasingly pervasive influence on unions of organized crime—in other words, the ascendancy of lumpen organization and the decline of working-class organization in the United States. Despite the change in leadership in the AFL-CIO in October 1995 and subsequent reforms in the associated unions, including the Teamsters, this tendency persists (New York Times, 24 January 1992, 22 June 1990, 9 April 1989, 21 February 1984, 28 April 1983, 12 December 1980, 9 February 1980; Los Angeles Times, 9 February 1984; Business Week, 14 February 1983; Wall Street Journal, 5 October 1982; U.S. News and World Report, 8 September 1980; National Law Journal, 29 February 1988). For example, Teamsters Local 817 in New York City, which represents many theater workers, is heavily influenced by the gang known as the Westies (English 1990, 155).

The movies and television, with their glamorizing of Goodfellas and The Last Don and The Krays, and the "Teflon Don" and "Sammy the Bull," continue to play a substantial role in sanitizing their partners, the mobsters. Of late, this trend has afflicted newspapers as well; the New York Times recently lauded pirates as true democrats—sure, they looted treasures from Africa and kidnapped Africans for slavery but, after all, they shared the booty among themselves (11 March 1997).

The projecting of glamorous images of gun-toting thugs has not only been instrumental in providing legitimacy to them at home, it has also served to spread lumpen organization and culture abroad, lubricating the path for U.S. imperialism by undermining domestic working-class oppositional culture. Jamaican gangsters, for example, "worshipped the gunfighters in Hollywood westerns"; in Kingston there was a "time honored tradition of gunmen modeling themselves on Hollywood desperadoes." There was a "secret symbiosis" between these Caribbean gunfighters cum "mercenaries" and "politicians"; this worked to the working-class opposition led in the 1980s by the social democratic leader Michael Manley (Gunst 1995, xiv, 9, 74, 81).

As the example of Jamaica suggests, it did not escape the attention of many Blacks that others had amassed enormous wealth and improved their status as a group under capitalism by taking the route of the lumpen. Blacks in the United States perhaps most notably in South Los Angeles—have not been blind to developments in the neighboring area of Hollywood. This led to the creation of "gangsta rap" and music moguls with plans as audacious as their lumpen brethren of the 1930s; yet somehow, in typical U.S. fashion, the discourse on this latter-day phenomenon has avoided making this obvious connection.

As early as the 1970s, African Americans had organized the Fairplay Committee—comprised of "an intimidating group of people" to improve their status in the music industry. They were trying to form a "black 'family' who would oppose the 'families'" that controlled the business. In response, music impresario Morris Levy hired an African American, Nat McCalla, "one of the first blacks ever to be admitted to the ranks of the Italian Mafia." But this entente did not calm racial tensions; one mobster was irate about the rise of Black-owned Stax Records: "We just took over their publishing company and we are going to take over the record company, put all those niggers out, and put that head nigger in jail." All of these racist dreams were not realized; however, in 1980 McCalla was "shot in the back of the head" in Fort Lauderdale and this early attempt of Blacks to take the lumpen route in the music industry was derailed (Picardie 1990, 173, 177, 192–93; 253).

Years ago, Max Weber defined the state as the agency which held a monopoly of legitimate violence in the area under its control. However, even in the days of Weber, this was rarely true in the absolute sense, as various lumpen—from mercenaries to pirates to mobsters—regularly used violence, particularly against enemies of elites, such as the unions. The ability of these lumpen to deploy violence is just another example of a traditional goal of right-wing elites—diminishing the role of the state and increasing the role of nonstate actors. One would think that creating two, three, or many Somalias, where the state was eviscerated and the ability to survive was often dependent on the protection to be received by families— organized crime or otherwise—is the ultimate goal of these elites.

The Economist, in the same story in which it cited Weber's familiar aphorism, noted the proliferation of private police forces in recent days.

Since 1970 a transformation has been under way. In that year, there were still more public policemen than private guards in America. The ratio of public to private was 14-1. Now there are three times as many private policemen as public ones; in California, four times as many. General Motors alone had a private police force of 4200 more than all but five American cities. (19 April 1997)

In Northern Ireland "punishment squads" have arisen, "gangs who beat up their victims with baseball bats to suppress crimes in Loyalist or Catholic areas." These squads have assumed the role that police departments have played (Johnson 1992; McKenzie 1994). Such developments are made to order for exploitation by organized crime factions, who are best able to fill the breach when the state withdraws (see, e.g., Horne 1995b). Such developments also provide unique career opportunities for those with a violent bent; Timothy McVeigh, convicted of blowing up the federal building in Oklahoma City in April 1995, is a former private security guard (Zielinski 1995, 50).

Meanwhile, the assault on the state and the decline of the Left, has opened rare and extraordinary opportunities for the lumpen. Often in conjunction with "legitimate" business, organized crime gangs have caused money laundering and drug dealing to expand exponentially (Chossudovsy 1996). It is almost as if the United States, which began as a nation with an enormous boost from England's deported lumpen, now, two hundred years later, is not only still the land of opportunity for gangsters but is exporting its model abroad and in the process is helping to create various "gangster republics."

In any event, as we confront the new millennium, a few points are obvious: certainly an acceleration of working-class ideology and organization is a must, but a condition precedent to this development is a better understanding—and subverting of—the lumpen ideology and organization that have become staples of U.S. imperialism.

HANDS ACROSS THE WATER: AFRO-AMERICAN LAWYERS AND THE DECOLONIZATION OF SOUTHERN AFRICA

The Guild Practitioner, Volume 45, 110 (1998)

NCBL's experience on the question of decolonization of Africa has been a little noticed watershed in Afro-American history. It has marked the resurgence of a trend initiated years before by Paul Robeson. The close connection between political action and the shaping of law is much more apparent in the context of international law. Shedding the tightly legalistic notion that dictated that lawyering should be confined only to the court-room, by becoming immersed in such issues as recognition of Angola, NCBL blazed a trail that others have followed.

From FSAM to NBA

When the National Bar Association (the largest organization of Afro-American attorneys in the U.S.) contributed $50,000 to prospective Democratic Party Presidential hopeful Jesse Jackson and promised $100,000 more, their major reason was that he would make elimination of apartheid "a critical issue in the 1987 and 1988" campaign debates. This provided further evidence of the key role that Black lawyers have played in the battle to liberate Southern Africa.[1]

This significant action, which took place during their annual convention at New York's Marriott Marquis Hotel in July 1987, demonstrated that the anti-apartheid impulse had reached what has been perceived to be the most staid and stand-pat sector of the Black bar and, by inference, showed the roots this movement has sunk in the Black community generally.

In a certain sense it was further confirmation of the vanguard role that Black lawyers have played on this crucial issue. Recall the day in November 1984 when Black lawyers Nary F. Berry, Eleanor Holmes Norton and Randall Robinson, joined by Congressman Walter Fauntroy, launched the Free South Africa Movement and ignited a new stage in the struggle against colonialism, imperial- ism and racism in Southern Africa. Though pregnant with hope, these relatively recent developments also highlighted some of the ongoing difficulties raised by Black intervention on the international stage.

The presence of Blacks in this country is a partial product of this nation's foreign policy, which serves to underline why historically Afro-Americans have taken a keen interest in international affairs. This is no recent development. The Negro conventions of the mid-19th century not only spoke out forcefully on questions of Africa but also on such issues as the colonization of Ireland. Willard Gatewood has shed light on the nascent anti-imperialism of the Afro-American community as the Spanish-Cuban-American War and the Anglo-Boer War were launched. The National Association for the Advancement of

---

1   *New York Amsterdam News*, August 1, 1987.

Colored People (NAACP), particularly during the time when
W.E.B. Du Bois was working in the national office continually
stressed international affairs.[2]

Council on African Affairs

Nevertheless, when Paul Robeson, a graduate of the law school
at Columbia University, initiated the Council on African Affairs
in 1937, a new stage in Black intervention in foreign affairs was
reached. CAA's purpose was to push for decolonization and
educate the U.S. populace about the issue. It was not a mass
membership organization: strikingly, a disproportionate part of
its leadership emerged from the Black bar: Hubert Delany of
New York City and Earl Dickerson of Chicago (future head of
the National Lawyers Guild), to name two.

CAA stood in close solidarity with the African National
Congress of South Africa, supported miners in Nigeria striking against transnational business interests, backed the liberation struggle in Kenya that was given the name "Mau Mau,"
etc. Inevitably, CAA's policy came into conflict with that of
the U.S. State Department and the trans-nationals. During the
Cold War, CAA was subpoenaed to appear in court and produce all correspondence with the African National Congress,
all books, records and accounts, everything: the Subversive

2   Philip S. Foner and George Walker, eds, *Proceedings of the Black State
    Conventions. 1840–1865*, 2 vols (Philadelphia: Temple University
    Press, 1979–1980); Willard Gatewood, "A Black Editor on American
    Imperialism: Edward Cooper of the Colored American, 1898–1901,"
    Mid-America, 57 (January 1975): 3.; Gerald Horne, *Black & Red:
    WEB DuBois & the Afro-American Response to the Cold War. 1944–
    1963* (Albany: SUNY Press, 1985).

Activities Control Board was charging CAA with being a "Communist front."[3]

CAA was forced into liquidation: its demise posed a sharp question for Afro-American lawyers and the Afro-American community. If they were to stand shoulder to shoulder with their brethren across the sea, this would often bring them into conflict with influential circles. If they were to stand apart from these progressive positions, Black lawyers would be "marginalized" within their own community because one of the most powerful and significant, yet little recognized, aspects of the U.S. political scene is that the Afro-American community stands far to the left on the U.S. political spectrum.[4] This particularly holds true for international affairs.

While the preponderance of Marxists in the leadership of a MPLA in Angola or an ANC in South Africa might pose problems for a weighty segment of the U.S. body politic, it is not a major issue among Blacks. Cries of "Soviet influence" are generally sufficient to make many in the U.S. stand down, but they do not have the same impact among Afro-Americans. As the

3   Hollis Lynch, "Black American Radicals and the Liberation of Africa: the Council on African Affairs, 1937–1955", unpublished paper, 1977; cf also Horne, *Black & Red*, passim.

4   Alfred O. Hero, Jr. and John Barratt, eds., *The American People and South Africa: Publics, Elites and Policymaking Processes* (Lexington: D.C. Heath, 1981); Alfred O. Hero, "American Negroes and U.S. Foreign Policy: 1937–1967." *Journal of Conflict Resolution* 8 (June 1969): 220–251; Steven Metz, "The Anti-Apartheid Movement and the Populist Instinct in American Politics," *Political Science Quarterly*, 101 (3, 1986): 379–395; Afro-Americans have also been found disproportionately in the top ranks of the Communist Party, U.S.A. Cf. Harvey Klehr, *Communist Cadre: The Social Background of the American Communist Party Elite.* (Stanford: Stanford University Press, 1978).

post-1960s heighten Afro-American identification with Africa, this community comes into increasing conflict with leading U.S. policy-makers because Africa has a disproportionate number of "Marxist-oriented" ruling parties. Congo, Ethiopia, Benin, Zimbabwe, Angola, Mozambique, are a few examples. This tendency is particularly salient in the area where interest is presently the greatest: Southern Africa.

Red-baiting NCBL and IADL

This tendency has not escaped the attention of the far-right critics of Black solidarity. One termed the National Conference of Black Lawyers a group of "Marxist lawyers," despite the inaccuracy of such an allegation. Lennox Hinds, former NCBL National Director, is now United Nations Representative of the International Association of Democratic Lawyers: this same critic termed IADL a "Soviet Communist Party front group." In an attempt to defame Randall Robinson, this Black lawyer and leaders of Trans-Africa was termed a "personal friend of Cuba's Fidel Castro (and) Nicaragua's Daniel Ortega . . . " Necessarily, the far-right has attempted to "red-bait" the liberation movements of Southern Africa in order to reduce their influence here; former Senator Jeremiah Denton of Alabama went as far as having full-scale hearings on this subject. An article written by UCLA political scientist Martin Weil, ironically placed in the Congressional Record by then Congressman Andrew Young, warned that "a successful black lobby for Africa must maintain a certain distance from the African liberation movements in order to maintain its own credibility with the American public . . . ." NSC-46, allegedly written by then National Security Advisor Zbigniew Brzezinki in 1978 and leaked to the press, worriedly pondered the impact of leftist

Southern African liberation movements on U.S. Blacks and ultimately U.S. policy.'[5]

South Africa, too, has been concerned about U.S. public opinion, particularly Afro-American. Their Department of Information has insinuated itself into the U.S. electoral process, working to defeat anti-apartheid legislators, and has hired a Black lobbyist, William Keyes, at $390,000 per year. The development of the Congressional Black Caucus, particularly the role of Black lawyers like John Conyers and George Crockett of Detroit, has been a noted bane for apartheid. The CBC also illustrates the overall progressive tilt of the Black community, for their positions are far more progressive on such questions as disarmament, labor rights, Southern Africa, etc., than their Euro-American counterparts.[6]

A Faustian Bargain

One reason Black lawyers have had to step forward on the Southern Africa question has been the reluctance of traditional civil rights organizations to do so. Beginning with the purge of W. E. B. Du Bois in 1948 from the NAACP, after he had been invited back in 1944 to become something of a "Minister of Foreign Affairs" for the organization, the onset of the "Red

5   Tomas D. Schuman, "Disinvestment Movement in the U.S. – A Proven Soviet Active Measure," *Family Protection Scoreboard* (Special Edition on South Africa, 1987): 52–53; Williams Keyes, "ANC: African Terrorists," *Lincoln Review* 6 (Fall 1985): 31–33; Zbigniew Brzezinski, "Black Africa and the U.S. Black Movement," *The Black American* 19 (July 18–24, 1980): 19–22.

6   Murray Waas, "South Africa Payoff! Congress, Press Involved," *National Leader* 2 (October 27, 1983): 1–20; *Washington Post*, November 21, 1985; *Business Week*, September 30, 1985.

Scare" was marked in the Black community. The NAACP, which was avowedly "anti-imperialist" during World War II, began to keep quiet on the increasingly anti-communist and interventionist foreign policy of the U.S. The National Urban League has traditionally been uninvolved in foreign policy.

Especially after World War II it seemed that civil rights groups had made something of a "Faustian" bargain with the rulers of the U.S.: in return for muteness or support of U.S. foreign policy, there would be civil rights concessions at home. With the coming to independence of African nations, Jim Crow at home was becoming an aching Achilles heel in winning "hearts and minds" abroad, so these concessions had to come in any case. Nevertheless, the NAACP not only backed the U.S. war against Vietnam but attacked others who deigned agree: the same held true earlier for the war in Korea.[7]

Two Blocs of Black Lawyers

Black lawyers have traditionally been key opinion solders in their communities: with the abdication of leading civil rights organizations, these lawyers' role in foreign policy has been heightened. But it is well to note there has not been unanimity among them on foreign policy positions.

On the one hand, there have been lawyers like Thurgood Marshall and William Hastie. Given certain objective conditions, these attorneys have been disposed to lean left. Both were members of the National Lawyers Guild and during the pre-war period, Marshall maintained close relations with the

---

7   Horne, *Black and Red*, passim.

Guild and these relations continued for a while after the war. But for the most part in the post-war period these lawyers have stuck closely to their domestic knitting: this group has been predisposed to align with the National Bar Association.

Then there are lawyers like George Crockett and Earl Dickerson. The former was defense counsel in the infamous 1949 frame-up of Communist Party leaders and was jailed for his vigorous defense; the latter wrote a stunning amicus brief in that case and rallied support from his post as head of the Guild. The lawyers symbolized by this pair have been predisposed to align with the National Conference of Black Lawyers and have been quite active in the international arena. The fact is that the NBA is a traditional bar association designed to defend the interests of Black members of the profession. Until the advent of the Free South Africa Movement, NBA has been loath to intervene internationally, while NCBL, designed to defend the interests of the Black community, has acted in an altogether different manner.[8]

These two blocs of attorneys can be seen as "center" and "left" of the Black bar. Of course, it must be recognized that what is "center" among Blacks would be "left" among the U.S. body politic. Still, if the left is those who see U.S. foreign policy toward Southern Africa inevitably dominated by transnationals and are keen on aligning with left if not Marxist-led organizations at

8   Percival Roberts Bailey, "Progressive Lawyers: A History of the National Lawyers Guild." PhD dissertation, (Rutgers University, 1979). For a 1942 report to the Guild by Hastie and Marshall, see Ann Fagan Ginger and Eugene M. Tobin, eds., *The National Lawyers Guild: From Roosevelt through Reagan* (Philadelphia: Temple University Press, 1987) 43–45. For the roles of Dickerson and Crockett in Guild work from 1940 on, see Ginger and Tobin, *National Lawyers Guild*, passim. This paper does not purport to address each and every facet of Black lawyers' activity on this issue of Southern Africa but primarily the organizational and significant aspects.

home and abroad, this is a serviceable definition. There has been a danger of center Black lawyers being "ghettoized" in terms of dealing with only Black issues, while the same has not held true for the left. It is symbolic that one of the few times the Reagan Administration stated that race was a factor in naming an ambassador was in the nomination for South Africa. Indeed, a disproportionate number of Black ambassadors have been sent to Africa, including Black lawyers Franklin William (Ghana) and Clyde Ferguson (Uganda). Moreover, Congressional hearings (conducted, appropriately enough, by Congressman Crockett), demonstrated that those center Blacks who have chosen to enter the State Department have faced a fate worse than mere "ghettoization": they have faced outright racism.

Black lawyers from the left have followed a difficult path. Robert Van Lierop, who has worked closely with NCBL and made a prize-winning film on the struggle led by FRELINO in Mozambique, went on from there to become—in a highly unusual move—Ambassador to the United Nations of Vanuatu (formerly the New Hebrides, a British-French condominium in the South Pacific). Lennox Hinds' role with IADL has involved him in all manner of international issues.[9]

Pre-eminent Role of Lawyers in Liberation of Southern Africa

Robert Mugabe, Prime Minister of Zimbabwe, holds two law degrees. Herbert Chitepo, a key founder of Mugabe's party, ZANU, read for the bar in London and returned home in

9   *TransAfrica News*, 2 (No 5, 1983): 3; *New York Amsterdam News*, August 15, 1987. Center lawyers in trying to integrate elite institutions run smack into a status quo highly resistant to change on any level.

1954 as Southern Rhodesia's first African barrister. He served as legal advisor to Joshua Nkomo at the Southern Rhodesia Constitutional Conference in 1961 and then went into exile in Dar es Salaam where he became the first African Director of Public Prosecutions before he was assassinated. ANC leaders Oliver Tambo and Nelson Mandela were law partners in South Africa. Thus, lawyers playing a leading role in the U.S. is consistent with the Southern African trend. Yet, the unfortunate fact is that the abdication by the civil rights groups and the inability to develop in the U.S. a mass membership organization akin to CISPES (Committee in Solidarity with the People of El Salvador) have meant that progressive Black lawyers have not only had to serve as advisors, but as mass organizers as well.[10]

The development of NCBL in 1968 meant that the National Lawyers Guild, historic home of progressive Black lawyers, had been usurped to an extent. Still, NCBL stalwarts like Haywood Burns (present NLG President), Gerald Horne (who formerly worked in the NLG national office and still serves on their Editorial Board) and Timothy Wright of Chicago (late of Mayor Harold Washington's staff) helped to carry aloft the anti-apartheid torch for the Guild in alliance with non-Black members. Often the Guild's work in this area has been in conjunction with NCBL, eg, mobilizing for the huge April 25, 1987 March on Washington concerning Southern Africa and central America. Another notable recent development was the New York City Guild chapter dedicating its major 1986 fund-raising event to Nelson Mandela. One of the more significant recent

10   David Martin and Phyllis Johnson, *The Struggle for Zimbabwe: The Chimurenga War* (New York: Monthly Review Press, 1981), 158.

products of NCBL-NM collaboration is the publication of The Legal Front, which covers law-related developments and has received favorable response.[11]

BALSA

The National Black Law Students Association obviously does not encompass attorneys, but it has served as a useful training ground for Black lawyers, often most fruitfully in conjunction with NCBL. Indeed, the saying in BALSA circles for some time has been: "We go to NBA for career advancement and NCBL for politics." Thus, the June 1982 issue of NCBL Notes reported that BALSA leaders had travelled to Zimbabwe for meetings with the Ministry of Legal and Parliamentary Affairs with the aim, inter alia, of sending Afro-American lawyers there be- cause of the "shortage of African lawyers presently in the country." As a result, the W. E. B. Du Bois International Legal Program was established at the NCBL national office.

The student divestment movement has also seen the conspicuous presence of BALSA. In 1985 Black law students at Georgetown made headlines when they and their allies forced the law library there to cancel the subscription of the University of South Africa to their law review, against the argument that the First Amendment barred this action. BALSA has continued its anti-apartheid solidarity, and in March 1986, in

11   Program of NLG Annual Dinner, March 7, 1986, New York City; *The Legal Front*, 1 (1987) (in possession of author). For the work of the NLG on Southern Africa generally, see the germinal collection of Guild materials and editorial comments by Ginger and Tobin, *National Lawyers Guild*, 189, 322, 326, 343, 385–86, 399; for the specific role of Black Guild members, 357, 369.

conjunction with NCBL, it, too, had a gala tribute to Nelson and Winnie Mandela.[12]

NCBL

It is impossible to analyze the subject of Southern Africa and Afro-American attorneys not to mention the Afro-American community itself—without devoting due attention to NCBL. From the time it was organized in 1968 as a progressive alternative to NBA, it tried to be on the cutting edge of politics. NCBL was a left-center organization from the beginning.

The problem for NCBL was that as time progressed, the kind of objective conditions that allowed center lawyers to align with the left in 1968 began to evaporate as the Age of Reagan set in. Increasingly, these center attorneys began to leave the organization and often international affairs were the reason given. For some, it was the Angola crisis of 1976. Others alleged that the organization spent too much time on international questions. Inevitably, the fact that NCBL's views conflicted with those of Foggy Bottom was seen as not a guarantee of career advancement. For example, NCBL sued the U.S. after the invasion of Grenada: it sent delegations to the West Bank and Gaza that sharply denounced Israeli policies; it sent delegations to both Iran and Libya at times of crisis and did not hesitate to hit U.S. policy toward those regimes. All of these policies were justifiable and certainly not controversial within the context of either the Afro-American community or the United Nations—but in

---

12   *NCBL Notes*, June 1982; *National Law Journal*, February 18, 1985; Eighteenth Annual Convention and General Assembly of BALSA, dinner March 28, 1986, Omni Park Central Hotel, New York City (in possession of author).

the U.S. as a whole this was not the case and center lawyers continued to flee.

Leadership in NCBL certainly was not oblivious to this tendency and prior to a high-level "retreat" in August 1984 invited long-time supporter Prof. Derrick Bell of Harvard Law School to comment. Typically, he was blunt:

I realize this suggestion will not be warmly received, but over the years I think black lawyers have perceived NCBL's major program was involvement in foreign arenas. There has been, I think, some alienation of black lawyers . . . I fear (without any proof) that NCBL's foreign adventures increase the difficulty of obtaining foundation grants.

No one in NCBL could disagree with his latter point about the foundations: particularly after NCBL's position on the Mid-East conflict became clear, foundations began to pull the plug on NCBL. But, in response, NCBL Board member Gerald Horne took issue with the import of Bell's contention:

The fact is that this work only engages a small part of the membership. The point is that this demarche is perceived as occupying a disproportionate percentage of our time because we are virtually unique in this regard—unfortunately. . . . Bi-partisan foreign policy and partisan disagreements ending at the water's edge have been key postulates for the conduct of U.S. politics in the post-World War II era. Swift retribution has befallen those courageous enough to sail into this biting wind.

Certainly NCBL would have a healthier bank balance if we were to de-emphasize or drop some of our positions on international affairs—but at what price?

Horne went on to aver that the military budget was the key domestic and international issue and that without slicing it drastically, solving problems of homelessness, education, poverty, etc. could not be successful. Still, even Horne had to concede that the organization's views on international affairs did not help to attract center lawyers.[13]

This contention over international affairs was not always the case. During the tenure of NCBL National Director Haywood Burns, 1968–1973, criminal justice was a major concern of NCBL: yet even here the emphasis was to the left, as clients like Angela Davis and the Black Panther Party demonstrated. But by the time Lennox Hinds assumed the helm after Burns, things had begun to change. As the election of 1972 approached, the first African American National Conference on Africa was held at Howard University, organized by the Congressional Black Caucus and chaired by Congressman Diggs, with significant NCBL participation. This Conference initiated an annual African Liberation Day march in Washington, which in 1972 attracted 10,000. By May 1973 these marches had spread to 30 cities, again with significant NCBL participation. In the fall of 1973, the National Anti-Imperialist Conference in Solidarity with African Liberation was held in Chicago, including Oliver Tambo and Angela Davis, along with a number of NCBL members. Illustrating once again how NCBL tended to reflect tendencies already present in the Black community, it was around this time that NCBL began speaking out more insistently on international issues.

13   Derrick Bell to NCBL Retreat Participants, August 2, 1984; Gerald Horne to NCBL Retreat Participants, August 13, 1984; *NCBL Papers.*

There were other factors. Watergate and the weakening of President Richard Nixon helped to create favorable conditions for advance on the Southern Africa front. The war in Vietnam forced more to ponder militarism and imperialism. The over-throw of the Portuguese fascist junta on April 25, 1974 signaled the impending liberation of Mozambique and Angola, and her-alded the demise of Rhodesia, which accelerated an already growing tendency. NCBL was well-placed to address the ques-tion of Southern Africa, with (then Judge) George Crockett in its ranks, as well as Hope Stevens, who had worked closely with Black Communist lawyers William Patterson and Ben Davis, and eventually served as Co-Chair.[14]

Legal Skills Against Colonialism

Over the years, NCBL devoted considerable effort to provid-ing legal skills to the struggle against colonialism in Southern Africa. But two factors militated against greater effort in this area. First, litigation and the like was expensive and NCBL's budget, even during the great days, rarely exceeded $100,000. The membership base probably never exceeded 1500, with the strongest chapters in Boston, New York, Washington, Philadelphia, Detroit, Mississippi, Seattle, San Francisco Bay Area and Los Angeles, though at various times there were chap-ters in virtually every major U.S. city, not to mention Toronto and the U.S. Virgin Islands. This base, mostly of law professors, public interest lawyers and Legal Services attorneys did not and could not provide the wherewithal to take on major litigation. Rare was the NCBL attorney from a big law firm.

14 *Washington Post*, May 27, 1972; *Southern Africa*, May 1973; *Southern Africa*, January 1974.

The second factor militating against greater effort was the absence of a CISPES-type organization on Southern Africa and the fact that NCBL was one of the few progressive nationally-based groupings meant they were drawn inexorably into more mass organizing work than they would have preferred.

Nonetheless, NCBL applied considerable legal skills over the years. In a 1975 memo Prof. Henry Richardson, then chairing NCBL's International Affairs Task Force, noted NCBL's participation in Diggs v. Schultz, 470 F2d 461 (DC Cir 1972), an attempt to enjoin importation of Rhodesian Chromium ore by Union Carbide in violation of various UN Security Council Resolutions.[15]

These efforts had led Gerald Horne in 1974 to unsuccessfully seek funding for a staffed International Affairs Division of NCBL. Therein the NCBL proposal noted:

The demands on our task force have simply become too varied and too enormous for them to render the painstaking and time-consuming attention that these issues warrant. Daily we are besieged with requests that have international ramifications which we are simply unable to fulfill. NCBL sought to monitor "U.S. State and Defense Department Policy as it Relates to Southern Africa, the Caribbean and Latin America" along with "conducting research and test-case litigation."

NCBL also worked in the legislative arena during this time. Gerald Horne drafted legislation with Roger Green (presently head of the New York State Black and Puerto Rican Legislative Caucus) that was introduced by Assemblyman Albert Vann seeking to restrict New York from doing business with

15 Henry Richardson, "Multinational Corporations, Southern Africa." See also "NCBL: A Sketch for a Future Program," October 30, 1975; "Proposal on International Affairs Division," July 1974; *NCBL Papers.*

corporations doing business with South Africa, Namibia and Rhodesia. Lennox Hinds and NCBL General Counsel Lewis Myers pioneered in writing and researching the legal repercussions of activities of armed mercenaries in Southern Africa; their research was circulated worldwide.

After representing NCBL at an international conference in Lisbon in solidarity with the front line states in March 1983 that was attended by Tambo, Nujoma and the Foreign Ministers of the regions, Horne proposed "a damage action against the U.S. government brought by Angolan plaintiffs, similar in conception and theory to the one brought by Nicaraguans: note also Filartiga . . . to the extent we can located South African military in the U.S., the Paraguayan case might be of value. The issue was also raised of investigating laws re: banning importation of goods made with slave labor and applying such to RSA. . . . [A] suit against 'Soldier and Fortune' magazine . . . is advisable given its recruitment of mercenaries. . . . What about an action to enforce the Clark Amendment?" Historically NCBL had brought much of its litigation in conjunction with the Center for Constitutional Rights, which included NCBL members, and Horne had directed a joint NCBL-CCR-NLG project earlier, but the Center—which brought and won Filartiga v. Pena-Irala, 630 F2d 876 (1980)—was then bogged down in Central American lawsuits and was not able to move.[16]

---

16   Lennox S. Hinds, "The Legal Status of Mercenaries: A Concept in International Humanitarian Law," Eighth Conference of the Law of the World Sponsored by the World Peace Through Law Center, August 21–27, 1977, World Peace Through Law Center, Manila; G.C. Horne to NCBL Chapters, NLG friends, et al, "Proposed Legal Action re: Southern Africa," March 30, 1983, *NCBL Papers*.

In 1983 NCBL's UN Delegate, Jeanne Woods, proposed that the UN Special Committee Against Apartheid fund a NCBL Anti-Apartheid Litigation Project. She called for litigation to enforce Decree No. 1 protecting Namibia's natural resources, to prevent the Export-Import Bank from extending credits to South Africa, to prevent South African Airways from landing at U.S. airports, to bar all importation of South African goods, to institute stockholders' derivative suits to prevent corporate investments in South Africa, to challenge Department of Justice demands for inspection of records of the UN Observer Missions of the ANC and SWAPO, to challenge delays and denials of visas for ANC and SWAPO militants, legislative drafting and monitoring, etc. Though Woods and NCBL subsequently did receive some funding from the UN it was not for this Project, which remained just another good idea on paper.

NCBL had more success in disseminating information about such advanced legal concepts. For example, in April 1984 at the University of Pennsylvania, NCBL sponsored a seminar on Foreign Intervention and the Law: Enforcing Domestic and International Standards of Conduct. Speakers included former U.S. Senator James Abourezk (of Lebanese descent, who came to work closely with NCBL on Mid-East questions), Francis Vendrell (Senior Political Affairs Officer at the Department of Political Affairs & Decolonization at the UN), Gay McDougall, Lucia Hamutenya (Associate Political Affairs Officer of the UN Council for Namibia), and Peter Weiss and Michael Ratner of CCR, who had been pivotal in Filartiga. Though a central focus here was the Mid-East and Central America, NCBL's primary foreign policy priority—Southern Africa—was highlighted. This priority took center stage the following year when a second seminar was held at Harvard Law School on Namibia that featured remarks by Prof Henry Richardson, Timothy Wright and Gerald Horne.[17]

NCBL Lobbied and Sued

NCBL also was involved in influencing the course of legislation concerning Southern Africa. This was true across the country but seemed most salient in New York City. Intro 619, which eventually passed, was introduced in 1984 and sought to bar the city from doing business with corporations involved in South Africa. But there was court action by NCBL. In 1985 both the Seattle and Boston chapters had to go beyond pro forma defense of Free South Africa Movement demonstrators— and won smashingly. In 1986 NCBL leader Nark Fancher of Camden, New Jersey filed suit to ensure that this city would live up to the call of a recent bill that barred dealings with corporations like IBN. NCBL in Detroit joined with NLG to force the Regents of the University of Michigan to divest the school of $51 million in investments in U.S. corporations doing business in South Africa.

In 1987, NCBL, along with Lennox Hinds and Black CCR attorney Frank Deale, brought suit in a controversial headline-grabbing case that in today's times only the left Black bar could have brought. Prof. Fred Dube is a direct descendant of the founder of the ANC and a leading member in the U.S., where he teaches at the State University of New York-Stony Brook. The suit charges that he was denied tenure principally because, in a class on racism, he discussed Zionism as a form of racism, consonant with the famous UN resolution. Governor

---

17   Jeanne Woods to Abdennous Abrous, September 8, 1983; Program, NCBL Seminar, April 13–14, 1984; *NCBL Papers.*

Mario Cuomo of New York joined Zionist organizations in denouncing Dube, as did an Afro-American who headed the SUNY system, Dr. Clifton Wharton; he now heads the teachers' pension fund that has adamantly resisted divestment. The Dube case is an example of the kind of case to which NCBL committed its meager resources and it illustrates how NCBL's alignment with the majority at the UN brought plaudits abroad and some derision at home.[18]

Indeed, NCBL's alignment with the majority at the UN was probably more developed and well-defined than any other national Black organization. NCBL delegations travelled frequently to the Soviet Union and Eastern Europe, Northern Ireland, the Caribbean, and elsewhere. NCBL delegations to Cuba, beginning in 1973 and continuing sporadically thereafter, had dramatic impact on the organization's involvement in foreign affairs. It may be no accident that this involvement increased dramatically in the post-1973 era: certainly many of the delegates were impressed at seeing Afro-Cubans at top levels of society, including high-ranking party leaders, heads of ministries, etc.

Though some of the membership thought otherwise, many of these trips were not simple junkets. For example, in 1980 Gerald Horne presented a paper to an Oil-Workers conference in Libya that grappled with the key question of nationalization of the oil industry and how this could be done even under U.S.

18 *New York Amsterdam News*, March 17, 1984; *Village Voice*, April 10, 1984; *Mississippi Enterprise*, June 14, 1986; *Camden Courier-Post*, July 16, 1986; *Dunbar v. Camden City Council*, et al L-045903-86 PW; *Regents of the University of Michigan v. State of Michigan*, 83-50309-CZ; *Stony Brook Statesman*, November 16, 1983; *Village Voice*, December 20, 1983; *Newsday*, May 7, 1986; *New York Amsterdam News*, May 14, 1977.

law. He went on to suggest that all of the hoopla about "Marxist regimes" in Africa shrouded the fact that trans-national corporations wield undue influence on U.S. foreign policy and that, in any event, public enterprise was perfectly legal. Still, there is no doubt that many in NCBL were not pleased by then National Director Victor Goode's stay in Iran just after the overthrow of the Pahlavi regime.[19]

A Brief Panoramic Look

The tone for NCBL's activity concerning the decolonization of Southern Africa was set in 1972 when the convention resolved, "NCBL should view itself in a Pan- African context and undertake to involve itself in African liberation struggles (on) behalf of African people wherever their struggle may occur." Thus, International Section Chair Henry Richardson, National Director Haywood Burns and Co-Chair Timothy Jenkins engaged in discussions on Southern Africa at the World Peace Through Law Conference in Cote d'Ivoire in August 1973. Shortly thereafter Richardson observed, "NCBL is simultaneously moving in several directions internationally. One is even tempted without much risk of overstatement, to say 'exploding' into the international arena." Evidence of this was the establishment by NCBL in 1976 of the Fred Hampton College of Law and International Diplomacy in Chicago. Developing skills to

19 Gerald Horne, "The Legality of Nationalization of the Oil Industry in the U.S.," Oil Workers Anti-Monopolist Conference, Tripoli, Libya, March 1980; cf Jonathan Boe, "American Business: The Response to the Soviet Union, 1933–1947," PhD dissertation, Stanford University, 1979. It is always ironic to hear ideological denunciations of state-owned enterprise on National Public Radio and Corporation for Public Broadcasting stations.

assist the brethren in Southern Africa was part of the mandate of this overly ambitious effort.[20]

1976 proved to be a turning point not only for NCBL but for the progressive movement in general, and perhaps for international peace and security, as reflected in the attack on detente. The critical issue was Angola.

The coming to independence of the Popular Movement for Liberation of Angola (MPLA) government on November 11, 1975, the collaboration between Pretoria and Washington to install UNITA's Jonas Savimbi in Luanda (as subsequently reported by then CIA station chief John Stockwell) and the dispatching of Cuban troops who sent the South Africans fleeing south energized the Afro-American community in a way hardly seen since the Italian invasion of Ethiopia in the 1930s. Though they tried to minimize the extent of the effort, even the New York Times could not help but detect the "interest and tension" among Blacks. Angola also marked the escalation of a trend that NCBL had long been concerned about the use of mercenaries, especially Afro-Americans, on the same side as South Africa. Roy Innis of CORE was the eminence grise here. Other Black devotees of Maoist China, e.g., Amiri Baraka, were de facto members of this alliance. On the other side, Judge Booth of the American Committee on Africa (ACOA) and the Congressional Black Caucus derided U.S. intervention.

The State Department howled that its willful fantasy— that detente with the USSR meant Moscow's reneging on aid to national liberation struggles, something the USSR had never stated—had been violated. The U.S. public opinion was confused. Some erstwhile supporters of African liberation,

20 Statement on the NCBL Task Force on International Affairs by Henry Richardson, August 14, 1973; NCBL Activities Report, 1973, *NCBL Papers; Bilalian News*, October 1, 1976.

too, were confused, if not frightened, as reflected in a letter to Horne: "I regret to inform you that the program scheduled for May 27, 1976, at the Harlem Hospital Center has been cancelled. Our committee has become disillusioned with the political atmosphere created by New York groups supporting African liberation. We feel that the risk of fiasco outweighs the benefit of bringing these groups to Harlem at this time."[21]

With a national office in Central Harlem and a membership of Black lawyers with an activist bent, inevitably the waves created by Angola swept into NCBL. By background and by nature, NCBL was not predisposed to be attracted to the anti-communist line on Angola. For example, Louis and Dorothy Burnham, father and mother of NCBL leader Margaret Burnham, were two of the most adept organizers the U.S. progressive movement has produced. Moreover, NCBL—then as now—found itself defending the right of MPLA, SWAPO, ANC, etc., to receive aid from the Soviet Union. But—then as now—there was a peculiar habit in the country as a whole, where anti-communism is the closest thing there is to a state

21 *New York Times*, December 14, 1975; CORE News Release, February 10, 1976: "As supposed political representatives of Black America, the communist dupes of the Black Caucus are urged to forego its schizophrenic and cowardly stance on the Angolan crisis." (in possession of author); *Jet*, January 8, 1975; *Bilalian News*, January 16, 1976; *Unity and Struggle*, August-September 1975 (this was the newspaper of Baraka's ill-fated Congress of African People); *New York Times*, January 18, 1976 (Booth's ACOA initiated this ad opposing U.S. intervention that was signed by Black lawyers like Franklin Williams, Congressman Charles Rangel, et al); Booth also led a rally on the steps of the Capitol (*Daily World*, January 15, 1976); *Africa*, February 1976; Dr. James Louis Davis to Gerald Horne, May 3, 1976 (in possession of author); Cf Soho *Weekly News*, February 12, 1976: "The battle over Africa is being fought on two fronts; the hot war in Angola and the cold war in New York City. In both cases it's American black vs African black, and the casualties are heavy."

religion: the attempt to figure out how many in the leading bodies of these liberation movements were "card-carrying Communists" in order to take appropriate action. But NCBL saw itself as a non-sectarian organization—"one house with many rooms" excluding only outright Nazis. NCBL encompassed nationalists, moderates, Marxists, and more. It saw no need to discriminate against Communists at home or abroad and certainly could find no legal justification for doing so.

In any event, NCBL's relationship with NPLA predated the 1975–76 crisis. On June 26, 1974, Hinds wrote Abel Guimararaes of HPLA in Dar es Salaam: "We are prepared to extend our assistance to you in any way that lawyers and the legal perspective may be of use to advance the national interest of the people of Angola in their struggle for liberation from colonialism. May we meet with you in New York or Dar es Salaam, at your convenience, to discuss the ways we can be of service?" Thus, Hinds was acerbic and consistent in 1976 when he castigated U.S. intervention: "Paradoxically while Nr. Moynihan . . . warns of such a Soviet takeover Americans witness Hr. Ford and family on TV being toasted by our alleged enemies in Peking and Nr. Kissinger dining on caviar in Moscow." He assailed the Pretoria-Washington alliance, warned against Blacks being used as mercenaries and called for a congressional investigation in a NCBL statement that typically received wide coverage in the Afro-American press.[22]

---

22 *Bilalian News*, February 13, 1976: Added Hinds: "The State Department sees Blacks as their 'trump-card' hoping to lure us into the battle to demoralize our African brothers and sisters by the spectacle of Blacks giving aid and assistance to South Africa, the arch enemy of Black people all over the world."

Horne, in an article widely circulated in the left press, was equally harsh, particular toward those "progressives" who opposed the MPLA simply because Peking did. As the battle was reaching intensity, Hinds travelled to Luanda in February 1976 and engaged in high-level discussions with MPLA officials and others similarly situated from Congo, Ethiopia, Sao Tome, ANC, Benin, etc. That same month the Cubans consulted with NCBL on what U.S. groups to invite to an emergency conference on Angola in Havana: Patricia Murray represented NCBL. Host controversial was the participation of Hinds, Hope Stevens and NCBL attorney Kermit Coleman of Chicago in the International Commission of Enquiry on Mercenarism held in Luanda in July 1976 that tried and convicted a number of white mercenaries. The Washington Post, other mainstream news organs, and the international press highlighted NCBL's role.[23]

NCBL Support for NPLA

There was not unanimity within the ranks about NCBL's avid support for the NPLA government. Prof. Richardson averred: "This issue is whether NCBL should (a) publicly urge the State Department to recognize the MPLA regime as the government of Angola, or (b) whether NCBL should take no public position at all on the issue. I am strongly inclined towards (b) . . . NCBL is not and should not be a bandwagon organization . . . our urging publicly recognition of MPLA takes NCBL into a public

23 Gerald Horne: "Maoism – Trojan Horse for Imperialism in Angola," *Black Liberation Journal* 1 (Winter 1976): 34; *New York Times*, February 28, 1976; Report of the National Director, 1975; Patricia Murray to Lennox Hinds, February 1976 (re: Seminar on Angola); "A Decade in Defense of Human Rights, 1968–1978" NCBL Report, 1978, *NCBL Papers; Washington Post*, June 29, 1976.

political position in favor of NPLA . . . it throws us into taking sides in what is still an African civil war. . . . I regret very much that you did not inform me, as Chairman of the appropriate Task Force, of your recent trip to Luanda. . . . If (Cuban troops) remain for any length of time, I believe there will be an African reaction to them as an alien occupying force eat will soon force the MPLA to ask them to leave."[24] NCBL member Prof. Emma C. Jones of the law school at the University of California at Davis was cautious. She urged recognition but questioned whether NCBL should urge criminal prosecution of CORE and wondered "what effect (all) this advocacy (will) have on our tax-exempt status." Swaying her was the fact that the Organization of African Unity had recognized the government.

In a thoughtful memo, Goler Butcher, like Prof. Jones a member of the Task Force, seemed to raise questions about Richardson's demarche and Jones' comment on CORE:

> It is no excuse for failing to issue such a statement to argue that such a pronouncement would be a call for prosecution of a Black group. First, if being a lawyer means anything, it means possessing the ingenuity to frame the issues so that undesirable conclusions are avoided, and the objective is achieved. Thus, in the case of the recruitment of mercenaries the issue is not the calling for prosecution of a Black group, but: advising Black Americans what the law is in order that they not fall afoul of it. . . . I certainly hope that NCBL will not flinch in speaking out on the legal issues.

24   Henry Richardson to Lennox Hinds, February 24, 1976, *NCBL Papers*.

Yet, she added: "I recommend that the Task Force and NCBL except in extraordinary situations, address those issues which arise in a legal context. This would normally exclude questions of recognition, since recognition is basically a political matter."

The dialogue did not stop there. Apparently, Hinds charged that Richardson was reluctant to take any "advanced position that challenges both U.S. racist and imperialist policy." Richardson demurred and questioned Hinds' reluctance to call for prosecution of CORE; he also recalled what he considered to be NCBL's flawed opposition to the U.S. embargo of Cuba . . . Patricia Murray "was distressed that such a discussion is occurring at this point and serve to delay that much longer our actual work . . . "[25]

Results of NCBL Work on Angola

Angola was not only a watershed for the left, the Black community and the US-USSR relationship; it marked a significant departure for NCBL. On the positive side, it was significant that Black lawyers were engaging in such sophisticated debate on Southern Africa's decolonization at this moment in history. On the negative side, it did introduce some strain in the organization and convinced some of what was perceived to be "adventurist" tendencies of the left elements within the leadership. In any case, within months Butcher had resigned from NCBL as she took a post with the Agency for International Development, and so did Richardson, as he joined the National Security

25   Prof Emma C Jones to Henry Richardson, April 6, 1976; Goler T Butcher to Lennox Hinds, April 5, 1976; Henry Richardson to Lennox Hinds, March 15, 1976; Patricia Murray to Henry Richardson, March 19, 1976; *NCBL Papers*.

Council in the Carter White House. Charles Roach of Toronto took his place. Shortly after, the bar of New Jersey, perhaps in an unrelated move, sought sanctions against Hinds for random comments made at a trial that wound up in the U.S. Supreme Court. Apparently this entire experience had a dramatic impact on the NCBL leadership, for it was at that time that a Political Affairs Task Force was formed that sought to discuss the larger questions raised, inter alia, by the Angola crisis.[26]

All this did not prevent NCBL from addressing other questions. For example, in May 1976 Gay McDougall issued a lengthy statement calling for commutation of the death sentences of the SWAPO 6 and freeing of South African political prisoners. The Soweto rebellion in June 1976 found Hinds hailing the Security Council resolution and calling on Washington to "fulfill its obligations under international law towards Black South Africa." Again, in September 1976 Hinds called on President Gerald Ford to "send an international commission of lawyers to visit South Africa . . . with the task of interviewing all prisoners presently being detained, in furtherance of (Security Council) resolution 392 . . . ." The Angola crisis followed closely by Soweto gave added impetus to NCBL decolonization efforts. Letters of protest were sent to Ford and presidential candidate Jimmy Carter.[27]

Thus, the stage was set for the Detroit convention in 1976 where, perhaps inspired by the presence of premier Black

26   Goler T Butcher to Lennox Hinds, June 30, 1977; Lennox Hinds to Charles Roach, April 1, 1977; Undated Press Release re: Hinds case; Lennox Hinds, "A Study in Contradictions: Black Radical Lawyers," November 1976; *NCBL Papers.*

27   Press release, May 17, 1976; press release, June 21, 1976; undated press release, circa September 1976; Gay McDougall to International Affairs Task Force, undated, regarding "Ford-Carter-Burke letters", *NCBL Papers.*

Caucus Africanist Charles Diggs, NCBL passed the most detailed and comprehensive resolution on Southern Africa to that point. It called on banks to refuse loans to South Africa. It urged city councils to emulate Gary, Indiana in boycotting corporations with South African ties. It demanded no recognition of Transkei. It advocated continued sanctions against Rhodesia by the UN. The range was both well-informed and impressive.

This was quickly followed by a typically portentous press release: "On March 21st, 1977, the anniversary of the infamous Sharpeville Massacre, one of the most significant moves ever taken in this country against South African apartheid and racism [will occur]." This was NCBL's way of announcing the drafting of legislation for the New York City Council and the state legislature on not doing business with South Africa-related corporations.

After that NCBL made a coordinated effort to have the membership deluge the Carter White House with telegrams on Southern Africa, particularly after the murder of Steven Biko and the unveiling of the Congressional Black Caucus plan on the region.

NCBL continued this trend in 1978 with the Nigerian Ambassador to the UN, Leslie O. Harriman, addressing the NCBL convention in New Orleans on Southern Africa. Suitably inspired, the Boston chapter soon thereafter sponsored a regional conference on Southern Africa Clyde Ferguson, Harriman, and Aggrey Nbere of the ANC.[28]

---

28   *NCBL Notes*, 3 [Spring 1977]: 8; press release, circa March 1977;
     brochure, NCBL Regional Conference, May 4–5, 1979, Boston; cf.
     also Philip John and Lauren Anderson to "Dear Brothers and Sisters."
     October 25, 1977, *NCBL Papers; New Orleans Times-Picayune*,
     August 13, 1978.

THINGS FALL APART: CHINA AND THE DECLINE OF US IMPERIALISM

Political Affairs, 2007

When historians of the future look back, they may very well conclude that 2007 marked the time when the crisis of US imperialism became so obvious that even the dimmest bulb could detect it. For it is evident that imperialism is about to suffer a staggering and transformative defeat in Iraq as this illegal and criminal invasion has stretched the military to the breaking point, alienated allies and emboldened the lengthening list of foes of US imperialism.

At the same time, China, still ruled by a Communist Party, has accumulated an eye-popping $1 trillion in foreign currencies, a figure never before attained by any nation. This sum is so formidable, so huge, that there is a palpable fear in Washington that Beijing may develop a version of the International Monetary Fund and World Bank, rendering both of these imperialist dominated vehicles irrelevant. In the so-called backyard of Washington, socialist Cuba has not been slowed down by the hospitalization of President Fidel Castro and continues to move from strength to strength. Cuba and China in turn serve as anchors for Africa, Asia and Latin America in their ongoing attempt to break the chains of imperialist bondage. All this suggests that the crisis of US imperialism continues unabated.

The declining prestige of Washington was no better revealed than when the human rights watchdog of the United Nations rebuked the US for violations of international law at home and abroad, especially in connection with its so-called war on terror. Adding to a growing cascade of criticism, singled out were the secret detention facilities where torture is the norm and the failure to provide prisoners at Guantanamo Bay, Cuba with due process of law. But what really captured attention were the sharp criticisms of US domestic policy. Washingtons draconian asylum and immigration policies, the promiscuous deployment of the death penalty and life imprisonment and police brutality, were all condemned in no uncertain terms.

This international body of experts seconded by the UN oversees implementation of the International Covenant on Civil and Political Rights and chose 2006 to examine US compliance with this document for the first time since 1995. Predictably Washington reacted angrily to this rebuke. Ironically, the nation that has taken it upon itself to evaluate nations near and far and the extent to which they have complied with Washingtons version of democracy and freedom, now cries foul when the script is flipped.

US imperialism finds it hard to ignore this complaint from the UN for George W. Bush recognizes that it is precisely his malfeasance in the global arena that may very well jeopardize not only his legacy but his freedom of movement as well. For as the noted University of Virginia law professor, Rosa Brooks, put it recently, the US Supreme Court ruling in the case of Hamdan vs. Rumsfeld, concerning a so-called enemy combatant, suggests that Common Article Three of the Geneva Convention applies to the conflict with al Qaeda. But more than this, the high court holding makes high-ranking Bush administration officials including the president—potentially subject to prosecution under the federal War Crimes Act.

What this suggests is that US imperialism cannot escape the grasp of global forces, no matter how well it is able to bludgeon domestic opposition. More than this, even sectors of the US ruling elite have come to recognize that conservatism, which has served this class so well to this point, may be very well incapable of protecting its interests as the 21st century unfolds. For example, how can one expect the US right wing to subdue the rudimentarily conservative force that is so-called Islamic fundamentalism when historically they have been in the same trench, e.g., during the war in the 1980s in Afghanistan that turbo-charged religiosity?

The bold posture of the UN is emblematic of how the international community has come to recognize that US imperialism is a primary threat to international peace and security. Similarly, this is suggestive of how the erosion of the strength of US imperialism has made Washington more susceptible to being influenced by global trends. In the first place, the tax cutting mania of the Republican right without the concomitant muscle to slash social programs proportionately has made this nation more dependent on capital flows from Asia in particular to curb escalating deficits. As foreign nations have grabbed a larger stake in the US government and economy, understandably they have become more concerned about their investments here which provides more incentive for them to rein in Washington.

Of late, China and Russia on the UN Security Council have banded together to curb the more horrific and lunatic plans of Washington, e.g., imposing severe sanctions on Iran due to its attempt to develop civilian nuclear energy. Still, disturbing plans continue to emerge about Washingtons plans to bomb Iran which would be akin to opening the gates of hell.

Resort to bloody war has been the ultimate sanction held out by US imperialism for those so bold as to ignore their diktat but the catastrophic conflict in Iraq has shown that this threat is not as meaningful as it seems. The puncturing of this threat has plunged sectors of the US ruling elite into crisis mode. This melancholy was not assuaged when Israel proved unable to overpower Lebanon during its disastrous 33-day war that unfolded during the summer of 2006. Israel was encouraged by US imperialism to contribute to its ill-conceived war on terrorism by seeking to eliminate Hezbollah with the conflict over detention of Israeli soldiers as a pretext. But Israel was unable to accomplish this task, which diluted its importance in the eyes of US imperialism, with consequences that continue to be tallied. In a column for the Israeli daily Haaretz, former Israeli Foreign Minister Shlomo Ben-Ami argued that since US deterrence and respect for the superpower have been eroded unrecognizably, this means that an exclusive Pax Americana in the Middle East is no longer possible because not only is the US not an inspiration today, it does not instill fear.

As regimes globally sense that US imperialism may be weakening, there is a ripple effect in diverse areas. In the first place, it has called into question the utility of the dollar, the viability of which has obviated the necessity of making the tough decisions on fiscal matters that this nation's debt and deficits would ordinarily mandate. For example, in 2006 the United Arab Emirates, which had accumulated a treasure trove of dollars, announced that it has moved 10 percent of its $29 billion in foreign exchange reserves into euros, the common currency of the European Union, the erstwhile ally cum competitor of US imperialism, which has dreams of global domination all its own. Certainly the controversy in March 2006 when Dubai Ports World was blocked from taking over the interests in the US of another foreign entity, Britain's P&O, soured many Arabs on the reliability of US imperialism.

Other sober analysts transnationally are weighing a flight from the dollar as well, which if implemented could have disastrous consequences for US imperialism. In August 2006, China and Japan, Asia's two economic giants and rivals, developed what was termed an unusual consensus in support of an ACU or an Asian currency unit to as noted in the Financial Times reduce their reliance on a weakening dollar. Speaking in Australia, Fan Gang, a leading Chinese economic theorist, called for a sharp devaluation of the dollar as a way to bring health to the global economy. Of course, this could mean a sharp rise in prices for all manner of US imports including toys, automobiles, clothes, consumer electronics, and the like. The ACU has many hurdles to overcome before becoming reality, but the fact that Tokyo and Beijing could agree on its importance is suggestive of the crisis of US imperialism.

Even sectors of the US ruling class are now joining with progressives in calling for the ouster of the Bush regime. Calling for the ouster of this criminal regime and actually accomplishing this task are two different matters. For like the towering government debt and deficits that have accumulated under his watch, Bush has left many land mines behind, which will be bedeviling this nation for decades to come and are quite susceptible of exploding at any moment. There are many examples of this but what quickly comes to mind is the fact that the overstretched US military, pressed for recruits, has allowed

the infiltration of their ranks by neo-Nazis. Such is the conclusion of the well respected Southern Poverty Law Center,
which has reported the disturbing news that Aryan Nations
graffiti can now be found in Baghdad, along with numerous
soldiers with fascist tattoos. As the neo-Nazis see it, joining
the military allows them to gain military training, which could
be critical in coming years. Moreover, it allows them to legally
slaughter those not of European descent. Purging the military
of this vermin and scum has to be seen by progressives as a
top priority.

Certainly their presence does little to halt the desper-
ate belligerence that today characterizes US imperialism and
increasingly this hostility is targeting China which is both
non-European and ruled by a Communist Party, thus attain-
ing the daily double of right-wing hate politics. It is true that
a number of Fortune 500 corporations have invested heavily
in China, which serves as a restraint on the bellicosity of US
imperialism toward Beijing. But it should not be forgotten that
as I write a roiling and fierce debate is unfolding in the ranks of
the elite National Association of Manufacturers over trade with
China. The split in their ranks pits smaller US manufacturers
who are being hammered as they see it by Chinese factories
against their larger counterparts, some of whom are benefiting
from what is seen as an undervalued Chinese currency. China
is waging a mercantile war, claimed M. Brian O'Shaugnessy,
President of Revere Cooper Products, Inc. of Rome, New York,
and were being pacifists. These smaller corporations are threatening to leave the NAM unless it takes a tougher stance against
Beijing; of course, though these smaller companies make up
74 percent of the NAM membership, they only contribute
23 percent of the dues so the whales are expected to prevail

over the guppies. Still, one cannot easily expect these forces to go silently into the night if they are defeated.

A weakened US imperialism inevitably will be seeking scapegoats for the decline of the self-proclaimed sole remaining superpower in Beijing, e.g., accusations about Chinas currency manipulations already have gained traction and, of late, led to serious debate in the Congress about slapping an astonishing 27.5 percent duty on their exports to this country. Moreover, Chinas relations with Iran and the Democratic People's Republic of Korea (North Korea), the remaining members of the so-called axis of evil, are already the cause for anguished commentary in Washington.

Beijing has strengthened its relations with Tehran significantly, for example, signing several long-term energy exploration production and delivery contracts since 2004 with Iran worth more than $100 billion. In 2006 China invested in Iran's domestic oil-refining industry, agreeing to expand the country's gasoline output significantly.

China and the DPRK have long been close allies. Recall, for example, the latter stages of US imperialisms bloodthirsty invasion of the Korean peninsula in the 1950s, when it was common wisdom that these two Asian nations were as close as lips and teeth. Concerns about the DPRKs attempt to develop nuclear energy have caused Washington to try cajoling China into pressuring its ally. The fact that South Korea is lukewarm at best about sanctioning its northern neighbor is suggestive of the point that Koreans from north to south are looking forward to reunification and have little interest in bending to the intimidation of Washington.

China and Syria also have strong commercial ties, as Beijing has invested substantially in the development of this Arab state's transportation infrastructure, as well as in energy exploration and production. China is also a key supplier of military equipment to Syria.

China has become a major investor in Venezuela's energy sector and is also investing in this nation's transportation infrastructure, including railroads, ports and crude oil tankers, not to mention telecommunications, mining and agriculture. Caracas is directing more and more of its oil exports to China, which has not made Washington happy. In 2004 this figure amounted to 12,000 barrels of oil per day to China but by 2006 this figure had jumped to 200,000 and is slated to rise to 500,000 by 2009. China also has supported the attempt by Venezuela to obtain a coveted seat on the UN Security Council.

China has invested heavily in US Treasury securities and other US assets to the tune of about $800 billion. It is also true that if China were to devalue its currency as some in Washington are demanding this could reduce the value of China's foreign assets by a hefty $200 billion. Why should China the creditor yield to the demands of the US, the debtor?

Drunk with national and racial chauvinism, there are those in Washington who have yet to understand fully the comparative decline of US imperialism and its inability to impose its diktat. There seems to be little realization that China possesses countermeasures of its own. Beijing could liquidate its massive holdings of US Treasury securities, pushing US interest rates higher and the value of the dollar much lower against other major currencies. This could mean higher taxes or dramatic slashes in government programs.

What is striking about this developing relationship between Beijing and Washington is that, in some ways, it is coming to mirror the cold war. Increasingly Washington is taking umbrage at the fact that the world's most populous nation is developing interests globally. Washington seems to be particularly concerned with Beijing's incursions in Africa, which the US and Western Europe alike have long seen as its own private preserve and has long been a major petroleum supplier to both. Of late, this tendency has been manifested in overheated press coverage in the US about China's role in Africa. Typical was an August 2006 New York Times article which spoke wondrously of Dakar, Senegal, long a bastion of French influence, but which now is home to Chinese merchants who sell shoes, electronics, plastic jewelry and toys. China, it seems, is suddenly everywhere in Africa, not just in oil-rich states. Trade between Africa and China has almost quadrupled since 2001 and last year reached almost $40 billion in Sierra Leone Chinese companies have built and renovated hotels and restaurants. In Mozambique, Chinese companies are investing in soybean processing and prawn production. At the African Union summit meeting in Banjul, Gambia last month, the Chinese delegation dwarfed the ones sent by France, Britain and the United States.

This reference to oil rich states was not coincidental since Nigeria, Gabon and Angola are among the major petroleum producers globally. Also, not coincidentally, the Supreme Commander of the North Atlantic Treaty Organization, General James Jones announced in May 2003 that in the future US naval forces under his command would spend much less time in the Mediterranean. Instead, he predicted: I will bet they will spend half the time going down the West Coast of Africa. That same year, a senior Pentagon official was quoted as saying that a key mission for US forces [in Africa] would be to ensure that Nigeria's oilfields, which in the future would account for as much as 25 percent of all US oil imports, are secure.

Unsurprisingly, in January 2005 the US Navy commenced a two-month Gulf of Guinea deployment with participation by the USS Emory, carrying about 1,400 sailors and marines; port calls were made in Douala, Cameroon (close to Nigeria); Sekondi, Ghana; and Port Gentil, Gabon. Reportedly being considered as a potential site for a US military base is the island state of Sao Tome and Principe, close by the major oil producers and a former entry point for the unlamented African slave trade.

The so-called war on terror is also the stated rationale for Washingtons increasingly large footprint in Africa. Algeria, the supplier of huge amounts of liquefied natural gas to North America, has been critical in this regard. Algiers has been the recipient of significant amounts of military assistance from the US but this has not quelled and, in fact, may be heightening regional instability, as suggested by the coup in Mauretania, Tuareg revolts in Mali and Niger and continuing unrest in southern Algeria itself.

Indeed, there is concern throughout Algeria about the peculations of Halliburton, which has been bleeding the nation white. Surely this misbehavior only serves to underscore why more and more African nations are looking to Beijing as a counterweight to US imperialism, just as they once looked to Moscow.

No doubt Zimbabwe is viewing things through this lens. Heavily sanctioned by London and Washington, not least due to its expropriation of farmers from the European minority, Harare has decided to look East and, as a result, China has become this African nation's second largest supplier of imported goods. In 1998 China ranked only 11th in Harare's roll call of importers. Now it accounts for 6 percent of Zimbabwe's imports. One informed estimate is that there are at least 15 to 20 sizable Zimbabwe-China business deals, mostly involving state enterprises.

This nervousness about the global reach of Beijing illuminates as well the panic about Venezuela that has gripped the US ruling class. Unquestionably, Caracas has sought to use its oil wealth for progressive purposes, e.g., its alliance with Argentina that has led to development of a regional bank targeting nations frustrated with the domineering International Monetary Fund. Caracas also has purchased $3 billion in Argentine bonds, not to mention $25 million in Ecuador's debt. Just as China has tightened ties with Iran, Venezuela has acted similarly. On the banks of the Orinoco River in this South American nation is a sprawling factory that churns out 40 tractors a week; this is a joint venture between Tehran and Caracas with a bus factory and a cement plant soon to come. Iran plans to invest a sizeable $9 billion in 125 projects in Venezuela.

Caracas's close ties to Havana are a matter of public record. Cuba, which has invested heavily in human capital, has supplied Venezuela with 14,000 doctors who now provide free treatment to the poor. This is not to mention the 3,000 Cuban medical staff who were deployed to South Asia recently in the wake of the 2005 earthquake in Pakistan. Within 48 hours of Hurricane Katrina Cuba offered to send 1,600 doctors to the Gulf Coast, plus 36 tons of medical supplies but this urgent offer went unanswered. Hundreds died, mostly poor and Black, due to a lack of aid and treatment. That China has tightened relations with Cuba of late, has provided Havana with even more flexibility in making such generous offers.

What is of ultimate concern to US imperialism is that an alternative power center is developing in Beijing, which makes it difficult for Washington to bring to heel nations like Venezuela, Iran, the DPRK, Cuba and Zimbabwe. Yet instead of a calm and calculated assessment that would reveal that this turn of events is due to the weakening position of US imperialism and the disastrous decisions it has made over the years, including invading Iraq, aligning with China against the former USSR some three decades ago and generally seeking to stem the inexorable tide of history, Washington has sought scapegoats and Chinas ascension inevitably has attracted jealous attention.

This mordant concern reached an apogee in October 2006 when Bush signed a new national space policy that rejects future arms control agreements that might limit US flexibility in space and asserts a right to deny access to space to anyone hostile to US interests. This chilling document, which reads like something out of bad science fiction, stresses national security, encourages private enterprise and characterizes the role of US space diplomacy largely in terms of persuading other nations to support US policy. Worried observers argued that this initiative was simply a prelude to introducing weapons systems into the orbit of planet Earth.

Thus, as recent as 2004 the Air Force announced a doctrine that detailed how protecting US satellites and spacecraft may require deception, disruption, denial, degradation, and destruction targeting various foes. When in September 2006 the US military leaked the alleged secret that Beijing supposedly had tried to disrupt the orbit of a US satellite, it came clear even to the most obtuse who this new space initiative was targeting: China, of course.

It is difficult to overestimate the abject danger of this latest turn in the military strategy of US imperialism. It is not enough to jeopardize life on Earth, now Washington seeks to place the entire solar system in peril. But like global bullies of the past, US imperialism will discover to its dismay that it is much too late to play King Canute seeking to stem the tides of history. Chinas rise is inexorable, as is the crisis of US imperialism.

FROM CRISIS TO CATASTROPHE? WHAT IS TO BE DONE IN EASTERN EUROPE

Political Affairs, March 2022

The end of the cold war was the beginning of the America unipolar moment. But the "end of history" was followed by contradiction and arrogance which brought the conflict in Ukraine into being.

The current crisis in the Ukraine will inevitably eventuate as that rarity: a turning point in world history. This involves a number of main points:

First, it clarifies that the preceding epoch, the Cold War, presumably ending in December 1991 with the collapse of the Soviet Union, will likely be seen in the future as a catastrophic success for U.S. imperialism.

A success to be sure—at least in the short term—as it inaugurated the rapidly receding era of "unipolarity" and the heyday of the "sole remaining superpower."

But to attain this success, Washington executed a trio of critical blunders: there was the turbo-charging of religious zealotry that led initially to the alliance in Afghanistan in the 1980s that contributed to the demise of the Soviet Union— then the attack on New York and Washington in 2001 and the ignominious ouster of the U.S. from that same South Asian nation in August 2021. Whatever the case, it is evident that we have not heard the last of the zealots, especially since they receive covert and overt aid from certain friendly regimes, Saudi Arabia not least.

Then, when Washington forced the dissolution of the USSR, this allowed Moscow to cease subsidizing Moldova, Turkestan, Georgia and formerly socialist regimes in the vicinity. This allowed Russia to husband its resources leading to what Stanford scholar, Kathryn Stoner terms in her latest tome: "Russia Resurrected," a self-explanatory title that speaks to the development of hypersonic missiles and an agricultural superpower and a nation that can turn geopolitical tides in Syria among other sites. Imperialism failed to acknowledge that Russia had outgrown the sellout years of Boris Yeltsin and adamantly refused to adapt accordingly. NATO should have collapsed in 1991 when the USSR did but instead extended its remit to Libya, along with destroying the former Yugoslavia and devastating Afghanistan.

And, above all—and ironically—the intervention in the Ukraine occurred as we were marking the 50th anniversary of yet another turning point: the U.S.-China entente of February 1972 on an anti-Soviet basis with the payoff to Beijing being massive direct foreign investment creating a juggernaut that bids fair to leave imperialism sprawling in the dust.

Indeed, arguably, it is the specter of China that drove imperialist strategy toward Russia. That is, confronting Beijing directly means a faceoff with Tesla and Apple and Microsoft and Starbucks and KFC and a slew of U.S. giants, whereas weakening China's major partner—Russia—is more palatable, at least for the time being.

That is why, as I write, it is not only regime change in Kiev that is at issue: imperialism seeks regime change in Moscow, with all the dangers attendant with regard to toppling a nuclear power.

The ostensible issue —Ukraine joining the U.S. dominated NATO—would mean a rise in the stock price of Raytheon (former home of Pentagon chief, Lloyd Austin) and Lockheed Martin, as member states are required to spend more on advanced weaponry, which inevitably comes from these corporations.

With Germany pledging to re-arm, we also witness the shortsightedness of world imperialism, which refuses to learn the lessons of the 20th century, especially the catastrophe of world war ending with the uncovering of industrial funeral pyres in 1945. Not only Washington but London, Brussels and Paris should be shuddering right now.

Of course, since Germany will now be buying natural gas from Texas—and not Russia—this will satiate Washington: for the time being.

France is particularly culpable since Paris blathers and bloviates constantly about "strategic autonomy" but is so dependent upon Washington for aerial and satellite assets to keep a lid on its neo-empire in Africa, that it is paralyzed.

Brussels, Paris and Berlin apparently are unfamiliar with the recent memoir by sacked National Security honcho for Trump—John Bolton—who admitted that the 45th U.S. President saw the European Union as second only to China as an antagonist.

And this crisis in Ukraine will reinvigorate EU vassalage to U.S. imperialism.

However, the underlying contradiction of this crisis is historical: a glance at the map reveals that much of European territory is Russian and this huge nation still has a population twice the size of that of the Number 2: Germany.

In sum, while Western Europe was getting fat from the plunder of the Americas and Africa in recent centuries, Russia was moving eastward—often at the expense of China—and establishing its window on the Pacific in 1860: Vladivostok.

Thus, Western Europe was becoming a global power at the same time that it did not necessarily rule its home continent. Two centuries ago, Napoleon sought to resolve this anomalous contradiction by invading Russia—and being soundly defeated. A few decades later in the 1850s there was the Crimean War as, again, France, Britain and Turkey ganged up on Russia.

Then there was the final self-inflicted wound when in 1905 London financed the Japanese attack on Russia, which backfired spectacularly in that it wounded white supremacy grievously as Du Bois, Ho Chi Minh, Sun Yat Sen and Nehru all recognized. But it also led to the transformative Bolshevik Revolution of 1917 that inaugurated the General Crisis of Capitalism itself— which has yet to dissipate—then was punctuated by the Tokyo payback in 1941–1942, when the British Empire was devastated when its cash cows of Hong Kong and Singapore were seized by Japan.

A few decades later, as noted, Washington repeated the blunder of building up Asia to confront Moscow when in 1972 the entente with China was brokered.

Russia is the equivalent of the "whale" in Melville's "Moby Dick," the pursuit of which drives the North Atlantic bloc into crazed self-destruction.

Of course, Russia was not standing still as it sought to weaken European colonialism in Africa when in the 1890s it armed Abyssinian/Ethiopia to the teeth as it defeated Italian invaders.

Then under Soviet rule doing the same in Southern Africa from the 1960s to Southern Africa independence culminating in 1994 with the election of Nelson Mandela.

Of course, the Black community—or at least many among us—are culpable in that since the "Compromise of 1954," anti-Jim Crow concessions in return for the ditching of our internationalists led by Paul Robeson, ill prepared us to understand global affairs or even capitalize upon an often-favorable international situation.

Then there is the U.S. left which during the Cold War, assured us that once the alleged albatross of the Soviet Union disappeared, radicals and progressives would be liberated: instead, we see the emergence of right-wing populists in Eastern Europe (Poland and Hungary particularly), not to mention Washington. In France, the presidential election is today characterized by a surfeit of these types with the once mighty Communists and Socialists on the back foot.

There are many lessons to draw from today's crisis but among them must be not only a better understanding of history and the international correlation of forces—but also stronger collectives by which we can take advantage of propitious moments.

PART III:
RESISTANCE

TOKYO BOUND: AFRICAN AMERICANS AND JAPAN CONFRONT WHITE SUPREMACY

Souls Journal, Volume 3 Issue 3, 2001.

In the period before World War II, Japan was probably the nation most admired among African Americans. Du Bois, Garvey, Booker T. Washington, and others may have had conflicts among themselves, but all looked to Tokyo as evidence that modernity was not solely the province of those of European descent and that the very predicates of white supremacy made no sense.

This is an important point to consider for many reasons. Those who have focused on the appeal of the former Soviet Union to Americans need to consider that the choice was not necessarily between the herrenvolk democracy of the United States and the imperfect socialism of Moscow, but Imperial Japan was also considered as an alternative. Furthermore, historians have increasingly begun to point to external factors as a major reason for why Jim Crow began to crumble in the United States; this is usually put in the context of the Cold War, Soviet aid to African liberation movements, and the indisputable point that Washington had difficulty winning hearts and minds in Africa and elsewhere among the world's majority as long as peoples of African descent were faced with Jim Crow. This focus on external factors as a cause for the erosion of Jim Crow is also important because it sheds light on why progress toward racial equality tends to flag when external pressure seems to lessen, for example, today. But in assessing this external factor, we must take into account the specter of Japan, particularly in the first four decades of the twentieth century, and not just the USSR from 1917 to 1991.

In addition, scholars on the left have been criticized for not treating race as an independent variable, as an unmediated factor. Bringing Japan into the equation suggests the difficulty of seeking to treat race as an independent variable, however, just as the fact that scholars doing historical research on race— even those examining the first four decades of the twentieth century—commit scholarly malpractice when they fail to take Tokyo into account.

To be fair, part of the difficulty in unravelling Japan's influence is the reticence of European and Euro-American elites when it came to confronting the race question beyond the black-white dyad. For example, in fighting the inaugural war of U.S. imperialism—the war against the Philippines at the turn of the twentieth century—one general order of the U.S. Army declared that "such delicate subjects as . . . the race question, etc. will not be discussed at all except among ourselves officially."[1] This trend continued during the Pacific War. Theodore White, one of the most highly regarded U.S. journalists of the twentieth century, acknowledged during his tenure in China

---

1   Brian McAllister Lin, *Guardians of Empire: The U.S. Army and the Pacific, 1902–1940* (Chapel Hill: University of North Carolina Press, 1997), p.60.

during the war that "the ethic of the time forbade one from reporting in terms of race."

Frank Furedi, who has authored one of the more salient books on race in recent years, writes that not only was there reticence, but, as well, "[It] is striking how little racist thinking was questioned before the Second World War. Even radical critics of imperialism were reluctant to criticize the racist justification for national expansion." Referring mostly to Europe, he adds "It is striking to note how much more willing writers were to discuss class rather than race." The fear of racial revenge, which, unlike class revenge, conceivably did not have limits, at least as far as Europeans were concerned, "was a major reason for this relative silence."[2]

James Belich, the leading scholar of the titanic wars that led to a stalemate between the British invaders and the indigenous people of New Zealand, argued that as a result of this humbling episode, Great Britain resorted to its "final safety net," which was "to forget."[3]

John Dower writes,

> If one asks Americans today in what ways World War II was racist and atrocious, they will point overwhelmingly to the Nazi genocide of the Jews. When the war was being fought, however, the enemy perceived to be most atrocious by Americans was not the Germans but the Japanese and the racial issues that provoked greatest emotion among Americans were associated with the

---

2   Frank Furedi, *The Silent War: Imperialism and the Changing Perception of Race* (London: Pluto Press, 1998), p.164.

3   Ibid., pp.6,101.

> war in Asia . . . Japan's aggression stirred the deepest
> recesses of white [supremacy] and provoked a response
> bordering on the apocalyptic.[4]

The war with Japan awakened the idea of racial revenge, that Japanese in league with African Americans and other Asians would seek retribution for a racialized colonialism and imperialism. So provoked, European and Euro-American elites moved, even as the war was unfolding, to begin the reluctant and agonized retreat from apartheid, though like a child awakening from a nightmare, they largely chose to forget a major reason why they were taking this monumental step.

Such a retreat was far from the mind of Commodore Matthew C. Perry of the U.S. military when he stepped onto the shores of Japan in 1853, prying that nation out of more than two centuries of self-imposed isolation. Interestingly, at this turning point in world history, Perry decided to wade ashore, "marching between two orderlies, both tall and stalwart Negroes."[5] Other than the fact that in the nineteenth century a disproportionate number of U.S. sailors were black, it is unclear why Perry chose to be accompanied by Negroes at this fraught moment. Perhaps he thought that the fact that Euro-Americans could subordinate and subjugate "tall and stalwart Negroes" would convince the Japanese of the invaders' power while warning them of what fate awaited them if they did not acquiesce.

---

4   James Belich, *The New Zealand Wars and the Victorian Interpretation of Racial Conflict* (Auckland: Auckland University Press), pp.321, 235.

5   John Dower, *Japan in War and Peace: Essays on History, Culture and Race* (London: Fontana, 1996), pp.258–259.

Japan took the hint and over the next few decades engineered an amazing turnaround that led to the construction of the first major non-European power by the end of the century.

Rather quickly, Japan became a beacon of attraction for African Americans, who thought they could learn lessons from Tokyo in how to subdue white supremacy. W.E.B. Du Bois was among the many Africans and Asians who saw the beginning of the end for white supremacy in Japan's defeat of Russia in 1905, since, as he wrote, "The Negro problem in America is but a local phase of a world problem."[6] In 1912, Booker T. Washington told an inquiring Japanese correspondent,

> Speaking for the masses of my own race in this country I think I am safe in saying that there is no other race outside of America whose fortunes the Negro peoples of this country have followed with greater interest or admiration . . . in no other part of the world have the Japanese people a larger number of admirers and well-wishers than among the black people of the United States.[7]

A few years later, the FBI reported nervously that Marcus Garvey "preached that the next war will be between the Negroes and the whites unless their demands for justice are

6   Samuel Eliot Morison, 'Old Bruin': Commodore Matthew C. Perry, 1794–1858 (Boston: Little, Brown, 1967), p.332.

7   W.E.B. Du Bois, "The Color Line Belts the World," in Herbert Aptheker, ed., Writings by W.E.B. Du Bois in Periodicals Edited by Others (Millwood, N.Y.: Kraus-Thomson, 1982), p.330 (from Collier's Weekly, October 20, 1906).

recognized, and that with the aid of the Negroes, they will be able to win such a war."[8]

Du Bois, Washington and Garvey were simply express-ing the widespread admiration for Japan that permeated Afro-America. To cite one example, members of the African Methodist Episcopal (AME) Church, according to one scholar, "believed that the ability of Japanese to compete with Europeans and Americans on their own terms dispelled the myth of white superiority. Thus, AME leaders wholeheartedly supported the Japanese in the war against Russia...Japan fasci-nated church members, who demanded information on every aspect of Japanese life and culture."[9]

Of course, the organization that was to become the Nation of Islam was probably the most zealous of the pro-Tokyo ele-ments in Black America, with its leader Elijah Muhammad even going so far as to claim that Negroes were "Asiatic", not African. But even before he arrived at this conclusion, others had beaten him to the punch. Harry Dean was a grandson of the legendary Paul Cuffee. In the early nineteenth century, Cuffee may have been the most prominent African American in the nation, and certainly one of the most affluent in that he controlled a num-ber of ships. In the late 1890s, Dean, who stressed, "I am an African and proud of it," sailed to southeast Africa, where he

8   Booker T. Washington to Naoichi Masaoka, December 5, 1912, in Louis Harlan and Raymond W. Smock eds., *Booker T. Washington Papers, Volume 12: 1912–1914* (Urbana: University of Illinois Press), p.84.

9   "Bureau of Investigation Reports," New York City, December 5, 1918, in Robert A. Hill, ed., *The Marcus Garvey and Universal Negro Improvement Association Papers, Volume 1, 1826-August 1919* (Berkeley: University of California Press, 1983), p.306.

encountered a chief whose "name was Teo Saga" ands who was "more Japanese than African." Dean was told that

> Before the cataclysm in South Africa, Madagascar, Sumatra, Java and even Korea and Japan were all connected by land, and formed a great, illustrious, and powerful empire. The people were highly cultured, the rulers rich and wise. When the great flood came over the land it left only the remote provinces. However that may be, one may still find such Japanese names as Teo Saga on the coast of Africa to this very day.[10]

This admiration for Japan was also reflected in literature. In 1913, *The Crisis*, journal of the NAACP, published a story that imagined a military alliance of Japan and Mexico against the United States, further supported by black deserters from the U.S. Army and the secession of Hawaii, led by angry Japanese Americans. The U.S. president was forced to appeal to Jed Blackburn, a Jack Johnson-type character who led a force of 10,000 black soldiers on a suicidal counterattack of Japan's invasion of Southern California.[11]

This literary provocation was matched across the Pacific. General Sato Kojiro's 1921 potboiler, *Japanese-American War*, imagined the surprise destruction of the U.S. Pacific fleet,

10 Lawrence C. Little, "A Quest for Self-Determination: The African Methodist Episcopal Church During the Age of Imperialism, 1884–1916," Ph.D. Dissertation, (Ohio State University, 1993), pp.227, 252.

11 Harry Dean, *Umbala: The New Adventures of a Negro Sea-Captain in Africa and on the Seven Seas in His Attempt to Found an Ethiopian Empire* (London: George G. Harrap, 1929), p.93.

occupation of Hawaii, and an invasion by Japanese forces of the U.S. mainland supported by 10 million Negroes led by Marcus Garvey. There was more about Garvey and black unrest in the 1924 nonfiction book *The Negro Problem* by Mitsukawa Kametaro.[12]

Interestingly, these stories mirrored real-life events. In 1916, the Plan of San Diego was revealed. This plan involved, it was alleged, an abortive attempt by Chicanos and Mexico, in league with Japan and other foreign powers, to dismember the United States—kill all white males in the West and Southwest and establish independent black and Indian republics while reclaiming territory for Mexico that had been lost to the United States when Mexico itself was dismembered seventy years earlier.

As this episode suggests, like other foreign nations seeking leverage over the United States, the Japanese catered to disaffected minorities. This was not a new tactic. France had a well merited reputation for brutality in colonizing West Africa, yet African Americans as ideologically diverse as Josephine Baker, Richard Wright, James Baldwin and others too numerous to mention viewed Paris as a welcoming second home. Of course, there are those in Tel Aviv today who view the Arab minority in that nation as something of a security threat, subject to being wooed by less than friendly neighbors.

The Diplomatic Archives in Tokyo reveal that the Japanese paid close attention to African Americans. They maintained details of blacks in the U.S. military; the racial breakdown of various states; and material on Negro illiteracy, death rates,

12   Kevin K. Gaines, *Uplifting the Race: Black Leadership, Politics and Culture in the Twentieth Century* (Chapel Hill: University of North Carolina Press, 1996), p.206.

occupational status, as well as lists of "influential Negro Leaders" and "important Negro publications."[13]

This attention from Japanese elites was mirrored among the Japanese masses. Walter White's novel *The Fire in the Flint* was translated into Japanese with the title changed to Lynching; this new edition was a best-seller due in no small part to a publicity campaign by the Japanese government pointing out that the novel pictured the kind of barbarian acts that were tolerated and even encouraged in a nation, the United States, that was then criticizing Japan's policies in China.[14] Even Japanese opposed to the policies of their government, for example, Katayama Sen—a founder of the Communist Parties of Japan, the United States, and Mexico, a man who had matriculated at Fisk University and was a friend of the Jamaican-American poet Claude McKay—likewise found U.S. racial policies abhorrent.

Increasingly, on both sides of the Pacific, a perception was growing among peoples of color that they had a common enemy in white supremacy. Certainly this was the viewpoint of W.E.B. Du Bois. He argued that the exclusion of Japanese from the United States had resulted from a deal between the South and the West in which the former endorsed the Oriental Exclusion Act of 1924 in exchange for the sacrifice of the Dyer federal anti-lynching bill. A similar analysis could be made concerning U.S. opposition to Japan's attempt to insert a clause concerning racial equality in the post-World War I Versailles treaty. White Southerners fearing what this might mean in terms of Negroes united with those in the Far West who were

---

13   David Levering Lewis, *W.E.B. Du Bois: The Fight for Equality and the American Century, 1919–1963* (New York: Henry Holt, 2000), p.392.

14   Reports, November 28, 1933, circa 1930s and 1940s, 1460-1-3, Diplomatic Archives, Tokyo.

concerned about what this might mean about Asian Americans and Native Americans. And of course Japan's bitter experiences at Versailles and with the 1924 anti-immigrant bill worsened relations between Tokyo and Washington.[15]

Of course, Japanese and Negroes faced similar racist rationales. Tom Ireland, a Euro-American who was regarded widely as one of Cleveland's finest men, with a B.A. from Princeton and an LL.B. from Harvard, wrote in 1935, "The Mongolian race is too divergent from a biological standpoint to intermarry or to assimilate with the Caucasian for the good of either."[16] "Such miscegenation," he added, is "invariably bad." Hence, unlike Europeans, Asians should be barred from the United States.[17]

Bruised by the indignities of white supremacy, Tokyo adroitly played on these sentiments and made a concerted and not unsuccessful attempt to win over the black community to pro-Japan positions. The popular historian of the black experience J.A. Rogers traveled to Ethiopia to cover the Italian invasion and brought the eager readers of his newspaper columns stories about a possible merger through marriage of the Japanese and Ethiopian royal families; of course, it would have been ludicrous—perhaps even an offense worthy of a lynching—to even suggest a comparable merger through marriage of, say, the British and Ethiopian royal families. Supposedly, Rogers was entertained royally in Japan and allegedly had

---

15   Walter White, *A Man Called White: The Autobiography of Walter White* (Athens: University of Georgia Press, 1995), p.69.

16   Lewis, *W.E.B. Du Bois*, p.416.

17   Tom Ireland, *War Clouds in the Skies of the Far East* (New York: G. P. Putnam, 1935), pp.288, 292.

promised Tokyo "favorable publicity" when he returned to the United States.[18]

On the other hand, Rogers may have had an incentive to provide favorable publicity, even setting aside the courting he supposedly received. Rogers wrote in the Amsterdam News in 1934, even before the Italian invasion of Ethiopia, that Japan was aiding Africa by selling cheap clothes there. Before the arrival of their cotton goods, he argued, Africans wore clothes until they were filthy, thus breeding "lice, typhus and other diseases." He quoted an "overworked doctor" in Tanganyika who said the "purchase of cheap Japanese rubber soled shoes has done more to check hookworm here than all the efforts of the health department." The flood of Japanese imports into British controlled territory was one of the many factors exacerbating tensions between the two island nations and accelerating the drive toward war.[19]

Because of their sympathy for Japan, many African Americans were less than sympathetic to China after the Japanese invasion in 1931. The Pittsburgh Courier writer Ira Lewis summed up the sentiments of many when he argued in a front-page article that "between the Japanese and the Chinese, the Negroes much prefer the Japanese. The Chinese are the worst 'Uncle Toms' and stooges that the white man has ever had." With barely concealed rancor, he added, "as soon as he gets a chop suey place which is anything like decent, the first

18 Patrick Washburn, *A Question of Sedition: The Federal Government's Investigation of the Black Press During World War II* (New York: Oxford University Press, 1986), p.261.

19 *New York Amsterdam News*, June 9, 1934.

thing he does is put up a color bar."[20] Du Bois tended to agree, as he contrasted invidiously what he saw as China's tepid response to racist U.S. immigration laws, compared with Japan's robust response. He too referred to Chinese as "Asian Uncle Toms" of "the same spirit that animates the 'white folks [Negro] in the United States.'"[21] Moreover, many African Americans in the Far West held firmly to the perception that Japanese Americans were much more willing to flout the dictates of Jim Crow and serve black customers in their restaurants and hotels than Chinese Americans, who were seen as much more willing to observe the dictates of antiblack racism.

Moreover, many blacks were overreacting to the denunciation in the mainstream U.S. press of the Japanese invasion in China, which they saw as hypocritical in light of these same papers' failure to condemn the white supremacy that Europe and the United States had imposed on Shanghai, for example. Du Bois summed up the thoughts of many African Americans when he posed this query on arriving in China in the 1930s: "Why is it," he inquired, "that you hate Japan more than Europe when you have suffered more from England, France and Germany than from Japan." Du Bois, for example, announced in late 1941, "The British Empire has caused more human misery than Hitler will cause if he lives a hundred years . . . it is idiotic to talk about a people who have brought the slave trade to its greatest development, who are the chief exploiters of Africa

---

20   Washburn, *A Question of Sedition*, p.110. *Pittsburgh Courier*, March 28, 1942.
21   *New York Amsterdam News*, November 18, 1931. Lewis, *W.E.B. Du Bois*, pp.413–415.

and who hold four hundred million Indians in subjection, as the great defenders of democracy."[22]

Months after Pearl Harbor, Adam Clayton Powell Jnr., concurred with Du Bois when he noted that the "difference between Nazism and crackerocracy is very small" since "crackerocracy [too] is a pattern of racial hatred."[23] Parenthetically, as I examine Chinese foreign policy in the 1970s in southern Africa, which featured alliances with apartheid South Africa and U.S. imperialism, it is difficult to escape the idea that African American intellectuals may have been on to something when they complained about China's willingness to collaborate with European and Euro-American imperialism.

Thus, as tensions rose between the United States and Japan in the 1930s, Tokyo came to realize that it might have an ally in the African Americans. This sentiment was cultivated assiduously by a number of Japanese nationals who resided in black communities, for example, Harlem. A keen example was Yasuichi Hikada, an animated, graying little man who always showed up at Negro social functions accompanied by a Negro woman. Like many Japanese nationals in New York who were collaborating with Tokyo, he worked for an affluent white family in Forest Hills while maintaining a residence in Harlem. He wrote an unpublished biography of Toussaint L'Ouverture and had one of the finest collections of books on blacks in New York, short of the Schomburg Library (he was also a close friend of Arthur Schomburg). As late as 1941 he appeared at a debate in Harlem where, as he put it idiomatically, "Chinese were Jim Crowed by whites"; he also referred to blacks as "our

22   *People's Voice*, May 2, 1942.
23   *People's Voice*, September 12, 1942.

darker brothers." Hikada was not unusual. W.C. Handy, composer of the "St. Louis Blues," recalled a Japanese cook who traveled about the country for five years as a member of his vaudeville troupe and who later turned out to be an eavesdropping Japanese army officer. The Japanese valet of actor Charlie Chaplin also turned out to be an agent of Tokyo.[24]

The U.S. government was not totally oblivious to these maneuvers. Before Pearl Harbor, U.S. intelligence agencies intercepted a Japanese message that spoke of their use of a "Negro literary critic" whose purpose was to "open a news service for Negro newspapers. The Negro press is so poor that it has no news service of its own and as I have told you in various messages, [we] had been getting relatively good results . . . because of the advantage we have in using men like this . . . as an experiment," the message went on ominously, "I am now instructing Mr. [name deleted] of the National Youth Administration, and a graduate of Amherst and Columbia to be a spy." The message continued, "in organizing our schemes among the Negroes . . . Washington . . . should be our hub"; though it was added, "in the arsenals of Philadelphia and Brooklyn there are also a few unskilled Negro laborers, so I would say that in the future there will be considerable profit in our getting Negroes to gather military intelligence for us . . . we have already established connections with very influential Negroes to keep us informed with regard to the Negro movement."[25] The scholar Tony Matthews has argued that Tokyo turned for spying to the

---

24 Roi Ottley, *Inside Black America* (London: Eyre & Spottiswoode, 1948), p.256.

25 Intercepted messages, July 2, 1941, May 9, 1941, Box 2, Frank D. Schuler Papers, Franklin D. Roosevelt Library, Hyde Park, New York.

"American Negroes, a massive force of largely disgruntled citizens, many of whom had a special racial axe to grind."[26]

Of course, the antifascist tendencies among African Americans should not be underestimated, though I should add that I find it striking that the man considered the "brains" of U.S. fascism—a man who met with Mussolini, attended the Nazi Party gathering at Nuremberg in 1937, and wrote voluminously—was a black graduate of Exeter and Harvard: I refer to Lawrence Dennis. On the other hand, it is arguable that pro-Japan organizations attracted many more adherents among blacks than their pro-Soviet counterparts. Thus, Robert Hill, the leading scholar of Garveyism, writes that the Pacific Movement of the Eastern World "gained a substantial black nationalist following during the 1930s. One longtime leader, David D. Erwin, claimed that it had forty thousand members in 1936, while other estimates went as high as one million."[27] Nor should we forget that one of the more influential organizations among African Americans today, the Nation of Islam, is a direct descendant of this pro-Tokyo movement.

Robert Leonard Jordan was one of the key leaders of this movement. Born in Jamaica in 1900, he moved to England at the age of fourteen, and at eighteen left on a Japanese ship; by 1920, like so many other Jamaicans, he was in Harlem. By 1936, he was President-General of the Ethiopia Pacific Movement, with an office at 204 Lenox Avenue in Harlem. That year he addressed a lengthy letter to the Japanese foreign minister, Hachiro Arita; the stationary listed one "T. Kikuchi," a Japanese

26   Tony Matthews, *Shadows Dancing: Japanese Espionage Against the West, 1939–1945* (London: Robert Hale, 1993), p.27.

27   Robert Hill, *The Marcus Garvey and Universal Negro Improvement Association Papers*, vol.7, p.506.

national, as the group's "chief business advisor." This letter, which can be found in the Diplomatic Archives in Tokyo, noted that "we the dark race of the Western Hemisphere through the Ethiopia Pacific Movement . . . are putting our entire confidence in the Japanese people with the hopes that in the very near future, we will desire a very close relationship with the Japanese government."[28]

Along with Elijah Muhammad, Jordan was among the most prominent of the pro-Tokyo spokesmen in the United States; certainly he was the most prominent of this group in Harlem. The FBI reported that while toiling for the aforementioned Japanese shipping company and residing in Japan he "found the Japanese to be very friendly to the Negroes and that he had the privilege of studying the customs of the Japanese and becoming a member of . . . society in Japan."[29]

By early 1942, Japan's largely successful invasion of Asia had revealed that many Asians saw no reason why they should fight for colonial masters who openly professed white supremacy in London and The Hague. African Americans like Jordan were arriving at the same conclusion. In January of that year, a meeting of black leaders voted thirty-six to five (with fifteen abstaining) that African Americans were not 100 percent behind the war. Before that, in 1939, the FBI reported that "'enlightened Negro leaders' had told them, that between eighty and ninety per cent of the American colored population who have any views on the subject at all, are pro-Japanese as a result of the

28 Robert Jordan to Hachiro Arita, November 18, 1936, A461, ET/ll, Diplomatic Archives, Tokyo.

29 J. Edgar Hoover to Jonathan Daniels, August 11, 1943, Box 6, 4245g, Official File, Franklin D. Roosevelt Papers, Franklin D. Roosevelt Library, Hyde Park, New York.

intensive Japanese propaganda among this racial group." Right after Pearl Harbor, one-half of the Negroes interviewed in New York City told black interviewers that they would be better off, or at least no worse off, under Japanese rule.[30]

Inferentially, on December 13, 1941—days after Pearl Harbor—the *Amsterdam News* revealed some of the linkages that tied blacks to Tokyo:

> Immediately following [Pearl Harbor, the NYPD] invaded Harlem and began rounding up all Japanese suspects. . . . In view of the fact that with the exception of marked facial distinction there is somewhat of a striking similarity in hue between the [Japanese] and many Harlemites . . . colored policemen played an invaluable role in the mass arrests. . . . the area on Lenox Avenue between 10th and 16th streets [is] noted for some [Japanese] restaurants . . . Many of the sons of Nippon . . . declared "me colored man, too" when they were tabbed.

Yet it was men like Jordan, and also Carlos Cooks, a man venerated by Elombe Brath, one of Harlem's leading black nationalists of today and a host of popular radio program on Pacifica Radio, who were in the vanguard of this trend. But as between Jordan and Cooks, it was the former who was probably better known in Harlem at the time. The People's Voice, a popular front newspaper that despised these nationalists, conceded that Jordan, whom it called the "Harlem Mikado," had

30 Marc Gallicchio, *The African American Encounter with Japan and China: Black Internationalism in Asia, 1895–1945* (Chapel Hill: University of North Carolina Press, 2000), pp.107,121,142.

an "eloquence [that] is said to have driven a number of competing street speakers to introduce [Japanese] propaganda in their
talks to hold audiences."

This evident ideological hegemony of Jordan apparently
drove the popular front in Harlem to distraction. *The People's
Voice* told its readers that Japan had a "BB Plan," that is

> Black Followers of Buddhism [which] preached
> Buddhism as the religion of people of color the world
> over [and] the key to racial success. . . . Under the
> BB Plan, American Negroes who become Buddhists
> automatically won Japanese citizenship, would get
> chances to visit Japan, study sciences and professions,
> receive military and naval training. . . . Success of the
> plan would mean establishment of a black empire in
> Africa. . . . *PV*'s investigations have uncovered the fact
> that there may be some connection between the world
> B plan and the activities of Duse Mohammed Ali.

In trumpeting this alliance between Buddhists and Muslims
and followers of Moorish Science, this left-wing paper noted
"the scope of the world B Plan of the Japanese is almost unbe-
lievable"; it scornfully denounced the "cunning of an Oriental
group" that has "gone back to the wars of the Crusaders in the
interest of Christianity."[31]

What had driven the popular front to the point of hysteria was the fear that pro-Japan sympathies among African
Americans, carefully cultivated over the years by Tokyo and
propelled by a vile white supremacy, could complicate the war

31   *People's Voice*, February 28, 1942, March 7, 1942, March 21, 1942.

effort and lead to the victory of the anti-Comintern Axis. In the fall of 1942, many of these pro-Tokyo blacks were arrested. The indictment of James Thornhill, one of these leaders in New York, charged that he said that "colored United States soldiers should not fight the Japanese" and that, like the man who became Malcolm X, he might "shoot the wrong man" if drafted and given a rifle. Thornhill was also born in the Caribbean, in the U.S. Virgin Islands; like Jordan he derisively referred to the United States as the "United Snakes of America." Repeatedly he told Harlemites, "you should learn Japanese"; "when they tell you to remember Pearl Harbor, you [should] reply, Remember Africa." With fervor he added, "the white man brought you to this country in 1619, not to christianize you but to enslave you. This thing called Christianity is not worth a damn. I am not a Christian, we should be . . . Moslems."[32]

With evident anxiety, the FBI reported in 1943 that "numerous complaints have been received that the American Negroes favor a Japanese victory in the present war."[33] This sentiment was not unique to black Americans. The Colonial Secretary in Kingston, Jamaica, was told in 1941 that at one "Cold Supper Shop" there was frequent "anti-British talk" heard via the "wireless."[34] It should not be forgotten, even when analyzing communists' approach to the war, that it was

32 *USA v. James Thornhill*, Southern District Court of New York, Box 1049, R33.18.2.5, C-113-264, 1942, National Archives and Records Administration, New York City.

33 Robert Hill, ed., *The FBI's RACON: Racial Conditions in the United States During World War II* (Boston: Northeastern University Press, 1995), p.81.

34 FBI to Colonial Secretary, September 4, 1941, "Fifth Column Activity", 1B/5/77/49, CSO 750, 1941, National Archives of Jamaica.

hard for many, particularly those of African descent, to accept the argument that Britain was the fountainhead of democracy, particularly when Churchill already had announced that the Atlantic Charter's promise of democracy did not apply to those subjected to a racialized colonialism. Even Hugh Mulzac, a member in good standing of the popular front, wrote that there was a "strong feeling among colored Americans in 1941 that the colonial powers be allowed to destroy each other. As a former British subject I felt this keenly."[35]

Thus, just as black nationalists expressed outright sympathy for Tokyo, some blacks on the left found it difficult to provide unalloyed support for the Allies in light of the latter's white supremacy. As Du Bois put it, "If Hitler wins, down with the blacks! If the democracies win, the blacks are already down."[36] The Allies were well aware of this black hostility to white supremacy that made Africans worldwide susceptible to Tokyo's siren call. Hence, during the war, the British Colonial Office was reluctant to initiate an anti-German campaign among West Africans because officials calculated that such propaganda might encourage a revolt against rule as such. "Having been encouraged to hate one branch of the white race, they may extend the feeling to others," warned one memorandum.[37]

Strikingly, the ideological ancestors of today's black conservatives also were both sympathetic to Tokyo and highly critical of the Allies. George Schuyler is Exhibit A in that regard. A prolific journalist and novelist, he too had been courted by

---

35   Hugh Mulzac, *A Start to Steer By* (New York: International Publishers, 1963), p.129.

36   Ibid.; Lewis *W.E.B. Du Bois*, p.467.

37   Ibid.; Furedi, *The Silent War*, p.184.

Tokyo and wrote a series of articles on Japan in the 1930s that were so pro-Nippon that his publisher refused to print them.[38]

In September 1940, as many black communists were scoring Tokyo because of its policies in China, Schuyler took an opposite tack; he saw this invitation as an exemplar of the progressive deflation of white supremacy and arrogance in the Orient. Where white men once strutted and kicked coolies into the street, they now tread softly and talk in whispers. . . . The Japanese have done a fine job in making the white man in Asia lose "face" and shattering the sedulously nurtured idea of white supremacy. Of course the white people hate them because they fear them.[39]

In his withering denunciation of white supremacy, the conservative Schuyler often used rhetoric that would have made black nationalists proud. By 1944, the fervor in the black community for the Double V campaign against fascism at home and abroad had dissipated as many shifted to a pro-Allies stance. But not George Schuyler. Days after D-Day in Europe, he wrote acerbically that

> the Europeans have been a menace to the rest of the world for the past four hundred years, carrying destruction and death wherever they went...True, their system of world fleecing directly benefited only a handful of Europeans, but indirectly it benefited millions of supernumeraries, labor officials and skilled workers... Europe has been a failure and a menace. The European

38 George Schuyler, *Black Empire* (Boston: Northeastern University Press, 1991), p.281.
39 *Pittsburgh Courier*, September 12,1940.

age is passing. One can derive a certain pleasure from observing its funeral.[40]

Schuyler was also probably the staunchest critic of the internment of Japanese Americans in the United States, returning to this subject again and again. That this internment, he asserted, was "a scheme to grab [Japanese-American] holdings and hand them over to white people is shown by the efforts to prevent Negroes from taking them over. . . . This may be a prelude to our own fate. Who knows? . . . Once the precedent is established with 70,000 Japanese-Americans," he added ominously, "it will be easy to denationalize millions of Afro-American citizens."[41]

Ironically, after the war concluded, U.S. elites cracked down on the black communists, who were harshest in their condemnation of Tokyo, whereas those like Schuyler who took an opposing position were promoted. Interestingly, black communists who were the most consistently anti-Tokyo force among blacks during the war suffered most after Tokyo was defeated. The assault on black Reds created favorable conditions for the rise of black nationalists, who had been pro-Tokyo; thus the organization that was to become the Nation of Islam rose, just as the popular front and the left in the black community diminished.

The end of the war also marked the decline of pro-Tokyo sentiments among African Americans as Japan became a reliable ally of Washington. Indeed, the kind of sympathy for Asia that these pro-Tokyo movements symbolized did not arise again until the era of Maoist China.

On the other hand, this veritable race war, in which those who defined themselves as "white" seemed to be losing in the

40 *Pittsburgh Courier,* June 17, 1944.
41 *Pittsburgh Courier,* April 25, 1942, May 29, 1943.

early stages of the conflict, helped to convince sober-minded elites in Washington to retreat from the more egregious aspects of white supremacy. Even as the war was unfolding the United States sought to do away with the "white primary," which limited black voting rights, and struck from the books most of the Chinese exclusion laws. There is nothing like the prospect of losing a race war to convince even the most obtuse of the necessity of eroding racism.

Still, in 1944, during the height of the war, Du Bois concluded, "The greatest and most dangerous race problem today is the problem of relations between Asia and Europe."[42] Yet in the United States today, the race discourse not only simply focuses on the just the black-white dyad but refuses to stray beyond the shores of this nation. Indeed, though black intellectuals of an earlier era wrote voluminously about Asia, few do so today. This may be because blacks of an earlier day, because they were effectively denied citizenship, perforce were compelled to be internationalist; ironically, part of the downside of full citizenship rights has been the erosion of black internationalism. Moreover, the decision made decades ago to shroud the race question in Asia has borne fruit in the form of helping some to think that the vaunted "color-blind" approach characterizes relations between those of Asian and European descent. This misconception is heightened by the use of the vague term "Westerner," which is used to describe Europeans who reside to the west of Asia as well as Australians and New Zealanders who live east of there. African Americans are no longer "Tokyo bound," but race remains a global concern.

---

42   W. E. B. Du Bois, "Prospect of a World Without Race Conflict," *American Journal of Sociology*, Vol. 49, no.5 (March 1944), pp.450–456; quote from p.451.

SHIRLEY GRAHAM DU BOIS: PORTRAIT OF THE BLACK WOMAN ARTIST AS A REVOLUTIONARY

NYU Press, 2009

Shirley Graham Du Bois pulled Malcolm X aside at a party in the Chinese embassy in Accra, Ghana, in 1964, only months after having met with him at Hotel Omar Khayyam in Cairo, Egypt.[1] When she spotted him at the embassy, she "immediately . . . guided him to a corner where they sat" and talked for "nearly an hour." Afterward, she declared proudly, "This man is brilliant. I am taking him for my son. He must meet Kwame [Nkrumah]. They have too much in common not to meet."[2] She personally saw to it that they did.

In Ghana during the 1960s, Black Nationalists, Pan-Africanists, and Marxists from around the world mingled in many of the same circles. Graham Du Bois figured prominently in this diverse—sometimes at odds—assemblage. On the personal level she informally adopted several "sons" of Pan-Africanism such as Malcolm X, Kwame Nkrumah, and

---

1   David Gallen, ed., *Malcolm X: The FBI File* (New York: Carroll and Graf, 1992), 331.

2   Maya Angelou, *All God's Children Need Traveling Shoe s* (New York: Random House, 1986), 138, 141.

Stokely Carmichael. On the political level she was a living per-
sonification of the "motherland" in the political consciousness
of a considerable number of African Americans engaged in
the Black Power movement. That is, if Black—mostly male—
radicals saw Africa as the geopolitical epicenter that would
"give birth" to the global struggle against racism and colonialism, Graham Du Bois served as a Pan-Africanist matriarch and
elder to help guide this process.

Yet Shirley Graham Du Bois's pioneering efforts as an
African American female artist, Pan-Africanist, and Marxist
have been marginalized in conventional discourse on the "Who's
Who" of twentieth-century Black radical figures. Graham Du
Bois's historical contribution is often delimited by her prominent status as the wife of W. E. B. Du Bois, towering African
American intellectual and honorary "Father of Pan-Africanism."
Indeed, her radicalism climaxed *after* the death of her husband
in 1963. Remaining in Ghana from 1963 to 1966, Graham Du
Bois played a central role in actively supporting Nkrumah's
political strategy: namely, gaining full and complete independence from the West by thwarting the economic domination of
the North Atlantic powers throughout Africa—and, moreover,
championing socialism as an alternative socioeconomic system
on the continent. Therefore, she might have been shocked,
but she was not necessarily surprised when, on the morning of
February 24, 1966, she found herself under house arrest after
the Ghanaian military staged a coup to oust Kwame Nkrumah
from power. At sixty-nine years of age, Graham Du Bois was
about to embark on another life—one of her many lives—by
resituating herself geographically, emotionally, and politically,
settling in Cairo and spending time intermittently in the United
States, China, and Tanzania.

The journey as a political activist began relatively late in Graham Du Bois's life, but the long road she had traveled as Shirley Graham, a working-class—albeit prolific—artist and mother, provided the existential basis for her subsequent commitment to transformative politics. Born in Indianapolis, Indiana, in 1896, Graham had spent much of her adulthood as a Black single mother whose later pursuit of antiracist activism and Marxism was undoubtedly influenced by the personal struggles she faced as a black woman in America's Jim Crow labor market based on the superexploitation of Black women. In short, as the Great Depression left millions of Americans without sufficient employment, shelter, or food, Graham was among the countless Black women who were compelled to work intermittently as household servants in order to feed their families.

As we shall see, in her efforts to become a renowned artist, she was continually negotiating within a dominant cultural apparatus in which she had to adhere to social mores of both "Negro" and female "respectability" if she hoped to secure any recognition from her peers, much less any financial compensation to be put toward her household. Yet she served as a composer, actor, director, producer, and musician all by the age of thirty eight. Certainly these achievements would be remarkable by any standard, but even more so for a working-class Black woman of her time. Further still, she was positioned from a working-class standpoint that, though not immediately reflected in her art, laid the basis for her intensifying angst with the class-based system of white supremacy in the United States.

But if the material basis for Graham's lifelong dedication to transformative politics was fundamentally rooted in her struggles as an adult, then some seeds of this incipient "race woman" were also sown during her childhood while under the influence of her father, David Graham. Reverend Graham was a "race man" in his own right, serving as a proud member of the National Association for the Advancement of Colored People and promulgating the cause of "racial uplift" championed by its leader and his daughter's future spouse, W. E. B. Du Bois. But her father's affinity for "talented tenth" leadership did not hinder his commitment to organizing everyday Black people for militant direct action against Jim Crow racism. Graham recalled her father once leading a prayer service with a loaded gun over his Bible while they were living in New Orleans, calling upon the women and children to clear the church while he and twenty-one men, locked and loaded, remained and prepared to ward off an encroaching lynch mob.[3]

Because she was a woman, Graham was encouraged by her father to revere the power of the pen over that of the sword to effect social change. Strikingly, in Graham's adulthood, she would come to champion the power of both the pen and the sword, ostensibly gender-bound forms of resistance. While residing in Colorado Springs at the age of thirteen, Graham wrote in to a local paper, unleashing her personal anger with racial segregation after having been denied entry into a Young Women's Christian Association site because she was Black. "You are now thirteen . . . young but not too young to speak out in protest against this kind of evil by a so-called Christian organization," her father advised. And she dutifully adhered.[4] If in her

---

3   Shirley Graham Du Bois article on coup, *Essence*, January 1971, Shirley Graham Du Bois Papers, courtesy of David Du Bois, Cairo, Egypt; Shirley Graham Du Bois, "What Happened in Ghana? The Inside Story," *Freedomways* (Spring 1966): 201–223, 220.

4   Shirley Graham Du Bois, "I Got Wings," short story (ts. draft), n.d., Shirley Graham Du Bois Papers, Subseries F, Fiction works,

later years Graham Du Bois tended to favor Pan-Africanism over Marxism, perhaps her eyewitness accounts of Black workers struggling against Jim Crow without the support of their white class brethren were an important causal factor; the white female companion who witnessed Graham being denied entry at the YWCA did not come to her defense.[5]

The contradiction, however, is that David Graham inculcated in the young Shirley a responsibility to challenge segregation in the "public sphere" only to enforce normative gender roles in the "private sphere." He instilled in his daughter the commonplace notion that a woman's primary social identity ought to be as a mother and caretaker. She was therefore taken hostage by the norms of "mothering," norms that reinforced the social division of labor between men and women, and thus she spent the better part of her youth caring for her siblings and assisting her mother in household tasks. In time, however, Graham turned her "mothering" skills into a political weapon through which she later—armed with ideologies of Marxism and Pan-Africanism—defended "race men" such as W. E. B. Du Bois and Kwame Nkrumah.

Anchored though she was in the domestic sphere, Graham found the leverage to excel intellectually and artistically as a

Schlesinger Library, Radcliffe Institute. See also Robert Dee Thompson Jr., "A Socio-biography of Shirley Graham Du Bois: A Life in the Struggle" (Ph.D. diss., University of California–Santa Cruz, 1997), 14–17.

5   Shirley Graham Du Bois, interview by Abigail Simon, April 10, 1974, Shirley Graham Du Bois Papers; Shirley Graham Du Bois, *His Day Is Marching On* (Philadelphia: Lippincott, 1971), 30, 31; Thompson, "A Socio-biography of Shirley Graham-Du Bois," 22–30.

young adult.[6] But opportunities for African American women, even those as brilliant as Shirley Graham, were slim in the Pacific Northwest during World War II, and after high school she attended a trade school where she qualified as an office clerk, eventually landing in Seattle. There she met and soon after married Shadrach T. McCants in 1921.[7] By the age of twenty-five she transitioned, albeit reluctantly, into the role of a wife and mother, and bore two sons, Robert in 1923 and David in 1925.

The details of her marriage to McCants from 1921 to 1927 are among the most obscure in her life, but she remained relatively stationary both geographically and professionally for the duration of the marriage. She retrospectively obscured her own biography during these years, proclaiming falsely that McCants had died in the 1920s. However, what emerges quite clearly is the fact that their two sons would remain the single most important personal and political anchors in her life. In her words, "Everything I did, everything I planned, everything I tried to do was motivated by my passionate desire to make a

6   She graduated as the class valedictorian at her Tennessee-based junior high school and later received high honors upon graduation from Lewis and Clark High School in the state of Washington, where her family had relocated in 1915. Too, she was recognized as the class poet and won an essay contest for a piece she composed on Booker T. Washington, indicating an interest in a figure to whom she would later dedicate an entire biography.

7   Elizabeth Brown-Guillory, ed., *Wines in the Wilderness: Plays by African-American Women from the Harlem Renaissance to the Present* (Westport, CT: Greenwood, 1990), 79. However, on her first passport application she listed her date of marriage as July 16, 1918; see file 100–99729– 84A, October 28, 1958, Federal Bureau of Investigation.

good life for my sons."[8] As a mother, Graham factored her sons into the equation of every subsequent calculation. Further still, as an analogue to this ideology of maternalism, she figured influential men into her life choices, making it her business to defend such leaders as Du Bois, Nkrumah, and Malcolm even when her efforts were met with harsh resistance.

But her anchor within the domestic sphere quickly gave way with Graham's divorce from McCants, and she at once became a globe-trotter, taking off for France in 1927, when, according to Tyler Stovall, "blackness became the rage in Paris during the 1920s." In Paris she became acquainted with prominent African Americans such as Eric Walrond, onetime editor of Marcus Garvey's newspaper, *Negro World*, and writer for the Urban League's journal, *Opportunity*.[9] Here too she encountered various forms of African music that she incorporated into her first opera entitled *TomTom*. But Graham remained a single mother who had financial responsibilities associated with her two sons, who remained in the United States under the care of her mother. Therefore, during her ventures in Paris with the Black artist community from 1927 to 1930, she returned to the States intermittently to tend to her children and augment her income, working as a music librarian at Howard University and as a music teacher at what now is Morgan State University, while taking summer classes at Columbia University.

Graham was not directly engaged with the political struggles at Howard that were sharpening in the wake of the Great

8   Graham Du Bois, *His Day Is Marching On*, 37–39.

9   Irma Watkins-Owens, *Blood Relations: Caribbean Immigrants and the Harlem Community, 1900–1930* (Bloomington: Indiana University Press, 1996), 156–157; Eric Walrond, *Tropic Death* (New York: Collier, 1972).

Depression in 1929, but she was there during a wave of student strikes in the late 1920s.[10] In the process of becoming a pioneering Black woman composer, she produced an early version of *Tom-Tom* in 1929 while at Morgan State with the teamwork of trailblazing Black male artists such as actor Roland Hayes, director Randolph Edmonds, and filmmaker Carlton Moss.[11] Most notable about the opera was the way in which it fused "Harlem cabarets" with African rhythm, representing the "beating heart of a people."[12] In a time when the Jim Crow United States was overwhelmingly averse to taking Africa seriously as an origin of modern culture, this opera boldly placed Africa at the center of the African American experience in North America from slavery to freedom.

But *Tom-Tom* also adhered to the predominant cultural norms of the society because it portrayed Africans as a fundamentally emotional, rather than intellectual, political—much less proletarian—people. Even her female dancers staged a protest prior to one performance by refusing to wear only rags for

---

10 She might have even crossed paths with Malcolm Nurse. Nurse, alias George Padmore, was a prominent student organizer on the campus, and, as a member of the Communist Party of the United States, he was soon to become a leading Black member of the Communist International commissioned with the task of organizing Black workers, particularly seamen. Differences of age, personal responsibilities to her children, and lack of political interest might have combined to prevent her from allying more closely with this student movement, but she would not have gone unaffected by its political presence.

11 When this opera reached full-scale production in 1932, it was a tremendous success, broadcast over the National Broadcast Company radio station and winning critical accolades in the pages of *Crisis*, the influential periodical of the NAACP.

12 Program for *Tom-Tom*, ca. 1932, Shirley Graham file, Oberlin College, Oberlin, Ohio.

their bottoms while dancing topless.[13] As we shall see, Graham later abandoned the "striptease" portrayal of women in her creative work only to reinforce such controversial theories as biological determinism and the women's sphere, both of which were evident in *Tom-Tom*.

Needless to say, *Tom-Tom*'s success did not pay the bills; therefore, Graham in the meantime enrolled at Oberlin College in 1931, where she worked at breakneck speed to complete both a B.A. and an M.A. by 1935 while also working part-time as a laundress like so many other Black working-class women of her day. Consider the amazing accomplishment of Graham as a single Black mother in her mid-thirties who completed college and graduate school while raising two sons and working for negligible pay. She then opted to keep her elevated credentials in the African American community by teaching fine arts at the historically black school now called Tennessee State University, rather than traveling to Vienna, which was an option for her at that time.

Teaching history, music theory, and French with insufficient supplies, little pay, little time for her sons, and even less time for her own artistic endeavors, however, left Graham thoroughly disillusioned. She remained at Tennessee State for only the 1935–1936 academic year, taking up a position in Chicago as director of the Negro Unit at the Federal Theatre Project (FTP), the government-funded sanctuary for progressive cultural workers during the Depression.

While working at the FTP from 1936 to 1938, Graham continued to grow as an artist, venturing away from opera and

13 *Afro-American*, July 9, 1932. See also *Washington Tribune*, July 8, 1932; *Boston Chronicle*, July 16, 1932.

into the world of theater by directing such critically acclaimed plays as *Swing Mikado* and *Little Black Sambo*. Leftists of the Popular Front milieu such as Black Communist writer Richard Wright, also in Chicago, dismissed her work as an example of the "waste of talent" in FTP productions, since it opted to depict "jungle scenes, spirituals and all" over proletarian struggle.[14] But when she directed Theodore Ward's play *The Big White Fog*, a now unfortunately obscure drama that grappled with Garveyism, African American families, and burgeoning Left, she was met with equal invective from Chicago elites— Black and white alike, including the local NAACP chapter, which dismissed the play as "communist propaganda."[15] With the subsequent disbandment of the FTP for alleged Communist subversive activity in 1938, Graham's later affinity toward the Communist Party was, quite ironically, anticipated—if not precipitated—by this early red scare. All the same, she emerged from the project with an enhanced reputation as a composer, director, and producer, as well as with a little acting experience. She was quickly accepted into the Yale Drama School to study theater even further.

Yale was "all that [she] expected and more," since she also studied German and Italian and even began contemplating a dissertation.[16] But despite the support from such prominent African Americans as Charles Johnson and Adam Clayton Powell Jr., she found that her white patrons,

14   Richard Wright, "I Tried to Be a Communist," *Atlantic Monthly*, September 1944, file 289882, Federal Bureau of Investigation.

15   Rena Fraden, *Blueprints for a Black Federal Theatre* (Cambridge: Cambridge University Press, 1994), 121–122, 134.

16   Shirley Graham to W. E. B. Du Bois, October 23, 1938, Shirley Graham Du Bois Papers, Amistad Research Center, Tulane University, New Orleans, Louisiana.

such as Mary White Ovington of the NAACP, were apologetic about her "Negro plays" when seeking investors for her. Moreover, when Graham attempted to perform her plays through African American theater companies, she found herself even more marginalized. Graham's *Coal Dust*, a play that signaled her growing interest in Marxism insofar as it was an "old fashioned type of play about workers," which was performed at the Black-run Karamu Theatre in Cleveland, Ohio, was quickly abandoned because it lacked the financial backing for major—read non-Black—advertising. At the time, white-owned theater houses had the monopoly of theatrical productions, and the emergence of Black-run theater projects was received with considerable hostility from the dominant cultural apparatus. Her work with the FTP prematurely aborted by the anticommunist suspicions of the House Un-American Activities Committee (HUAC), and efforts at Yale frustrated by the racism of her purported mentors, it is no wonder that she would later spend a significant portion of her life fighting the political repression thrust upon "Red" and Black people. Exasperated with the obstacles associated with producing African American theater, by 1941 she had abandoned her work at Yale and her artistic career altogether for a job with the YWCA in Indianapolis.

Graham's transition away from theater, however, was not a political retreat in the face of racism and sexism. Quite pragmatically, she needed a salary increase to support her children, and a change of careers was in order. In 1942, after a brief tenure at the Phyllis Wheatley YWCA in Indianapolis, where she served as a director of adult activities, she was awarded a position as the YWCA-USO director at Fort Huachuca, Arizona, where

5,000 Black enlisted men and 6,000 Black officers formed the "largest contingent of Negro soldiers in the country."[17]

She arrived at Fort Huachuca at an opportune moment; the Black soldiers were in an uproar against a rash of police brutality cases inflicted by the white military police on post. The NAACP was quite active in organizing these soldiers, focusing on the case of Ollie D. North, who was charged with mutiny for using a loaded rifle to terminate a military police beating of a fellow Black soldier.[18] Graham also intervened on behalf of North and "reached the General and influenced him to reopen the case and by military ruling had the soldier's sentence changed to ten years." In the process she was endearingly referred to as "mama" by the Black troops whom she, apparently, both mothered emotionally and defended politically.[19.] Needless to say, her Christian employers were far from enamored with her maternal-turned-political actions; she was dismissed shortly thereafter.

Graham understood her dismissal quite clearly (if not literally) in black-and-white terms: "My ladies at the YWCA-USO . . . ordered me to come into New York City for a conference. When I got here they coolly informed me that the USO was not interested in some of my activities which were

17   Graham Du Bois, *His Day Is Marching On*, 52. See also Judith Weisenfeld, *African American Women and Christian Activism: New York's Black YWCA, 1905–1945* (Cambridge, MA: Harvard University Press, 1997).

18   *New York Times*, November 28, 1942, February 17, 1943; Leopold Johnson to NAACP, April 8, 1943; Ottis Burns to James Davis, May 5, 1943; Leslie Perry to Charles Browning, September 29, 1944, box b159, group 2, NAACP papers

19   Albert McKee to Shirley Graham, March 3, 1942, Shirley Graham Du Bois Papers, courtesy of David Du Bois, Cairo, Egypt.

outside the recreation program of the USO." Her own evaluation of the firing was that "in the final analysis white supremacy has us by [the] throat because the white man has the money. Yet I'll be damned if I'm sorry."[20] Again she had witnessed a scenario in which the militant self-defense against racist terror was carried out by Black people while the perpetrators were white. On a personal level, her reactions to the firing revealed a deep-seated anger that pitted "us" against "the white man," which was a key tenet of the Black Nationalist ideology she would later profess.

As a result of her experience in Arizona, Graham deepened her commitment to the NAACP because it had been the primary organizational ally in her own struggles against racism. Therefore, upon her dismissal from the USO she immediately packed her bags for New York City to work as an assistant field director for the NAACP. She became active in the group when its membership was in the process of reaching an all-time high, from 40,000 in 1940 to 400,000 in 1945, but she was convinced that it could reach "one million."[21]

Her experience organizing NAACP chapters was significant for several reasons. First, it demonstrates that Graham was part of the "long" civil rights movement dating back to the Communist and NAACP organizing campaigns in the South during the Great Depression. Second, it unearths a political transition in her own perspective that would augur her growing affinity for the Communist Party during the war. She was

---

20   Shirley Graham to W. E. B. Du Bois, October 30, 1942, reel 53, no. 1047, W. E. B. Du Bois Papers, University of Massachusetts–Amherst Library.

21   Shirley Graham to Walter White, July 14, 1943, box a585, group 2, NAACP Papers.

frustrated by what she saw as the capitulation of the southern church constituency to Jim Crow; this was compounded by what she perceived to be chicanery and chauvinism of the preachers, who were far from the legacy of Reverend Graham. "Believe me," she declared, "I can see more clearly why the Russians closed all the churches! Come the revolution—that would be the first thing I should advise—*throughout the south.* These fat, thieving, ignorant preachers! All of them should be put to work" (emphasis in original).[22] By 1943 Graham was not only thinking in terms of a "revolution" in the United States but also sympathizing with the Russian variety of social transformation and even imagining that she might play more than an advisory role. This was a self-fulfilling prophecy. But Graham's decision to resign from her NAACP position despite the fact that she had raised more than $8,000 in 1943 alone was not the apparent result of an ideological pull toward Communism; rather, she felt the "urge to do creative work."[23]

While working at the Open Door Community Center in Brooklyn, she began participating in political campaigns against police misconduct and for better housing, health care, and jobs for the local residents. Remarkably, she also found time to turn out a series of "biographical novels," as she called them, on such figures as George Washington Carver, Paul Robeson,

22 Shirley Graham to Mary White Ovington, August 1943, Mary White Ovington Papers, Wayne State University Library, Detroit, Michigan; Nat Brandt, *Harlem at War: The Black Experience in World War II* (Syracuse, NY: Syracuse University Press, 1996); Neil Wynn, *Afro Americans and the Second World War* (New York: Holmes and Meir, 1976).

23 Arthur Spingarn to Shirley Graham, October 5, 1943; Shirley Graham to Walter White, September 8, 1943, box a585, group II, NAACP Papers.

and Frederick Douglass. While these popular biographies had helped Graham accumulate more money than she had ever made to that point, they also placed her more closely in circles with local and international Communist figures who were guiding her artistically and politically. Among these prominent men were actor Paul Robeson, writer Howard Fast, city councilman from Brooklyn Pete Cacchione, and, most notably, W. E. B. Du Bois, who though still far from being a Communist, was also taking an increasing interest in Red activity in the United States.

Cacchione was also there as an emotional comfort to Graham when her son Robert died while living in California in 1944. This devastation propelled Graham into a more intense work frenzy, since she continued churning out biographies and even entered a doctoral program at New York University (though she did not finish). As she noted in a letter, "My entire life was work."[24] Her close interaction with these Communist men was critical to winning her political loyalty to the Communist Party, becoming more overt by 1947. In that year not only was she on a HUAC list of Red "fronts," but she was also photographed at a rally alongside Fast and Cacchione to save the Communist-initiated *New Masses* from being discontinued during the post–World War II crackdown on Communists in the United States, commonly referred to as the McCarthy period.[25]

Graham's personal and political affinities for the Communist movement became increasingly intertwined as

24 Shirley Graham to Roselyn Richardson, July 3, 1946, Roselyn Richardson Papers, Indiana Historical Society, Indianapolis, Indiana.

25 *New Masses*, May 13, 1947.

Du Bois—her intimate "flame" since she had returned to New York in 1943—was marginalized and altogether ousted from the NAACP in 1948 for challenging the Cold War thrust of the organization's leadership. Relentlessly attacking the United States for human rights violations, W. E. B. Du Bois and Shirley Graham both supported third-party candidate Henry Wallace of the Progressive Party over Harry Truman in the 1948 election, all to the dismay of the NAACP. Graham came to Du Bois's defense, unequivocally decrying what she saw as the NAACP's "'brazen act' of 'sheer persecution' that illuminated the archaic and anti-democratic character of the NAACP's structure," toward her political comrade and lover.[26] This personal commitment to Du Bois aside, Graham's own support for the Progressive Party shows how her maternal experiences spoke to her newfound leftist politics. At the July 1948 convention that nominated Wallace (where she played a leading role), she stated, "I am only one Negro mother who has seen the doors of a great hospital closed against her dying son...What do we want? That our children may dwell in peace."[27]

Du Bois and Graham were increasingly operating as a two-person united front against U.S. foreign policy; the political repercussions of their activity were imminent. In 1949, the couple sent a greeting to Joseph Stalin, Communist leader of the Soviet Union, lauding his "leadership in uprooting racial

26   Shirley Graham speech, "National Founding Convention of the New Political Party at Convention Hall, Philadelphia, July 23–25, 1948," reel 2, Third Party Presidential Nominating Conventions, Proceedings, Records, etc.

27   Memorandum, September 11, 1950, no. 100–370965–8, FBI; *Daily Worker*, March 26, 1948, May 31, 1948, December 23, 1949; *New York Amsterdam News*, December 31, 1949; *CounterAttack*, July 1, 1949.

discrimination." To this statement they alone were signatories, but it reflected the fact that a considerable number of African Americans had an increased affinity for the Soviet Union—not least because it was most directly responsible for wiping the world's most racist dictator, Hitler, off the map. And in 1949, at a rally sponsored by the Communist-led Civil Rights Congress in Peekskill, New York, she was hit with a rock by an anticommunist heckler. Du Bois, too, was suffering the repercussions of being increasingly seen as a Communist "agent," specifically because of his anti–nuclear weapons stance. So when he and Graham attended the Paris Peace Conference to discuss the prospects for nuclear disarmament, this was no doubt to the chagrin of U.S. authorities. Therefore, when she and Du Bois married in 1951 after the death of his first wife, they did so secretly and hurriedly on February 14 because, only two days later, he was to be charged in court with attempting to aid a foreign power, that is, the Soviet Union. Just as she had been his avid defender in 1948 against the NAACP, so too did she aid him in rallying financial support for his trial after he made bail.

Noteworthy about their whirlwind tour for his case is the fact that her prestige, in fact, enhanced his credibility. For example, in St. Paul, her mother's original home, the arrival of Du Bois drew the largest interracial meeting ever held in that city because he was "Lizzie Etta's little girl Shirley's husband."[28] Fortunately, though indicted, Du Bois was able to escape conviction. After the turmoil of Du Bois's case had passed, Shirley Graham Du Bois and her husband began to settle into a seemingly pacific life in their chic Brooklyn Heights home, formerly owned by writer Arthur Miller, receiving frequent guests from

28 Graham Du Bois, *His Day Is Marching On*, 157–164.

across the globe, ranging from UN representatives to African anticolonialists. Since they were confined to domestic affairs because both of their passports had been revoked throughout most of the 1950s, Graham Du Bois busied herself by caring for her husband and staying in the circle of Black Communists also living in New York at the time.

In particular, Graham Du Bois co-led a feminist collective alongside two other leading Black women of her period, Eslanda Robeson and Louise Thompson Patterson, also betrothed to two of the most prominent Black Communist figures of the twentieth century: Paul Robeson and William Patterson. Graham Du Bois, along with Eslanda Robeson and Louise Thompson Patterson, started a group called the Sojourners for Truth and Justice, which intended to inspire leadership of women of color across the globe.[29] Challenging barriers of race and nation alike, the work of these Black Communist women "sojourners" indeed helped pave the way for the women's liberation movement of the 1960s that thrived on American college campuses and in the workplace, a movement so often attributed summarily to the leadership of such figures as Gloria Steinem.

But above and beyond her work within this Black Marxist feminist collective, Graham Du Bois was also beginning to perform as a key actor on the global stage in this very period when the civil rights movement in the United States was gaining strength. When leftist forces around the world were riled by the execution of alleged Soviet spies Julius and Ethel Rosenberg in the United States, she called upon her mothering skills and directly oversaw the process whereby their children

---

29   Gerald Horne, *Communist Front? The Civil Rights Congress, 1946–1956* (London: Associated University Presses, 1988), 208.

were successfully adopted.[30] These domestic political engage-
ments notwithstanding, the Du Boises leapt at the opportunity
to leave the country when, in 1958, their passports were rein-
stated. For the better part of 1959 and 1960, the couple stayed
in Europe, the Soviet Union and China—Graham Du Bois even
venturing into Africa.

While the Du Boises were being wined and dined in
Moscow, African Americans ought to contemplate more deeply
Communism as a viable socioeconomic system because such
blatant forms of racial degradation were negligible in the Soviet
Union.[31] The caveat, of course, is that the Du Boises were
given royal treatment in a supposedly egalitarian state not least
because the Soviets understood the positive propaganda associated with catering to such influential African Americans.

Graham Du Bois, reluctantly though excitedly, left her
aged spouse in Russia and departed for Africa, visiting Ghana,
Egypt, Sudan, and Nigeria with a Soviet delegation. While
in Ghana she gave a stirring presentation based on her husband's essay "The Future of All Africa Lies in Socialism," and
at an important Pan-African gathering she replaced the flag of
Taiwan with that of the Communist regime in Beijing.[32] After

30   Robert Meeropol and Michael Meeropol, *We Are Your Sons: The
     Legacy of Julius and Ethel Rosenberg* (Boston: Houghton Mifflin,
     1975).

31   *Pittsburgh Courier*, June 20, 1959; Martin Bauml Duberman, *Paul
     Robeson: A Biography* (New York: Knopf, 1988), 473. See also Shirley
     Graham Du Bois, "Heartwarming Memories," in *Paul Robeson*,
     ed. Brigitte Moegelsack (Berlin: Academy of Arts of the German
     Democratic Republic, 1978), 56.

32   W. E. B. Du Bois, *The Autobiography: A Soliloquy on Viewing My Life
     from the Last Decade of its First Century* (New York: International
     Publishers, 1968); Graham Du Bois, *His Day Is Marching On*, 301.

having traveled to China and met its Communist leader, Mao
Tse-tung, Graham Du Bois proclaimed, "Wonderful! I didn't
think any place could be better than the Soviet Union but
I must say China takes my breath away."[33] This indicated that
she was moving toward a deeper engagement with Beijing's
version of socialism. Moreover, her pro-Maoist sympathies in
fact anticipated the political association of the militant Black
Panther Party in the 1960s with Maoism.

Subsequently, Graham Du Bois's relations with her
U.S.-based, pro-Moscow comrades, even those in the Black
feminist circles, were to become increasingly strained. Upon
returning to the United States to help edit the upcoming
Communist-inspired magazine *Freedomways*, a spinoff of
the newspaper *Freedom*, she reported in the *Afro American*
that even European women had "more guts" than those in
the United States.[34] Convinced, apparently, that she might
be of more use to international movements than to those in
the United States, Graham Du Bois was off again in 1961 (this
time without her husband) and back to Ghana to attend the
conference "African Women and Women of African Descent."[35]

---

33   Shirley Graham Du Bois to Cedric Belfrage, April 4, 1959, box 2,
     Cedric Belfrage Papers, New York University Library.

34   *Baltimore Afro-American*, September 20, 1959. See also Annelise
     Orieck, *Common Sense and a Little Fire: Women and Working-Class
     Politics in the U.S., 1900–1965* (Chapel Hill: University of North
     Carolina Press, 1995).

35   From there she went to another conference while in Cairo called the
     "Extraordinary Session of the Afro-Asian Solidarity Council," which
     was specifically focused on the Congo crisis. In Cairo she signed onto
     an ad in a Trotskyite paper that denounced U.S. foreign policy activity
     in the increasingly Soviet-aligned Cuba, evidently less worried about
     undermining the political tensions between the Socialist Workers'
     Party and the CPUSA than in challenging U.S. imperialism.

Back in the States, W. E. B. Du Bois had made the decision to join the CPUSA, which he did in 1961. At first glance, it is curious that the couple would then turn around and move to Ghana that same year, effectively denying them the chance to organize for the American party. And yet, considering Graham Du Bois's inclination toward building an international movement based in Africa coupled with their general resentment of the U.S. government, their move to Accra was entirely fitting. Moreover, Kwame Nkrumah had arranged it so that they would have a house on the hill, complete with a steward, cook, driver, and night watchman, and in close proximity to Flagstaff House, his own home. Graham Du Bois's son David recalled that it was "like living in a glass house when you went to the home there in Ghana because it was a place of pilgrimage for people from all over the world and particularly all over Africa," as well as for Chinese diplomats and African Americans enthralled with Ghanaian state.[36] The prominent Du Bois family, it seems, was also so enthralled with the Ghanaian state that they failed to counsel Nkrumah on the potentially negative repercussion of marginalizing the Left, much to the chagrin of American and Ghanaian Marxists. On the ideological level, Nkrumah sought to "inculcate in" the Ghanaian "working people the love for labour and increased productivity."[37] In so doing, however, he declared trade unions "obsolete," since to "struggle against

---

36   David Du Bois, interview, June 3, 1992, Louis Massiah Papers, courtesy of Louis Massiah, Philadelphia, Pennsylvania.

37   Jeff Crisp, *The Story of an African Working Class: Ghanaian Miners' Struggles, 1870–1980* (London: Zed, 1984), 134. See also Ebenezer Oiri Addo, "Kwame Nkrumah: A Case Study of Religion and Politics in Ghana" (Ph.D. diss., Drew University, 1994); W. Scott Thompson, *Ghana's Foreign Policy: 1957–1966* (Princeton, NJ: Princeton University Press, 1969).

capitalists" was now, he felt, an irrelevant matter, and finally mandated that Communists be "banned from entering the civil service in the Gold Coast."[38] Charged with the task of remapping Ghana's entire educational system in support of the new regime, Graham Du Bois was in no position to challenge official policies of the state. In the coming period this would further alienate Graham Du Bois from the "old school" Marxists of the Moscow milieu while deepening her influence on the "new school" radical youth of the Maoist and Pan-Africanist varieties.

Graham, however, would soon be left to wage such battles on her own since, in 1963, W. E. B. Du Bois died. If Graham had remarkably mustered the energy to work throughout the pain after the loss of her son, Graham Du Bois managed to work even harder after the loss of her husband. She was already in the process of embarking on the most politically engaged and professionally productive position in her entire life: directing the television industry in Ghana while indirectly acting as a "first lady" to Nkrumah. Remarkably, Ghana TV would not have any commercials in that its primary function was not to serve big business; instead, Graham Du Bois stated that "the television we are planning will be a tremendous channel for education, for increased understanding and for developing and unifying the peoples of Africa."[39] Though in some ways this education did little to challenge traditional understandings of gender norms insofar as it offered "demonstrations of cooking, dressmaking, exercises, fashion shows, hints," and "interior

38   Hakim Adi, *West Africans in Britain: 1900–1960 Nationalism, Pan Africanism and Communism* (London: Lawrence and Wishart, 1998), 163.

39   Shirley Graham Du Bois to Gladys, December 16, 1964, courtesy of David Du Bois, Cairo, Egypt.

decorations," it also quite nobly offered an "evening programme for illiterates."[40]

To learn how to run such an operation, Graham Du Bois traveled across Europe from east to west, also stopping in Japan, where she finally brokered a deal with the Japanese electronics company Sanyo to supply Ghana with the televisions for this enterprise. As a result, Graham Du Bois facilitated the effective displacement of the Philips electronics company of the Netherlands, Ghana's colonial era television supplier, and furthered Nkrumah's hope that Ghana might avoid the road toward "neocolonialism" that was the fate of so many postindependence regimes. Graham Du Bois's political ascendancy upset the self-interested Ghanaian elites, since this was the first time that anyone—much less an African American woman and "outsider"—had been given free reign to sever the traditional colonial ties that had sustained their own class positions. Moreover, they were angered by her personal oversight of Nkrumah's health and well-being, reflected in the evening telephone calls to Nkrumah "each night at bedtime" along with advising him on such matters as his dietary needs.[41] Again, she had elided the personal with the political. As if her interventions in the economic and personal affairs of leading officials were not enough to incite discontent, Graham Du Bois additionally tested her political clout by using her influence within the Ghanaian publishing industry to praise African American Communists such as her comrade William Patterson. Given the wide reach of the Ghanaian press across the continent, Graham

---

40 Shirley Graham Du Bois to Mikhail Kotov, November 7, 1965, courtesy of David Du Bois, Cairo, Egypt.

41 Angelou, *All God's Children Need Traveling Shoes*, 138.

Du Bois helped grant distinction to a political milieu that could hardly expect the slightest praise from its own government. On her off time she also took occasion to meet with Black CPUSA leaders Claude Lightfoot and James Jackson when they came to Ghana, often discussing the content of *Freedomways* and its ideological direction in relationship to the civil rights movement in the States.[42]

But the ties to her CPUSA comrades, especially those involved in the production of *Freedomways*, were noticeably weakened as a result of her political shifts while in Ghana. On a global level, Graham Du Bois's loyalties to the Soviet Union were becoming increasingly strained as she gravitated away from what she saw as the Moscow/King approach to "peaceful coexistence" and toward the Beijing/Black Power call for militant national liberation. She was increasingly vocal in defending China to the point that in 1963 she wrote into the Nation of Islam journal *Muhammad Speaks*, taking both Roy Wilkins of the NAACP and James Farmer to task for their anti-Chinese positions.[43] But the CPUSA had continued to remain committed to the Soviet Union, while China—and by association Graham Du Bois—was becoming anti-Soviet.

Undoubtedly, she was fundamental to shaping the internationalist perspective of *Freedomways* insofar as it was she who solicited Tom Mboya of Kenya, Oliver Tambo of South Africa, and Julius Nyere of Tanzania to submit articles for the magazine. This all-star cast of African leaders was placed squarely before an ambivalent "old guard" base of leading Black activists

---

42 Shirley Graham Du Bois to John Henrik Clarke, January 24, 1965, John Henrik Clarke Papers, Schomburg Center, New York Public Library.

43 *Muhammad Speaks*, November 22, 1963.

involved with this journal just as a "new guard" representing the Black Power movement in the United States was looking increasingly to Africa and Asia as the centers of national and anticolonial struggles for liberation from Western imperialism. But Du Bois's death in 1963 placed Graham Du Bois and Esther Jackson Cooper, another editor, at odds, since Graham was enraged that Roy Wilkins was allowed to write on Du Bois though they were archenemies, whereas Graham Du Bois's picks such as Malcolm X were not accepted for submission.[44] This apparent hesitation on the part of the Old Left to break with leading Black activists of the time—even those such as Wilkins with whom they were once at odds—rather than embrace the emergent Third World leaders who were inspiring the youth of the Diaspora, would only further distance Graham from her longtime comrades in the CPUSA.

It was not simply that Graham Du Bois's "left Nationalist" tendencies complicated her position in the U.S.-based *Freedomways* circles; additionally, she challenged her political alliances with the left forces within Ghana by hiring only "professional experts" from the United States to work in the Volta region of that country. She confessed, "My heart bleeds when talented young Afro-Americans are brought to my attention and I am asked to give them an opportunity to use their abilities!" Even Robert Williams, the author of *Negroes with Guns*, who helped jump-start the militant self-defense movement as opposed to the nonviolent philosophy of King, did not make the cut because, she said, "Africa doesn't need 'leaders.' It does need the help of skilled technicians, experienced and exceedingly

44 Esther Jackson to Shirley Graham Du Bois, June 20, 1964, Esther Jackson Papers, courtesy of Esther Jackson, Brooklyn, New York.

welltrained."[45] Not only did this approach upset Ghanaian—
and non-Ghanaian—leftists, but additionally Graham found
herself politically defending Malcolm X's perceived "racialist"
viewpoint from attacks by Marxist Ghanaians, stating that he
was opposed to the "White government and the White ruling
class" of the United States.[46]

But Graham Du Bois was also aware of the fact that many
of the African American "skilled technicians" who were making their way into Ghana were "well-trained" by the State
Department and other government agencies, functioning as
self-interested surrogates of imperialism who, in her words,
sought "better and easier living and quick profits to take back
[to the United States]."[47] These "surrogates of imperialism,"
coupled with the anti-Nkrumah forces within Ghana, were
building their political and military force, growing such that on
February 24, 1966, Nkrumah's power was involuntarily abdi-
cated; so too was that of the honorary "first lady."

Graham Du Bois guarded Nkrumah's legacy as she had
done for Du Bois after his NAACP ouster. The litmus test for
the political righteousness of any self-proclaimed revolutionary
was their position on whether or not Nkrumah was unjustly
overthrown. Graham Du Bois was to answer, of course, that
he was, but many of her CPUSA friends were not quite so
decisive. In particular, prominent Communist writer Anna
Louise Strong enraged her when she raised the contention that

---

45   Shirley Graham Du Bois to John Henrik Clarke, December 20,
     1964, John Henrik Clarke Papers; Shirley Graham Du Bois to Cedric
     Belfrage, June 7, 1963, box 2, Cedric Belfrage Papers.

46   *Ghanaian Times*, May 18, 1974.

47   Shirley Graham Du Bois to George Murphy, May 5, 1963, George
     Murphy Papers, Howard University Library, Washington, DC.

Nkrumah was rumored to have been exceedingly corrupt.[48] But for Graham Du Bois there was no such thing as opposing Nkrumah from the left; to support his overthrow—or even to question his bona fides—was to aid and abet U.S. imperialism. Her days as a "comrade" in the CPUSA were numbered. Her defense of the African national liberation struggle was becoming increasingly unequivocal.

Apparently exasperated with U.S. nationals of many stripes—Red included—Graham decisively hedged her bets on Africa and lowered her political anchor in Maoist China. Although she kept her eye on the developments occurring in the United States, particularly events involving the Black Panthers on the West Coast (where her son David was to edit their newspaper) and the Student Nonviolent Coordinating Committee (SNCC) in the South, Graham Du Bois was now off to Cairo, Egypt, where she would be based for the duration of her life, residing intermittently in China, Tanzania, and the United States.

Cairo was in the midst of its 1967–1968 conflict with Israel when she arrived, and Graham Du Bois had decided to support a regime that, in her words, had quite appropriately "raised a blockade against white imperialism and aggression rather than against Zionism or the Jewish people."[49] As her political hatred of "white" imperialist foreign policy intensified,

---

48 Anna Louise Strong to Shirley Graham Du Bois, December 12, 1969. See also Shirley Graham Du Bois, "Nkrumah's Record Speaks for Itself"; Shirley Graham Du Bois, "Kwame Nkrumah: African Liberator," Shirley Graham Du Bois Papers, Subseries G. Clippings and Other Material Collected by SGD, Schlesinger Library, Radcliffe Institute.

49 Shirley Graham Du Bois to Kwame Nkrumah, June 1, 1967, Shirley Graham Du Bois Papers, courtesy of David Du Bois, Cairo, Egypt.

her political affinities became more "Egypt-centric." Indeed, Egypt in particular and Afro-Centrism in general would become a major theme in the lectures she would deliver to American students when she returned to the United States in the 1970s.

Supporting Egypt's leader, Gamal Nasser, however, also put Graham Du Bois in a delicate and sensitive position as a Red—analogous to her support for Nkrumah in Ghana—precisely because Nasser was receiving aid from Moscow while suppressing the oxygen supply to the Communist movement in Egypt. This occurred as her relations with Beijing became even closer. Because she was never lacking in vanity, it did not hurt that China had not only given her spouse ample airtime on Radio Peking while in Ghana—and most recently, Chinese officials had met her in Tanzania after Nkrumah's overthrow and pulled out the red carpet for her.[50] Transitioning into a stalwart defender of China was not, however, without its own contradictions for Graham Du Bois, whether or not she recognized this fact. The Chinese-U.S. normalization of diplomatic relations during the Nixon era at first frustrated her. But apparently she opted not to challenge the mandates of Beijing (which was her normal response of late). Perhaps she was wary of once again courting the wrath of a powerful state whose political repression might have been too much at her age. But more likely, she truly believed that China, with all its flaws, promised the one and only "third way" as a state alternative to Soviet and U.S. influence over the "darker races" of the world.

---

50   Mrs. Huang Hua to Shirley Graham Du Bois, August 31, 1962, reel 75, no. 900, W. E. B. Du Bois Papers; Bill Sutherland, interview by author, March 3, 1995.

By the 1970s, Graham Du Bois was back in the United States after a huge left-liberal spectrum—including, ironically, Roy Wilkins—garnered support for her right to return and lecture at campuses across the country. While she had refused to sever ties with her CPUSA friends leading the W. E. B. Du Bois Clubs—considered "revisionist" by her newly minted Beijing allies—she did quite pragmatically (perhaps even willingly) disavow her ties to the CPUSA itself in order to regain entry to the United States. This would seem to contradict all of the recent work she had contributed to *Freedomways* and her membership—if only nominal—to the Party; however, her desire to reach out to the youth in the Black Power movement in the States required that she make political concessions to the same government apparatus whose repression of political dissent had at one time driven her to the left. On her U.S. tour she spoke as a nationalist on questions related to Africa and Afrocentrism, not on class or socialism. Her Afrocentric leanings were also reflected in her novel *Zulu Heart*, which depicted the plight of the South African indigenes in their struggle against apartheid: this book included a European who, upon receiving a heart transplant from a Zulu, emerged from the operation with a new life rhythm. He could even dance! Needless to say, the *New York Amsterdam News*, a prominent Harlem-based weekly paper loved it, biological determinist implications notwithstanding.[51] Indeed, Graham Du Bois was treading the waters of cultural nationalism in the States that would become most associated with such figures as Ron Karenga, founder of the African American ritual Kwanzaa in 1967.

51   *New York Amsterdam News*, May 18, 1974.

As late as 1975 she was still lecturing in the United States, even working for brief stints in New England at both the University of Massachusetts in Amherst and Harvard University teaching literature. But she could also be found on the West Coast attending gatherings sponsored by the Black Panthers in Oakland and also speaking before the US China People's Friendship Association on "Africa and China."[52] For Graham Du Bois, defending China and Africa was a matter of life and death, quite literally in her case. In April 1977, after fighting the last of her many battles—this time with cancer— Shirley Graham Du Bois was laid to rest in China, a citizen of Tanzania, ending a series of her many lives in only one of her many homes.

52   *Guardian*, July 9, 1975.

"THE WHITE REPUBLIC": RESPONSE BY GERALD HORNE

Convergence Magazine, May 2021

The good news is that Comrade Bob Wing's analysis represents a step forward in terms of the U.S. Left's understanding of the nation—"republic"—in which it struggles.

The bad news is that the U.S. left has not necessarily kept pace with the U.S. ruling class in terms of similar issues, or even with non-radical African Americans, for that matter.

Consider the multi-part series on HBO Max (a member in good standing of the much reviled "corporate media") that premiered recently, i.e., Black filmmaker Raoul Peck's "Exterminate All the Brutes," a sweeping analysis and condemnation of settler colonialism (a term curiously absent from ordinary discourse on the left) and white supremacy. His other credits include the superb docu-drama "The Young Karl Marx."

Consider the 1619 Project of The New York Times, spearheaded by Black journalist Nikole Hannah-Jones, which—interalia—had the audacity to suggest that a settlers' revolt in 1776 led by slaveholders may have had something to do with maintaining slavery. Revealingly, the assault on this estimable initiative was mounted by self-described "socialists," liberals and conservatives: in essence, The White Republic.

Consider the book by Black scholar Tyler Stovall (published by an Ivy League press), *White Freedom: The Racial History of an Idea*, which is more advanced ideologically than comparable analyses on the U.S. left.

Consider the response to the concerted effort to deodorize the smelly roots of the vaunted "Founding Fathers": I speak of the Broadway/Disney extravaganza, "Hamilton," celebrated by the Cheneys and Obamas alike, not to mention some to their left—but skewered by paramount Black intellectual, Ishmael Reed.

How and why the U.S. left has tailed the ruling class on such a bedrock matter as conceptualizing white supremacy soars far beyond the confines of this brief response. Suffice it to say for now that misconception begins with the origins of the slaveholders' republic in 1776, a creation myth that Comrade Wing does not challenge explicitly. Those who consider themselves to be sophisticated refer to an "Incomplete Revolution," as if the founders had in mind "others" not defined as "white" but, perhaps, forgot to include them. This is akin to referring to implanting apartheid in 1948 as an "Incomplete Reform," as if these founders, perhaps, forgot to include Africans in the bounty that was accorded to poorer Afrikaners. Even the supposedly perceptive term "bourgeois democracy" as a descriptor for 1776 and its fruits is misleading at best since "rights" definitely did not include any not defined as "white" and, thus, this term becomes part of the massive misdirection that now has us on the brink of fascism.

Settler Colonialism and the Construction of Whiteness First

Consider the confluence of settler colonialism and the construction of "whiteness." When settlers arrived in what is now North Carolina in the 1580s it was a multi-class venture—shopkeepers, smiths, etc.—sponsored by the London elite. This was in the midst of religious wars between Catholics and Protestants. Catholic Spain, which came within a whisker of toppling the London monarchy in 1588, imposed religion as a qualifier for settlement. England, the scrappy Protestant underdog, moved toward Pan-Europeanism—or "whiteness"— incorporating Scots and Irish and Welsh in the first instance, those with whom they had been warring for centuries, and then moved toward incorporating others who had been warring: British v. German; German v. Pole; Pole v. Russian; Serb v. Croat—the list is long. All of a sudden when crossing the Atlantic, in a manner that would make Madison Avenue blush, all are rebranded as "white," which subsumes many of the tensions, ethnic and class among them, in a new monetized and militarized "identity politics" of "whiteness" based on expropriation of the Indigenous and mass enslavement of the Africans.

As the 17th century roots of Maryland suggest, London was willing to sponsor Catholic settlers, while inquisitorial Madrid continued to bar and expel those not deemed to be religiously correct. Thus, from the inception in the early 1500s, Havana contained African conquistadors who professed Catholicism (a sharp divergence from racialized settlements in the "Anglo-sphere," leaving a legacy which continues to wrongfoot those seeking to comprehend socialist Cuba) and as late as 200 years ago, settler Stephen F. Austin professed a nominal Catholicism in order to engage in his land grab in Mexican Texas.

Of course, Ottoman—and heavily Islamic–Turkey was an igniting factor in this process. Their seizure of what is now Istanbul in 1453 impelled an existential crisis in Western European Christendom: as Columbus headed westward in

1492, on behalf of Catholics he was seeking to circumvent the Ottomans; 1492 also marks the accelerated weakening of Islamic rule in Iberia, followed by many fleeing to North Africa and to Ottoman jurisdiction, along with the Jewish minority.

Tellingly, London had expelled its own Jewish minority circa 1290–1291 but in the contestation with Catholics, this Protestant power embraced this minority—as did Protestant Holland—and the victorious republicans did so too by 1776. The philosophically idealistic and credulous tried to convince the rest of us that this was a result of "Enlightenment," as opposed to seeking to broaden the base of settler colonialism in order to confront obstreperous Africans and the mighty Indigenous.

Interestingly, in the late 1930s, the Dominican dictator Rafael Trujillo also embraced a fleeing European Jewish minority and only the naïve would ascribe this decision to "Enlightenment"—as opposed to a crude attempt to "whiten" the population in the ongoing conflict with the bête noire that was neighboring Haiti, whose nationals were simultaneously being massacred along the border.

Speaking of neighbors, it is similarly informative that patriotic U.S. analysts of the left generally refuse to scrutinize the "control group" due north. Canada did not rebel against London and yet now has a health care system that is the envy of the so-called "revolutionary republic"—should not one expect the opposite?

Actually, settlers' revolts—be they in Southern Rhodesia in 1965 or Algeria in the late 1950s—are generally problematic, especially when driven by white supremacy and/or religious bigotry. To the "credit" of the North American settlers' revolt, unlike their French counterparts in Algiers, they were not as advanced in seeking to liquidate the monarch himself, as was the case in Paris in April 1961 with Charles de Gaulle in the crosshairs. (For the naïve who continue to guzzle the Kool-Aid and propaganda of "liberal democracy," on the 50th anniversary of this plot, French military men threatened a coup against President Macron, just as the elite U.S. publication Foreign Affairs reported a disturbing trend of the military bucking civilian rule: see also 6 January 2021 and the recent open letter signed by dozens of retired military brass in the U.S. echoing MAGA talking points and warning ominously against the purported "socialism" of the current regime in Washington.)

Given the troubling roots of this republic, it was inevitable that at a certain point what are described as "cultural" issues—immigration; reproductive and LGBTQ rights—would leap to the fore as these are perceived as natal matters essential to an apartheid state: maintaining a presumed "white" majority.

Left-Wing White Nationalism

This transition from religion to "race" was occurring in the context of a bumpy transition from feudalism to capitalism. "Bloody Mary," the English monarch in the mid-16th century, received her moniker as a result of reports of Catholics burning Protestants at the stake. Unsurprisingly, as capitalism attained liftoff as a direct result of the plunder of the Indigenous and the mass enslavement of the Africans, by the end of the 19th century, Africans were being immolated (in enslaved form representing the essence of capitalism)—with either Catholics or Protestants of European descent, often of British origin (at times jointly) lighting the torch.

The attempt to build "class unity" without confronting these underlying tensions often has meant coercing oppressed nationalities—Blacks in the first place—to co-sign a kind of "left wing white nationalism," as reflected in the lengthy attempt to convert slaveholder, Thomas Jefferson, into a unifying symbol. Black failure to do so leads to our denunciation—in today's terms as "identitarian" [sic], in previous decades, as "narrow nationalist." Actually, the class collaboration embodied in "whiteness" was seeking to impose "class collaboration" on the descendants of the enslaved, inducing us to align with enslavers and their descendants. And given that pre-1865 U.S. history—and to a degree the era thereafter—involved deputizing Euro-American settlers as a class to patrol and coerce the Indigenous and the Africans, this too involved an often-undetected class collaboration. It also involved often lush material incentives for those settlers who complied and harsh disincentives for those who did not.

In sum, unlike Raoul Peck, the U.S. left parachuted into the 20th century and sought to impose an ersatz "class unity" brutally at odds with historical reality. They were akin to cineastes entering the theatre halfway through the film, while thinking they had a firm grasp of the plot. Indeed, Peck's work and that of other Blacks represents an attempt to wrest the powerful searchlight of Marxism away from those who have strived to convert it into a feeble flashlight.

When reality does not correspond to the facts on the ground, the U.S. left often responds like the fictional French intellectual who maunders: "I know what you are saying is true in fact, the question is—'is it true in theory?'" That is, a detailed knowledge of history and contemporary trends is the meat to be placed on the skeleton that is theory—without that meat one is left with a putrefying cadaver.

Thus, when Euro-Americans vote across class lines for faux billionaires, we are instructed that the reason is that the opposition did not meet their exacting progressive standards—hence, they voted for the right. (Once when I was explaining to a prominent left-leaning scribe that the citadel of the elite, the Upper East Side of Manhattan, and the citadel of the Euro-American working and middle classes, Staten Island, are the bastions of the right wing in Gotham, he demurred seeking to point out that the latter borough voted thusly because of liberal failings: and, yes, he had never heard of John Marchi, Staten Island's decades long proto-fascist GOP boss, re-elected repeatedly.) Of course, this miscomprehension begs the question as to why descendants of the enslaved even in the same borough and nationwide—marinated in the ultimate class struggle of slaves versus slaveholder—vote against the right wing in extraordinarily high numbers.

This misanalysis also neatly elides the instructive 1991 gubernatorial election in Louisiana when well over half of Euro-Americans across class lines voted for a Nazi and Klansman, David Duke, for governor—who would have prevailed but for the staggering blow delivered to his onrushing campaign by the mailed fist that was the Black vote.

Forge Alliances Beyond U.S. Borders

African Americans in particular sliced neatly the Gordian knot of oppression historically by forging alliances beyond the confines of settler colonialism, with ties to the Indigenous (e.g., antebellum Florida) or Haiti (post-1804) or London (1776–1865) or Tokyo (pre-1945) or Moscow (post-1917) or independent Africa and the Caribbean (post-1960).

What does this mean for today? It means rejecting the new Cold War against Russians and Chinese and, instead, forging alliances with both. It means linking demands for reparations nationally with like-minded struggles in the Caribbean and Africa. It means realizing that the uncanny ability of some on the U.S. left to hand rhetorical weapons to the right to bash the oppressed—from "political correctness" to "cancel culture"—is hardly a coincidence or accident but simply another expression of a "cross-class alliance" that has propped up settler colonialism from its inception. (Truth be told, these weapons were honed principally by "white" leftists in internecine conflicts that led—objectively and unsurprisingly—to a dearth of questioning of the legitimacy of settler colonialism.) It also means forcing class initiatives as a solvent against the pestilence that is white supremacy—for example, the PRO law or right to organize unions, now before Congress.

Per Comrade Wing, it also means seeking to deepen our understanding of the fundamentals of U.S. imperialism, white supremacy not least. Congratulations to Comrade Wing for seeking to rescue virtually every sector of the "radical" U.S. left from a swamp of Right Opportunism.

PERMISSIONS

"The Dawning of the Apocalypse: The Roots of Slavery, White Supremacy, Settler Colonialism, and Capitalism in the Long Sixteenth Century" reproduced with permission of *Monthly Review*.

"Hell in the City of Angels: 1965 and 1992" and "Hands Across the Water: Afro-American Lawyers and the Decolonization of Southern Africa" reproduced with permission of *Guild Practitioner*.

"'Myth' and the Making of 'Malcolm X'" reproduced with permission of *American Historical Review*.

"Shirley Graham Du Bois: Portrait of the Black Woman Artist as a Revolutionary" reproduced with permission of NYU Press.

"Things Fall Apart: China and the Decline of US Imperialism" and "From Crisis to Catastrophe? What is to be Done in Eastern Europe" reproduced with permission of *Political Affairs*.

"Tokyo Bound: African Americans and Japan Confront White Supremacy" reproduced with permission of *Souls*.

"'The White Republic': Response by Gerald Horne" reproduced with permission of *Convergence Magazine*.

"Who Lost the Cold War? Africans and African Americans" reproduced with permission of Oxford University Press.

Gerald Horne is Moores Professor of History and African American Studies at the University of Houston. His research has addressed issues of racism in a variety of fields including labor, politics, civil rights, international relations and war. Dr. Horne is the author of more than thirty books, including *The Counter Revolution of 1836: Texas slavery & Jim Crow and the roots of American Fascism* and *The Apocalypse of Settler Colonialism: The Roots of Slavery, White Supremacy, and Capitalism in 17th Century North America and the Caribbean.*

Tionne Alliyah Parris is a PhD candidate at the University of Hertfordshire who received a 1st Class Undergraduate degree and a Masters degree from the University of Dundee in Scotland. She is a specialist in African American history, and specifically in the Black Power Movement of the 1960s and 1970s. Her research is focused on American society's response to race-based political protests—as well as Communist ideology within Black Radical protests.

www.ingramcontent.com/pod-product-compliance
Lightning Source LLC
Chambersburg PA
CBHW020533030426
42337CB00013B/840